Richard H. Oehm
'72

THE ALPHA AUTOMATIC
PROGRAMMING SYSTEM

A.P.I.C. Studies in Data Processing
General Editor: Stuart Summersbee

A.P.I.C. Studies in Data Processing
No. 7

THE ALPHA AUTOMATIC PROGRAMMING SYSTEM

Edited by
A. P. YERSHOV
Computer Centre, Novosibirsk,
U.S.S.R.

Translated by
J. McWILLIAM

1971
ACADEMIC PRESS
LONDON AND NEW YORK

ACADEMIC PRESS INC. (LONDON) LTD.
Berkeley Square House
Berkeley Square
London, W1X 6BA

U.S. Edition published by
ACADEMIC PRESS INC.
111 Fifth Avenue
New York, New York 10003

Library of Congress Catalog Card Number: 72-149698

ISBN: 0-12-770840-5

PRINTED IN GREAT BRITAIN BY
WILLIAM CLOWES AND SONS LIMITED
LONDON, COLCHESTER AND BECCLES

PREFACE
TO THE ENGLISH EDITION

The author of any translator of a problem-oriented language to machine language, is faced with two major considerations: fast translation from the source language to the object language, and fast execution of the object language. There is usually a third consideration in the background: the provision of good diagnostics, for the program author in the source language. It may well be that these considerations represent incompatible constraints on the construction of a source language translator, and that, in practice, any translator is a compromise within these constraints, and the result represents the author's solution to a systems-engineering problem within these constraints. There are, of course, further considerations which determine the effectiveness of the ultimate product e.g. the machine configuration on which the proposed algorithms of translation are to be implemented. This book summarizes the efforts of one group of computer scientists to provide an effective (efficient) translator for a language closely resembling ALGOL 60.

The ALPHA-translator is the work of a group of Soviet scientists under the leadership of Professor A. P. Yershov. It represents the results of at least thirty man-years of work and while it is impossible to evaluate the final result in the Western world, nevertheless the book should be of interest to all those working in the field of language translators. Each group of workers has described in detail the algorithms used for their particular part of the general task, and reference to machine language has been kept to a minimum. The book should also be of interest to post-graduate students of computer science, for it provides an example of the structure of a complete translator.

The translation from Russian to English has not been an easy task. From the beginning two major considerations were borne in mind: first, the result had to be technically accurate, and secondly, it had to read smoothly in English with the current technical terms replacing the Russian ones (rather than the translated Russian ones). Inevitably, there will be some mistakes but we hope they are few, and comments will be welcomed. If the present work helps the detailed study of one completed project in a difficult and developing field, we shall be well satisfied.

SEPTEMBER 1971   S. SUMMERSBEE

EDITOR'S NOTE

The main aim of the collection is to give the reader a clear idea—without going into excessive detail—of the fundamental algorithms of translation, which have been developed or used by the authors and implemented in the ALPHA system. The book also discusses the problem of selecting a suitable input language for automatic programming systems and deals with the construction of a system for program modification at source language level and with the development of complex programming systems.

The book describes a specific programming system designed for a specific machine. However, the authors have tried to describe the algorithms of translation in the most general terms possible, clearly indicating points of contact between individual algorithms and the remaining part of the translator or features involved in calculating individual characteristics of the machine. Special attention has been given to the motivation and basis of the solutions used.

The authors have tried in particular to stress the difficulties arising in working out programming algorithms and to analyse mistakes and incorrect solutions encountered in developing the system.

This volume is therefore primarily addressed to our colleagues, i.e. to professional programmers, concerned with developing programming systems for computers. The book will also be of value to users of the ALPHA system, as familiarity with the algorithms of translation will allow them to solve problems more efficiently.

Since it covers practically all aspects of programming automation with the aid of translators and also thanks to the simple way in which most of the articles are written, the book may serve as an introduction to the problems and methods of automatic programming.

Since the present publication is a collection of articles and not a collectively written monograph, the style of the various authors and their individual approach to the problems under discussion are preserved. The editor has taken it upon himself merely to ensure that the articles are uniform in lay-out, that repetition is avoided by introducing appropriate cross-references, and that terminology is consistent.

The articles are presented in the order recommended to the reader. However, the expert can turn immediately to any specific article of interest to him, since cross-references provide a link up with other articles. Three types of reference are used in the articles: external—[10]; internal—1.2; and cross-references—[III.4.5]. External ones relate to papers included in the list of references at the end of the article. Internal ones relate to a section of the given article. Cross-references relate to the section indicated of one of the other articles in the book, the number of which is given in Roman numerals (as in the index).

It is assumed that the reader is familiar with the publication "Source Language for Automatic Programming Systems" by A. P. Yershov, G. I. Kozhukin and T. M. Voloshin, (Novosibirsk 1964), which describes the source language of the ALPHA system at standard language level. Algol and additional terminology used in the above book are not defined afresh in the present book and references to "Source language . . ." and descriptions of ALGOL 60 are omitted. All other terminology, apart from general programming and mathematical terminology, is defined in the book or cross-referenced. It should be noted that the Russian translations of official ALGOL 60 and source language words are used in the book.

The appendix includes two articles which at the beginning of 1961 formed the basis of work on the ALPHA system. They might be of interest to the reader as documentary proof of the degree of correlation between the original plans and the formulation of the problem for the final results.

Computer Centre,   A. P. YERSHOV
Novosibirsk,
U.S.S.R.

CONTENTS

CONTENTS

I ALPHA—A SYSTEM FOR AUTOMATIC PROGRAMMING

G. I. Babetskii, M. M. Bezhanova, A. P. Yershov,
G. I. Kozhukhin, S. K. Kozhukhina, Yu. I. Mikhalevich,
R. D. Mishkovich, I. V. Pottosin, L. K. Trokhan,
Yu. M. Voloshin, B. A. Zagatskii and L. L. Zmievskaya

ALPHA—a system for the automation of programming by translation from an ALGOL-type language—was developed by the authors at the Computer Centre† of the Siberian branch of the Academy of Sciences of the U.S.S.R. for the M-20 computer.

The main features of the machine are as follows: it has a three-address system, with a floating decimal point, one index register, a core memory of 4,096 45-bit words, three magnetic drums with a total capacity of 12,288 words, four magnetic tapes each with a capacity of 75,000 words, input and output on punched cards and an average speed of 20,000 operations per second.

The following are the component parts of the system. The ALPHA-*language* is the source language of the system in which problems to be programmed are written. The ALPHA-language[1] is a hardware representation of Input language[1] a somewhat modified version of the international programming language ALGOL 60.[2]

The ALPHA-*translator* is the compiler program which translates the text of the problem in ALPHA-language (of the ALPHA-program) into the computer object program of the problem, ready for processing.

The ALPHA-*debugger*—is a debugging program, making it possible to debug the ALPHA-program without having to examine the object program.

The ALPHA-system was developed during the period 1959 to 1964. The fundamental principles forming the basis for developing the system were worked out in 1959.[3] By the middle of 1960, preliminary information about the Input language[4] had been collected and towards the beginning of 1961 an experimental project was carried out on the system.[5] In autumn 1960, work on the fundamental algorithms of programming was completed and the Input language[1] was defined more precisely. Coding and block debugging were completed towards the middle of 1963 and complex debugging towards the end of 1963. In the course of 1964 an experimental trial run was carried out on the ALPHA-translator and the ALPHA-debugger was developed. The work involved in developing the ALPHA-system is estimated at 35 man-years.

The main scientific problem arising during the development of the ALPHA-system was to investigate the possibility of creating for medium size computers a system for automation programming of problems involving mainly numerical analysis based on a rich source language and giving a high quality of programming, closely approaching that achieved by the skilled programmer.

† Formerly a department of the Institute of Mathematics of the Siberian Branch of the Academy of Sciences of the U.S.S.R.

1 The ALPHA-Language

As has been mentioned, ALPHA-language is a hardware representation of Input language, described at reference language level in Paper 2. In addition to ALGOL 60, Input language makes use of complex quantities; the possibility of considering simple variables as vectors, matrices or in fact any multi-dimensional quantities and also the possibility of deriving multi-dimensional quantities from quantities of a simpler structure with the help of special "geometrical operations"; in addition it involves the admission of recurrence relations with upper time index, the admission of chains of inequalities, the possibility of describing the initial values of the variables and the possibility of a simpler description of the procedure declarations, to be calculated with the help of expressions.

Some simplifications were made in the hardware representation as compared with the reference language. The main simplifications introduced in ALPHA-language as compared with ALGOL-60 are as follows:

(a) the absence of any recursive procedures and recursive calls;
(b) the specification of the formal parameters which are labels;
(c) all the actual parameters corresponding to a given formal parameter be the same kind, type (to within the nearest **integer** or **real** number), and dimension;
(d) the absence of side effects when computing statements;
(e) *GO TO* switches must be explicitly defined.

In addition, in contrast to Input language, variables may have a single upper index. Contrary to the limitations normally encountered, dynamic own and integer labels may be used in ALPHA-language.

Supplementary to the reference language, ALPHA-language allows for declarations directing that certain variables should be stored on the drum or certain blocks of the ALPHA-program on external memory (tape, drum or punched cards). There are standard input—output procedures for variables from the external memory and the ALPHA-system can also include a library of sub-routines, based on the IS-2 standard interpretive system. The ALPHA-program includes computer instructions and variables in symbolic code for implementing non-standard actions. There is also a system for incorporating independently translated modules into one single program.

2 The ALPHA-Translator

During the development of the ALPHA-translator, special attention was paid to achieving a high efficiency of programming whilst maintaining an acceptable translation speed. The phrase "efficiency of programming" means the producing of as compact and fast a program as possible. Where shortening the program conflicted with shortening the operating time, preference was usually given to achieving a short operating time.

2.1 Optimization of the Program

The basic means of achieving programming quality is the application of formal transformations and a "mixed programming strategy" based on the principle of multi-phase translation. In multi-phase translation yet another language level is introduced in between source language and object language—the so-called *internal language*. Like the source language, the internal language is practically independent of the computer instruction code, but unlike source language it has a simple structure of statements and declarations which make the implementation of formal transformations easier. In connection with this, the work of the translator consists of two large parts or phases: translation from ALPHA-language into the internal language (translation phase) and translation from the internal language into the object language (coding phase). In each phase, the work of the translator involves the actual translation from a higher language level to a lower one, followed by a series of formal transformations at the lower language level, aimed at optimization of the object program.

2.1.1   The main optimizing transformations in the translation phase are the following:

(1) elimination of the "geometrical operations" on multi-dimensional variables by an appropriate distribution of the components of these variables in memory;

(2) amalgamation of the neighbouring *FOR*-statements having identical *FOR*-clauses and which occur when implementing component operations on the arrays;

(3) reducing subscript expressions to a canonical form, in which the subscript is expressed in a linear form of control variables with the appriate change of the control variable by adding a constant step together with an optional random term.

(4) "cleaning up" of *FOR*-statements involving the removal of the calculation of the expressions which are not recalculated within a *FOR*-statement is moved outside the *FOR*-statement;

(5) elimination of redundant expressions along the unbranched parts of the ALPHA-program.

2.1.2   In the coding phase, the chief transformation of the program consists of the so-called global memory economy, which involves determining for any pair of variables in the program (excluding dynamic arrays) whether it is possible in the allocation of core memory to allocate one and the same section of the memory for these variables. On the basis of this information, gathered in the form of an "inconsistency matrix" the ALPHA-translator produces an allocation of the memory which closely approaches an optimal one. During this phase local improvements in the program are carried out by taking account of the special features of the computer instruction code.

2.1.3   A mixed programming strategy is used when translating grammatical units of the ALPHA-language which have a rich syntactical structure—the procedures and *FOR*-statements. When using a mixed programming strategy, the universal algorithm of translation is supplemented by a series of algorithms, based on simpler constructions of a given grammatical unit and therefore giving a more economical program. The choice of the algorithm of translation is made on the basis of a preliminary analysis of the object program.

The following cases may occur when programming procedures:

(1) there is only one call to the procedure (in this case the procedure body is substituted for the procedure statement in the translation);
(2) all actual parameters, corresponding to some formal parameter, co-incide with one another (in this case, the actual parameter is submitted for the formal one in the procedure body during translation);
(3) all the arguments of a given actual parameter are not recalculated in the procedure body (in this case the call for the actual parameter is not produced every time the corresponding formal parameter appears, but only once, prior to entry into the procedure body);
(4) an array called by value can be called by name and on the other hand a scalar called by name can be called by value (in this case the corre-sponding variables are called by the simplest method).

Generally, the universal algorithm of translation described in the Paper 7 is used.

When programming *FOR*-statements the following cases arise:

(1) an integer control variable is changed only by the *FOR* clause by addition of a fixed step to the control variable (in this case checking for completion is effected very simply, whereas index expressions are calculated by adding a linear increase with the help of either the index register or the instructions for re-addressing);
(2) an integer control variable of a *FOR*-statement is changed only by the *FOR*-clause but arbitrarily (in this case the subscript expressions are calculated with the help of the index register, which can be changed only by passing to another repetition of the *FOR*-statement).

In the general case, *FOR*-statements are replaced by basic statements in literal accordance with the definition of *FOR*-statements in ALGOL 60.

2.2 Optimization of the Translator

The chief means of increasing the speed on the ALPHA-translator are tag-and-address encoding of the identifiers and basic symbols of the language, a broad application of "hash addressing", a semidynamic allocation of core memory for the translator blocks and use of the list structure for files.

Tag-and-address encoding signifies that a part of the code of a given element (the identifying part) is taken as equal to the relative address of the information relating to the given element in some file. The other part of the code of the element (the tag part) contains flags which define the class to which the given element belongs (a simple variable, an array, a constant, a procedure or an operational symbol, etc.) and also some information about the given element which is often required (e.g. the type of variable).

"Hash addressing", which makes it possible to eliminate table search when solving a problem of identifying identical elements in a set[8] is used in the

ALPHA-translator for translating identifiers of the ALPHA-language, when eliminating identical constants and expressions.

For a fuller utilization of core memory when working on the translator, each block, before its operation, allocates memory, leaving in core memory only those tables which will be used by it and allocating memory for tables to be reconstructed (wherever this is possible in principle) end to end without reserve by previous counting of the necessary quantitative characteristics of the program to be translated (for example the number of procedures, the number and depth of nesting of the *FOR*-statements and so on). Therefore, during operation each block utilizes to the full the advantages of the fixed and economic allocation of memory. But the allocation of memory varies from one problem to the next.

For new files of indefinite length or with items of information of different length a list structure for storing them in the memory has been used, making it possible for the number of memory fields with floating bounds to be reduced.

2.3 Using the Translator

The ALPHA-translator is arranged in a block system with sequential and repetitiveless operation of the blocks. The blocks are on magnetic tape and are read sequentially. The program to be translated is stored on a drum and is read off for processing into core memory in portions of the greatest possible size. Each block carries out only a strictly linear scan of the symbols of the program to be translated.

The ALPHA-translator consists of 24 blocks which are as follows.

2.3.1 *The translation phase.* Block 1 reads in the ALPHA-program, deletes comments and performs a partial syntactical check by examining pairs of adjacent symbols for compatibility and counting the number of brackets. Blocks 2 and 3 translate the identifiers and extract information about the identifiers from declarations, transferring it into tables and tag digits of codes, and also perform a partial semantic control, issuing lists of nondeclared identifiers. Blocks 4 and 5 program the expressions and conditional statements. Block 6 analyses procedure bodies and statements and Block 7 programs the procedures on the basis of the analysis. Block 8 carries out intermediate re-encoding of information, while Blocks 9 and 10 program the operations on complex numbers and multidimensional arrays and also carry out optimizations 1 and 2 in the abovementioned list of transformations. Blocks 11 and 12 clean up *FOR*-statements, reduce the subscript expressions to a canonical form and analyse *FOR*-statements. Block 14 minimizes redundant expressions.

2.3.2 *The programming phase.* Block 15 compiles computer instructions for all the statements of the internal language, except *FOR*-statements. Block 16 programs the operations (connected with the computation of subscript expressions) with the index register. Blocks 17 and 18 compile the instructions for controlling *FOR*-statements and instructions for readdressing. Blocks 19, 20 and 21 minimize the constants and temporary locations, and construct the inconsistency matrix. Block 22 performs the global economy of memory on the basis of the inconsistency matrix. Block 23 carries out local improvements in the program via the special features of the computer instruction code.

Block 24 assembles the program and loads it ready for execution or issues it on punched cards.

If necessary an interpretive system is attached to the object program—for calling standard library subroutines—and an administrative system. Its purpose is to reserve and clearout sections of memory for dynamic arrays and program blocks, which are required to be held in external memory and which are read into operative memory when called. In addition, the administrative system stores and loads values of dynamic own arrays.

The total capacity of the ALPHA-translator is 45,000 words.

3 The ALPHA-Debugger

The purpose of the ALPHA-debugger is to debug ALPHA-programs at source language level and to carry out a few other operations. The programs are debugged without an interpretive system, by the "insertion" method, in which additional operations which need to be carried out when altering the program are put into the ALPHA-program before it is translated on the basis of "debugging information", to be added to the text of the ALPHA-program to be debugged.

The debugging information is an arbitrary set of debugging instructions. Each instruction contains its range of operation, which might be the whole of the ALPHA-program or else any section or point in the text. The segment bounds are defined from a context rule, i.e. if the words P and Q are given as segment bounds, the range of operation will be a part of the text between the first P entry from the left in the ALPHA-program and the first Q entry from the left in the program, following the P. If $P = Q$, the section becomes a point.

The following are the debugging instructions.

(1) Replace all the A entries by B, throughout the range of operation.
(2) Print the variable x in position P.
(3) Print values of the variable x for any of its assignments in any given range of operation.
(4) Note the features of the path of all the labels in the given range of operation.
(5) Print the actual number of times the Nth *FOR*-statement is repeated, where N is the *FOR*-statement number, counting from the beginning of the ALPHA-program.

The ALPHA-debugger was designed as the zero block of the ALPHA-translator and is stored with it on the same tape. Analysing the ALPHA-program and the debugging information, it makes the indicated substitutions and also inserts the necessary calls to the standard subroutine of print in the ALPHA-program where required. As certain identifiers of the ALPHA-program must be printed in the debugging run, they are all rewritten into a special "code-array" stored on the working tape, the components of which will be used by the print subroutine when required.

The capacity of the ALPHA-debugger is about 2,000 words.

4   Operational Data

The ALPHA-system has been used experimentally since January 1964. During the course of the year more than 500 various working problems of 100 to 3,000 instructions were programmed. The average translation speed (without outputting onto punched cards) was 150 instructions per minute. The ALPHA-translator automatically detects 95% of all the errors made by the programmer when compiling the ALPHA-programs; 93% of the errors detected by the ALPHA-translators are found by the first (60%) and third (33%) blocks of the translator. The average number of runs required to achieve an object program, free from grammatical errors, is two.

A test was carried out on 17 numerical analysis problems, comparing the quality of automatic and manual coding. The results of the comparison in

TABLE I

Regis-tration No. of the problem	Type of problem	Length of program		Variant calculation time	
		Manual program-ming	ALPHA	Manual program-ming	ALPHA
T1	A system of simple differential equations	438	454	5′ 25″	4′
0042	Formula calculations	400	504	5′	6′
0054	Matrix calculations by formula	100	140	1′ 45″	1′ 45″
0056	Calculations by formula	135	335	3′	4′
0073	4-dimensional integration	168	324	4′	6′
0077	Double integration	165	312	4′	6′ 20″
0101	Calculations by formula	115	125	1′	1′
0105	Calculations by formula	78	128	54″	50″
0152	Root finding by the Newton method	204	262	18″	21″
0165	Formula calculations	131	171	4′ 41″	4′ 48″
0275	Monte Carlo method for algebraic equations	77	121	3′ 05″	3′ 35″
0300	Root finding by direct scan	156	236	1′ 49″	2′
0312	Transport problem	222	386	1′ 40″	2′ 10″
0513	Integral equation	64	84	4′	4′
0514	Boundary problem by the Random Walk method	93	144	9′ 12″	12′ 45″
0516	Matrix calculation of Markov chains	290	293	45″	35″
		290	293	45″	35″
0730	Universal program for singular integral equations	243	315	5′ 18″	6′ 05″
	TOTAL	3079	4334	55′ 52″	66′ 14″

terms of operation time and program length (without an interpretive system) are given in Table I.

On 8 problems a test was carried out to compare the quality of programming using the ALPHA-translator, the TA-1 translator[9] and a TA-2 translator.[10] The results of the comparison in terms of operation time and program length (without an interpretive system) are given in Table II (the translation was carried out on identical source programs).

TABLE II

Regis- tration No. of the problem	Time						Length of program		
	of translation			of calculation of the variant			TA-1	TA-2	ALPHA
	TA-1	TA-2	ALPHA	TA-1	TA-2	ALPHA			
T1	1′ 55″	11′	3′	7′ 50″	16′ 7″	4′	755	618	454
0052	1′ 15″	2′ 35″	1′ 20″	53″	48″	44″	315	126	116
0064	1′ 5″	2′ 40″	1′ 20″	2′ 30″	2′ 45″	2′ 29″	311	101	163
0101	1′ 15″	4′	1′ 20″	9′ 35″	1′ 35″	1′	544	166	125
0110	1′ 30″	4′ 20″	1′ 25″	24′ 10″	3′ 7″	1′ 40″	495	139	94
0131	1′ 28″	4′ 25″	1′ 13″	3′ 5″	3′	2′ 31″	295	102	85
0141	1′ 22″	3′ 15″	1′ 34″	74′	13′ 40″	8′ 26″	280	80	57
0257	1′ 38″	6′ 20″	2′ 35″	24″	25″	22″	603	278	213

The authors would like to point out that the results of the experiments tabulated here are of a preliminary nature and cannot form the basis of any final or conclusive judgments about the comparative efficiency of the translators, the more so as, upon slight revision of the texts of the problems, which would take into account the specific characteristics of the translators, the difference in operation time of the variant can be eliminated in some cases.

5 Acknowledgements

Work on the development of the ALPHA-system was a collective venture and many major decisions were taken jointly at a working seminar of the authors as an associated body. Therefore, the list given below which apportions how much each author contributed to the creation of the system is only approximate.

G. I. Babetskii developed Block 3 and took part in the development of Block 15. M. M. Bezhanova developed Blocks 11, 12 and 13 and worked out the idea and some of the algorithms of the ALPHA-debugger. Yu. M. Voloshin participated in the development of Input language and developed Blocks 9 and 10. A. P. Ershov was the instigator and scientific supervisor for the whole project. He participated in the development of Input language and developed the project task on the translator, as well as Block 8 and took part in the work on Blocks 19 to 22. B. A. Zagatskii worked on Blocks 1, 6 and 7. L. L. Zmievskaya developed Blocks 19 and 24. G. I. Kozhukhin helped to formulate

Input language and participated in the development of a project task on the translator, was the coordinator of the work on the translation phase, devised the administrative system, Block 2 and the algorithms of Blocks 4 and 5. S. K. Kozhukhina programmed Blocks 4 and 5 and developed Block 15. Yu. M. Mikhalevich programmed the ALPHA-debugger and maintained the software of the ALPHA-translator in a period of complex modifications. R. D. Mishkovich worked out Blocks 20 and 21. I. V. Pottosin was the coordinator of the work on the coding phase, developed Block 14 and the algorithms of Blocks 16, 17 and 18, and took part in the work on the algorithms of Blocks 12. L. K. Trokhan developed Blocks 22 and 23.

Apart from the authors, other sources also contributed to the formation of the system. V. A. Yankov took part in the preliminary development of Input language. R. N. Klyushkova compiled the program of Blocks 17 and 18; V. V. Voitishek compiled the preliminary variant of the compatibility matrix for pairs of symbols of the ALPHA-language. F. K. Ivanova did some preliminary work on part of the algorithms of the global economy of memory. I. A. Vitkina compiled a series of algorithms for the programming of subscript expressions. V. P. Minayev organized the experimental operation of the ALPHA-translator.

REFERENCES

1. YERSHOV, A. P., KOZHUKHIN, G. I. and VOLOSHIN, Yu. M. (1964). Input language for automatic programming systems. Novosibirsk.
2. BACKUS, J. W. *et al.* (1962). Revised report on the algorithmic language ALGOL 60. International Federation for Information Processing.
3. YERSHOV, A. P. (1961). Basic principles in the construction of a compiler program at the Institute of Mathematics, Siberian Branch of the Academy of Sciences of the U.S.S.R. *Sib. mat. Zh.* 2, No. 6.
4. YERSHOV, A. P., KOZHUKHIN, G. I. and VOLOSHIN, Yu. M. (1961). Input language for an automatic programming system. A preliminary report. Computer Centre of the Academy of Sciences of the U.S.S.R., Moscow.
5. YERSHOV, A. P. and KOZHUKHIN, G. I. (1961). A compiler program project of the Institute of Mathematics, the Siberian Branch of the Academy of Sciences of the U.S.S.R. A report from the Computing Centre of the Siberian Branch of the Academy of Sciences of the U.S.S.R. Novosibirsk. (Appendix 1, this volume.)
6. YERSHOV, A. P. (1961). Basic problems encountered when constructing a compiler program at the Institute of Mathematics of the Siberian Department of the Academy of Sciences of the U.S.S.R. A report of the Computer centre of the Siberian Department of the Academy of Sciences of the U.S.S.R., Novosibirsk. (Appendix II, this volume.)
7. INGERMAN, P. Z. (1961). *Thunks. Communs Ass. comput. Mach.* 4, No. 1.
8. YERSHOV, A. P. (1958). The programming of arithmetical operations. Academy of Sciences of the U.S.S.R. 118, No. 3.
9. POPOV, V. N. and STEPANOV, V. A. (1964). The compiler program. *J. Comput., Maths, math. Phys.* 4, No. 1.
10. SHURA-BURA, M. R. and LYUBIMSKII, E. Z. (1964). The ALGOL 60 translator. *J. Comput., Maths, math. Phys.* 4, No. 1.

II REVIEW OF THE CHARACTERISTICS OF THE ALPHA-LANGUAGE

A. P. YERSHOV, G. I. KOZHUKHIN AND I. V. POTTOSIN

As previously pointed out ALPHA-language is a hardware representation of the source language of the ALPHA-system, described at reference language level[1] as the Input language. A detailed description of the ALPHA-language can be found in "Guide to the use of the ALPHA-system"[2] and the present article is therefore merely intended to give a review of the differences between the ALPHA-language and the reference language arising partly out of some simplifications of the Input language and partly as a result of the introduction in the Input language of a series of complementary facilities, typical of other systems of automatic programming, and the reasons for introducing these differences.

We shall refer to the first group of differences provisionally as "limitations" and to those of the second group as "additions". It should be noted that the reasons for some of the limitations may become completely clear only after perusal of other articles contained in this book, in which those algorithms of translation, the logic of which requires these limitations, are described in more detail.

1 Limitations

1.1 Types of Limitations

All limitations inherent in the ALPHA-language as opposed to the standard specification may be divided into two types, a priori limitations and enforced limitations. The *a priori* limitations were introduced deliberately when designing the translator; the enforced limitations arose out of an analysis of the algorithms of translation, which showed that the algorithms developed did not cover all cases, admissible in Input language. In the majority of cases these limitations were introduced without hesitation since they appeared to relate to such contrived uses of the Input language that their occurrence in a reasonably written program seemed rather unlikely. However, some of the enforced limitations find their explanation in certain errors, committed in planning the algorithms, the elimination of which would have required an excessive amount of modification to be carried out on the translator. Naturally, limitations of this nature are not an object of pride for the designers of the ALPHA-translator. We consider it, however, to be rather important to make a detailed assessment both of these types of limitations and of the factors giving rise to them, partly to advise other would-be designers of translators of the necessity for an accurate and logical analysis of the algorithms of translation as regards their suitability for the volume of constructions to be translated, and partly to draw attention of future authors of algorithmic languages to the fact that they should not neglect to analyse problems arising when carrying out translation using the language devised by them.

1.2 A Priori Limitations

Since ALGOL 60[3] forms the basic constituent part of the Input language most of the limitations will be formulated in relation to ALGOL 60.

1.2.1   Recursive procedures and calls to recursive procedures are not permitted in the ALPHA-language.

The basic reason for adopting this limitation was the impracticability, from the point of view of the designers of the ALPHA-translator, of recursive procedures for all programming algorithms known to them, especially in the case of a deep recursion. Violation of this limitation in the ALPHA-program is discovered during translation and is blocked by transmitting the instruction "stop" (the so-called control stop).

1.2.2   The form, type (here integer type is not distinguished from real type) and dimensions of the identifiers and (or) expressions, serving as the actual parameters, corresponding to a given formal parameter must coincide.

The necessity for this limitation is dictated by the fundamental characteristics of the method employed in the ALPHA-translator for procedure programming, in which all substitution and utilizations of actual parameters are programmed beforehand on the basis of a statistical analysis of the procedure statements and declarations. This limitation could be overcome by introducing a "fix" for the procedure bodies, by providing each individual form, type or duplicate of the actual parameters with its own copy of procedure body. It was, however, realized that the complexities introduced by such a "fix" are too high a price to pay for eliminating this limitation. In translation, infringement of this limitation is prevented by a control stop.

1.2.3   Side-effects in procedure functions are disregarded. This is one out of a small number of limitations applied by the compilers without hesitation since a strict observance of all rules of calculation required for calculating side effects would excessively complicate carrying out optimizing transformations in the ALPHA-translator.

This limitation, of the ALPHA-language is not a categorical one. The change in the non-localized variables or the actual parameters in the body of the procedure function or removal from the procedure body by means of a *GO TO* statement is actually programmed into the ALPHA-translator. The result of these operations may, however, not correspond to the rules of the revised ALGOL 60 in some cases.

1.2.4   In contrast to ALGOL 60, the result of using a switch in the ALPHA-language is not definite if the switch deisgnator has an indeterminate value.

This limitation, which is exceedingly common in translators operating with ALGOL 60, was adopted since it was not desired to include in the object program the recursive mechanism for analysing values of subscript expressions and their comparison with the length of the switch list.

1.2.5   In the ALPHA-language, the order of calculation of subscript expressions when working out the assignment statement using the left-hand list, which consists of more than one variable, differs from that adopted in ALGOL 60. This difference is shown when making use of constructions of the type

$$i := j := 1; a[i,j] := i := j := 2$$

in the programs.

In ALGOL 60, the value 2 is assigned to the variable $a[1,1]$, whilst in the ALPHA-language this value corresponds to the variable $a[2,2]$. This is due to the fact that it was decided to program in all cases assignment statements of the following form (for the example given above):

$$j := 1;$$
$$i := j;$$
$$j := 2;$$
$$i := j;$$
$$a[i,j] := i$$

in the ALPHA-translator, whilst the corresponding programs used in ALGOL 60 are of the form:

$$j := 1;$$
$$i := j;$$
$$n := i;$$
$$m := j;$$
$$j := 2;$$
$$i := j;$$
$$a[n,m] := i$$

The following alternatives presented themselves for observing the rules of ALGOL 60:

(1) to carry out the calculation of subscript expressions from the subscript positions of the variables, forming the left-hand lists, into additional assignment statements placed in front of the compiled statement; and

(2) to carry out such an operation by analysing the assignment statement only where this is unavoidable.

The first of these two possibilities was rejected because changing the subscript expression taken out, to symbols of intermediate variables destroys information, for instance, that calculating the subscript of the given variable is bound up with using a parameter of some *FOR*-statement. Loss of information of this nature impairs the quality of the translation. The second alternative was not adopted because the designers were unable to find algorithms for the analysis which were sufficiently simple to be included in the translator blocks required to carry out this analysis.

1.2.6 In the ALPHA-language, identifiers of standard functions cannot be actual parameters of procedure statements. This limitation which is fairly typical for translators employing ALGOL 60, is due to the fact that the mechanism involved in the call to standard functions differs greatly from that involved in the call to standard procedures and the uniformity attained by tying up these mechanisms does not make up for the complexity of this agreement introduced. Unfortunately an infringement of this limitation is not always blocked by the ALPHA-translator.

1.3   Enforced Limitations

1.3.1   As previously mentioned in Section 1.2.2, it was decided to make use of a principle according to which the rules for programming the formal parameters contained in the procedure body are established on the basis of information relating to the corresponding actual parameters in the procedure call.

The realization of this principle which offers significant advantages, also entails certain difficulties bound up with programming designational expressions, functions of a transformation type and also with the possible presence of cross references in parallel procedures. Not all these difficulties were discovered in time and overcome, and this led to the introduction of some limitations.

The following limitations arise out of the use of designational expressions as actual parameters.

1.3.1.1   Formal parameter labels must be specified in the procedure heading.

1.3.1.2   Integers without a sign serving as the labels cannot be used as actual parameters for a procedure statement which has a formal parameter as its identifier.

1.3.1.3   Conditional designational expressions cannot serve as actual parameters in a procedure statement.

It should be noted that these limitations are excessive in their totality, but since each of them has its own, independent reason of existence they must all be formulated together. Transgressions against the limitation 1.3.1.3 are prevented by the control stop.

1.3.1.4   There is one limitation, bound up with the presence of cross references, which is difficult to formulate exactly. We shall only state here that such cases of cross references which appear in parallel procedures may occur when an existing translation algorithm enters into the compilation of expressions in the procedure body without an analysis of all call statements for the given procedure having first been carried out, which may lead to an error with some combinations of types of actual parameters in the call statements. An example of a situation of this type is given below:

Begin
    Procedure ϕ (1); **Begin**
                    F (0·5)
                End;

    Procedure F (x); **Begin**
                        ·
                        ·
                End;
    ϕ (L); F (1)
End

If no limitation is imposed on the ALPHA-translator in this case, the procedure body F will be programmed in the calculation for integer arithmetic with respect to x, although F should be programmed for real number arithmetic to maintain the correctness of the calculation. In the ALPHA-translator inadmissible combinations of types of actual parameters in such situations are blocked by the control stop.

1.3.1.5   A final characteristic related to the realization of the principle laid down in Section 1.3.1 involves some deviation from ALGOL 60 lying in the fact that irrespective of the type declaration of a formal parameter called by value (or result), this will be programmed in the arithmetic of its substituents, the actual parameters, i.e. in integer arithmetic if these are integers or in real arithmetic in the opposite case.

1.3.2   As regards the Input language, only one superscript is permitted in the ALPHA-language. In essence this limitation must be extended to the reference language, since it was brought about by demonstrating the impossibility of giving comprehensible and accurate semantics for the case of several superscripts. An infringement of this limitation is blocked by the ALPHA-translator.

1.3.3   In connection with the algorithms of programming FOR-statements in the ALPHA-language the following two limitations occurred.

1.3.3.1   A subscripted variable can serve as a control variable of a FOR-statement only if the subscript is an integral variable, and if the variable itself denotes a component of an array with constant boundary pairs. This limitation may also be formulated as follows: a control variable of a FOR-statement can only be a variable having subscripts such that their calculation leads only to a selection of values of integral variables. If the calculation of the subscript of the control variable involves carrying out a whole group of instructions, this will give rise to difficulties bound up with the necessity of having to multiply this group of instructions at all positions in which the control variable enters the FOR-statement.

1.3.3.2   The body of some FOR-statement having a control variable, the FOR-statement may not be statically included with the same control variable. This limitation is caused by the fact that in the programming of nested FOR statements a table is compiled for each FOR-statement, entry into which is effected by means of the identifier of the control variable.

Violation of each of these limitations is blocked by the control stops.

1.3.4   The last of the limitations known to the authors relates to the mechanism of the economy of expressions and lies in the fact that the ALPHA-translator does not guarantee the correct programming of expressions of the form

$$E - E \text{ or } E/E$$

where E is an expression more complex than the variable.

In conclusion of the section on limitations it should be noted that the so-called quantitative or technical limitations bound up with the volume of programs to be translated or other quantitative characteristics have not been dealt with. A more detailed account of limitations of this type will be given in the next chapter (III.4.4).

2 Additions

2.1 Preliminary Remarks

Before coming to the heart of the matter it must be mentioned that whereas in the preceding section we, the authors of this chapter, acted merely as "go-betweens" between the reader and the designers of the ALPHA-translator, we must accept full responsibility for all basic solutions adopted in respect of the additions made to the standard specification of the Input language, dealt with in the present section.

The concept of "addition" constitutes the conversion of an "abstract" system of programming in the reference language, which describes the algorithms for solving problems under conditions of a potentially unlimited memory and time, to a "hybrid" system of programming in which the means of the reference language are supplemented by an instrument which makes it possible to utilize more exactly the operational possibilities of the machine or to ascertain the limits and the number of levels of memory.

It should be noted that by contrast with macro-assemblers in which macro-operations are additions to the machine instructions rather than a basic part of the source language, it is found that in translators using languages such as ALGOL the implementation of a hybrid system of programming entails certain difficulties. A considerable portion of these difficulties mirrors the more fundamental contradiction which lies in the fact that the logic involved in *formulating* a problem by no means always corresponds to the logic of its *algorithmic solution*.

It would be most tempting to overcome this contradiction by a complete automation of the consideration of all specific machine characteristics, necessary for solving the problem. This would make it possible throughout to define the "abstract" formulation of the problem, without having to be concerned, for instance, with the allocation of the program or the processing of information between several levels of memory. We are, however, of the opinion that this method can only be employed if the algorithms used (e.g. segmentation) have a high effectiveness and do not cause the contradiction mentioned above to become concealed rather than overcome, leading to a loss in the capacity of the machine which cannot be controlled by the programmer. The authors, therefore, while still in the process of working out the ALPHA-system, adopted a solution[4] according to which the programmer (allowing for the special characteristics of memory where necessary) would bear full responsibility for making use of these special characteristics, clearly programming all the necessary operations or clearly imparting to the ALPHA-translator all the information required.

At the same time the authors considered that programming effectively, taking full account of the characteristics of the machine, must for the majority of problems engage a comparatively limited space. The introduction of machine characteristics into Input language was therefore arrived at by the "method of simple solutions" according to which the number of points of engagement between the computer and the system is reduced to a minimum, as far as possible, whilst the solutions themselves are obtained to a considerable degree during the period of experimental exploitation of the system on the basis of an analysis of concrete situations, encountered in the problems, presented for programming.

The whole set of additions may be divided into the following groups:

additions bound up with the use of libraries of standard programs and standard procedures;

additions related to the use of certain levels of memory of the computer and input–output operations;

additions making it possible to include machine code in the text of the ALPHA-program;

additions making it possible to combine independently translated programs in a single complex.

2.2   Standard Programs and Procedures

Standard programs are library sub-routines automatically called into the main program from tape or drum storage by means of the interpreting system IS-2.[5] Although IS-2 was developed for use under conditions of manual programming and although its inclusion in the ALPHA-system necessitated some artificial methods placing an additional load on the ALPHA-translator, it was decided to retain the library of the IS-2 system, allowing for its comparatively large volume, to enable the programmers to continue making use of it.

Call to a sub-routine taken from IS-2 is described in the form of a procedure statement

$$SP\langle\text{integer without sign}\rangle(\langle\text{list of actual parameters}\rangle)$$

where the $\langle$integer without sign$\rangle$ is the four-digit number to the base 8 of the sub-routine in the library, whilst the actual parameters may be scalar variables (including subscripts), integers without sign and labels.

Procedure identifiers cannot serve as actual parameters so some sub-routines of IS-2 (for instance the Runge-Kutta or the Adams method) cannot be used in the ALPHA-system.

The difficulties involved in incorporating the IS-2 library in the system lie in the fact that the ALPHA-translator must be able to analyse standard sub-routines similarly to procedures written in Input language. In particular, it would be necessary to obtain information on which actual parameters of the sub-routine are arguments and which results, and also on the positions in which the null-order address or direct argument (i.e. the parameter is a value and not a name) is used. So-called SP *tables* containing the necessary information about the actual parameters in the form of a binary scale, are therefore incorporated in all blocks of the ALPHA-translator which require this type of information. Entering the tables is carried out by means of the library number of the sub-routine.

This method reduced the number of points of contact of the IS-2 library with the translator and rendered it substantially invariant relative to the composition of the library. However, a limitation is imposed on the overall amount of available numbers of the sub-routine (up to 128) and an operation as delicate though quite practicable as a change of SP tables is required when changing the composition of the library.

The ALPHA-translator makes possible the use of library procedures described in Input language, automatically including in the ALPHA-program procedure declarations, stored on tape. Identifiers of standard library procedures must not exceed a length of five symbols. Incorporation procedure declarations into the ALPHA-program are carried out by the ALPHA-debugger which, on having discovered an indicator of a library procedure in the text reads from the tape the corresponding declaration placing it at the highest level of the program, enclosing it in additional statement brackets. This ensures that those declarations already contained in the ALPHA-program receive priority if the programmer accidentally uses library procedure identifiers for other purposes.

Tests carried out on the ALPHA-system make it possible to surmise that the high quality of procedure programming achieved by the ALPHA-translator in combination with the use of machine code contained in the text of the ALPHA-program will lead to a gradual replacement of the IS-2 library by a library of declared procedures.

2.3   Connection with External Memory

The connection with external memory is provided by descriptive means contained in the ALPHA-language, which supply the ALPHA-translator with cross references, on the basis of which the necessary instructions for change will be formulated together with the operational means giving the exchange operation in a clear form.

2.3.1   The declarations make it possible to declare some static arrays of the ALPHA-program to be *drum* arrays and some blocks to be *external* ones. All quantities and blocks not declared as being located on the drum or as being external ones, are placed into core memory when programming. The drum array is stored on a drum. Reading drum array B in memory is given in the form of an assignment statement, assuming the form of transfer B in some suitable array A, $A:=B$.

If B is declared as a subscripted variable, it will be mentioned with empty subscripts in this statement. Writing into the drum array is recorded in the form $B:=A$. The drum arrays cannot be mentioned in any other form in the ALPHA-program, except for standard procedures for exchange (cf. below). The drum arrays are located on the drum by the ALPHA-translator itself in the order of arrangement of their declarations.

The declarations of external blocks prescribe to some labelled block of the ALPHA-program to be located before the start of the object program, in external memory, i.e. on a drum, tape or on punched cards. The translator (depending on the mode of operation) either automatically arranges the coding of the external block at the corresponding external memory or else issues a subsidiary program relating to the recording the external blocks from punched cards to external memory, prior to carrying out the object program. For drum and punched-card blocks, only the form of memory is indicated but for tapes, the number of the tape (marked beforehand) is also given and the zone into which the block must be placed. When it is necessary to enter the external block while running the object program, a call to an administrative system is carried out, reserving a position for the block in memory, following which the instructions for carrying out the exchange, previously inserted in the object program by the ALPHA-translator, introduce the external block to the position reserved for it. Leaving the block, the occupied part of memory becomes free.

2.3.2   Operational means for carrying out exchange are standard procedures which are not declared and the statements which are formulated in the form of calls to standard IS-2 library programs with the numbers 0175 (for exchange with a tape), 0176 (for input–output) and 0177 (for exchange with a drum).

The structure of these calls approaches that of machine code for carrying out an exchange and has, therefore, a somewhat artificial appearance:

SP 0175 ($\langle$CN$\rangle$, A [init], A [final], $\langle$number of tape$\rangle$, $\langle$number of zone$\rangle$)
SP 0176 ($\langle$CN'$\rangle$, A [init], A [final], 0, 0)
SP 0177 ($\langle$CN'$\rangle$, A [init], A [final], 0, B [init])

where CN is a conditional number, indicating the exchange mode and the nature of the processing carried out on the information during input–output;

A [init] and A [final] denote the initial and final component of the portion of the array A in the memory, participating in the exchange.

It is assumed that the exchange is carried out on all components of the array A, starting from A [init] and finishing with A [final], issuing from the lexico-graphical arrangement of the components of the array. In doing so it is assumed in addition that all these components are contiguous in memory.

B [init] is the first component of the drum array B, with which the exchange is started.

To simplify the input procedure from punched cards (for complex, real and integral numbers with a conversion of the type $10 \rightarrow 2$, for logical ones without conversion) and output in digital print (with analogous conversion) simpler exchange statements are employed:

input ($\langle$list of identifiers$\rangle$)
output ($\langle$list of identifiers$\rangle$)

In the lists the identifiers may be referred to both as simple variables and as arrays. In the initial blocks of the ALPHA-translator these calls are replaced by standard ones.

2.4   Representation of Variables in the Computer

Real numbers are depicted by the usual normalized machine numbers. Complex numbers occupy two neighbouring cells: the first for the real part and the second for the imaginary part. Integers are shown in units of the second address, negative integers in a supplementary code. The difference in the representation of integral and real numbers is based on the point of view that integers are used most widely in index arithmetic, for which this form of representation is most convenient, in view of the special characteristics of the instruction code. It should, however, be realized that the difference between integral and real arithmetic, which requires clearly defined programming of the transfer functions gave rise to difficulties which have been alluded to in Chapter I.

Logical scalar quantities are represented by the constituent on the extreme left in the order of the machine word (1—**truth**, 0—**false**). Logical arrays are packed into the machine words in double rows from left to right in the order of lexicographic increase of the values of the subscripts.

2.5 *Machine Instructions in the* ALPHA-*Program*

Machine instructions have the following form:

Θ	$A1$	$A2$	$A3$

where Θ is the nine bits.

$A1$, $A2$ and $A3$ are the twelve-bit first, second and third addresses respectively.

When including the machine instructions in the ALPHA-program, the operation code is written in the octal system and the address either in the octal system or else is symbolized by scalar variables (including subscripts) or labels. The instruction itself is placed at the required position in the ALPHA-program, in the form of a statement of an undeclared procedure CODE:

$$\text{CODE}\,(\Theta, A1, A2, A3)$$

Fulfilment of this statement signifies carrying out the instruction in question.

If all three addresses of the instruction are numerical ones, it is treated as an actual machine constant. In this case the corresponding procedure statement CODE must be labelled by a label playing the role of the address of the constant. During the translation the machine constants are taken from the ALPHA-program and placed together with the remaining constants of the program. In the ALPHA-program, machine constants must precede instructions mentioned by them.

When using machine instructions in the ALPHA-program, limitations are imposed which are aimed at making these randomly introduced instructions conform to the general laws obeyed by machine instructions produced in connection with the translation of standard statements of Input language. Observance of these laws makes it possible to analyse the topological and informational structure of a program and also to maintain control over the change of the index-register. Practice has shown that these limitations are comparatively easily overcome if full use is made of the admissibility of arbitrary alternation between machine instructions and standard statements when loading the ALPHA-program.

In the opinion of the authors, the basic object of machine instructions in the ALPHA-program is the implementation of non-standard operations such as "unpacking" and "packing" of numbers in some cell, operations on parts of machine words and other local transformations of information not expressed by the means of Input language.

When working out the method for including machine instructions in the ALPHA-program we made use of the ideas put forward in paper.[6]

2.6 Incorporation of Programs in a Complex

In designing the ALPHA-translator it was assumed that the basic mechanism for compiling a complex of programs alternating with one another when working out the solution of a program would be that of external blocks. In practice it was, however, found that this mechanism must be supplemented by a means for incorporating independently translated programs.

The mechanism for incorporating object programs makes use of one special characteristic of the ALPHA-language, namely that although the memory allocation is completely "in the hands of" the ALPHA-translator, there exists a *signal cell* with the address 7776_8, which the programmer can connect with a simple scalar variable x in the ALPHA-program should he so desire. For this purpose the type declaration of x must first be made in the ALPHA-program (more exactly, x must be last in the list of identifiers of the first type declaration). The signal cell was introduced to create an address known beforehand, from the content of which a statement could be traced from the console of the machine while solution of a problem is in progress.

Let it be required to incorporate in a single complex the independently translated programs $P_1, P_2, \ldots P_n$.

They may be combined provided the programs completely interchange with one another in memory during their operation. This signifies that memory is only charged with one program at any given moment and that the information link between the programs is only realized via a drum or tape. It is moreover necessary that some integral variable is declared in each block, which is fixed in the signal cell, its conversion being arranged in such a way that on completion of some program P_i, the number j of the program P_j which is required to start work after completion of P_i, is located in the signal cell. Finally, programs which are not terminators for the whole process must finish their operation by leaving the outer closing end whilst the concluding program should complete its work by passing on instructions to the stop operator which is clearly indicated in the program.

During translation, the final block of the ALPHA-translator issues information relating to the address of the first instruction for the object program, the length of the program and the address of the stop instruction, appearing at the position of the outer closing end program, the so-called *last stop*.

To incorporate the programs $P_1, \ldots P_n$ in a complex, external memory of the machine must be allocated so as to preserve these programs. Information relating to the allocation of memory is combined with the above-mentioned information, and (with indication as to which program will operate first) is introduced into the machine as initial information for a special program, the *linkage editor*.† On the basis of this information, the linkage editor arranges on the drum a small *control program*, the basic part of which is a table of exchange instructions initiating programs $P_1, \ldots P_n$ at the required position of memory. In addition, the linkage-editor produces and issues cards for

† Translators note: the Russian says, literally, complexator.

2

introducing the programs $P_1, \ldots P_n$ from punched cards and from their loading at the indicated position of external memory.

To initiate the working of the complex, the incorporated programs must be introduced into the machine by means of the cards obtained. Following this, the initial call to the control program which belongs to memory, carried out first in the program, is implemented, as a result of which the so-called *super-control program* is introduced into the reserve cells of the IS-2 (from 7770 to 7777) and control is transferred to this.

The super-control program has two entries. At the first entry instructions are passed after introduction of the next program of the complex, prior to the starting of its work, whilst at the second entry this is done after completion of the work of the next program. Transfer to the first entry is carried out from the control program. When working via the first entry the survey-control changes the final stop of the introduced program to transmission of instructions to the second entry of the super-control following which it passes instructions to the first instruction of the introduced program.

When operating via the second entry point (when the next program has been completed) the super-control brings into operation the control program and passes instructions to it. The control program in accordance with the contents of the signal cell introduces the following program from the complex and again passes instructions to the first access point of the super control.

2.7 *Arrangement of the Operating Panel*

The arrangement of the operating panel also forms a constituent part of ALPHA-language. This is carried out prior to loading the ALPHA-translator and indicates the mode of the operation of the translator. The most important part is the tumbler, the position of which determines whether the object program after completion of the translation is run immediately without putting it on punched cards or whether the translator completes the work by punching out the object program.

The remaining processes of the ALPHA-translator are bound up with artificial "forcing through" of the program to be translated when the required program cannot be obtained by the standard operation mode.

These processes are as follows:

(a) Inclusion of a method of double calculation when carrying out the translation. This method is realized by including any desired combination of 24 tumblers (included in the number of blocks of the ALPHA-translator). Blocks, whose tumblers are included are considered to be supporting blocks. Translation between all pairs of neighbouring supporting blocks is carried out twice with preservation of the whole preceding state of the object program on a supplementary tape.

(b) Compulsory inclusion or, conversely, compulsory exclusion of blocks, carried out on the global economy of memory.

(c) Inclusion of simplifying cleaning up of *FOR*-statements, this being carried out only on internal *FOR*-statements and on two *FOR*-statements enveloping them.

(d) Artificial increase of the IS-2 working field in order to preserve arising library programs at maximum dimensions (the translator has some internal strategy for selection between maximum and minimum dimensions of the working field which cannot always be determined by the programmer).

In conclusion the authors wish to express their appreciation to G. Liman, L. V. Maiorov, M. V. Stepanova, and L. I. Fryazinova, whose experiments on using the ALPHA-translator stimulated the development of the linkage editor.

REFERENCES

1. YERSHOV, A. P., KOZHUKHIN, G. I. and VOLOSHIN, Yu. M. (1964). Source language for a System of Automatic Programming, Novosibirsk, 1964. No. 3 APIC Series in Data Processing.
2. POTTOSIN, I. V. (Ed.) (1967). Guide for using the ALPHA-system of automatic programming. Novosibirsk.
3. BACKUS, J. W. et al. (1962). Revised report on the algorithmic language ALGOL 60. International Federation for Information Processing.
4. KOZHUKHIN, G. I. (1961). Exchange operations with external means in Source language. Otchet instituta matem., Siberian Branch of the Academy of Sciences of the U.S.S.R., Novosibirsk.
5. SHURA-BURA, M. R. (1961). The IS-2 system of interpretation. In "Library of standard programmes," Ts.B.T.I., Moscow.
6. FABIAN, V. and HAJEK, O. (1962). Specific representation of ALGOL 60 and algorithms of translation for MSP computers. No. 209, Výzkumný ústav matematických strojů (Computer Research Institute), Prague.

III ORGANIZATION OF THE ALPHA-TRANSLATOR

A. P. YERSHOV

1 General Structure

1.1 Requirements and Possibilities

Difficulties involved in making decisions regarding the organization of the ALPHA-translator are typical of those encountered in developing any complex system: the conflict which always exists between the actual characteristics of the system and the resources available for its implementation must be overcome.

In the case of the ALPHA-translator the project required a high standard of programming, closely approaching the quality of large-scale production attained by a skilled programmer whilst maintaining an acceptable translation speed (at least 100 instructions of the object program per minute of execution time of the translator.) The complexity of the ALPHA-language and the limitations of the computer also had to be taken into consideration: the low capacity of core memory (4,096 words), the comparatively low capacity and unreliability of the magnetic drums (12,288 words) and the relatively low speed of the magnetic tape (about 3,000 words per second). The only favourable factor was the high speed of the computer when carrying out logical operations in core memory—40,000 three-address operations per second.

From a logical point of view, the programming process is translation from a higher level language (ALPHA-language) to a lower level language (the machine language). The concept of language level cannot be accurately defined but it does comprise some properties of the language which characterize the degree of its complexity: an abundance of syntactical constructions, the degree of divergence of information formats, the size and number of types of statement, etc. It is of fundamental importance that in translation from a higher level language to a lower one some information, contained in the higher level program, is lost. In fact, even with a thorough knowledge of the algorithms of translation, it is usually impossible in principle to recall the original ALPHA-program from the object program.

The basis of the programming process consists of direct universal algorithms of translation, which yield some syntax unit of a higher level in the form of a set of lower level language statements. However, the universal algorithms determined for the general case do not take into account the true statistics of the application of higher level syntax constructions and in the majority of cases produce superfluous constructions in the lower level program which lower its quality. In ALGOL 60, which constitutes the bulk of ALPHA-language, this will in the first instance affect procedures and *FOR*-statements.

One method of raising the quality of translation is to develop programming algorithms which take into account the special features of the program to be translated. For this the universal translation algorithm is supplemented by a series of the simpler programming "strategies", destined for more specific circumstances, but on the other hand producing more compact constructions in the object program. The "strategy" is chosen on the basis of an analysis made earlier to establish the practical complexity of using higher level syntactical constructions in the program.

Another way of improving the programming quality is the implementation of optimizing transformations of the program to be translated, i.e. transformations which preserve the language level in which the program is written, but improve those of its characteristics which are bound up with memory capacity or with the time required for it to be carried out.

An analysis of ALPHA-language shows that it is not at all suited for the implementation of formal optimizing transformations because of the variability of the format of the identifiers and variables, the recursive structure of expressions and statements, the contextual significance of many symbols and the abundance of algorithmic operations which are implied but not clearly specified. However, the lower level language (the machine language) which has the necessary simplicity of syntax and semantics, consists of excessively small operational units and—this is the main point—no longer contains that part of its information about the program which was lost in the translation but which would be useful for a greater efficiency of optimizing transformations.

1.2 Multiphase Translation

In connection with what has been stated above, the introduction of the intermediate language at the level of which those optimizing transformations could be implemented, which are not feasible at the lower level, naturally comes into consideration when planning the ALPHA-translator. This language, which in the ALPHA-translator is referred to as *internal language*, is also a barrier separating the algorithms of translation which are orientated towards the ALPHA-language and are independent of the working computer, from those algorithms of translation which relate to the machine language and are to a significant degree dependent on the specific features of the working computer.

Consequently, the work of the ALPHA-translator acquires the character of a multiphase process.

The process of translation from the ALPHA-language into the internal language has been called the *translation phase* whilst translation from the internal language to the machine language is known as the *coding phase*. This splitting up of the translation process serves not only as a means of improving the programming quality but also provides the chief opportunity of subdividing the program of the ALPHA-translator into consecutively operating blocks, each sufficiently small to fit into memory together with the necessary operating instructions.

As a result of an analysis of the correlation between memory capacity and speed of the computer and their comparison with the size of the ALPHA-translator and the admissible size of the programs to be translated, the following decisions were taken.

All 24 blocks of the ALPHA-translator with lengths of 500 to 3,000 words are stored on separate sections of the magnetic tape, which operate in the absence of an instruction indicating the necessity for double calculation when translating in a system involving only reading in and one-way pass. All the information about the program to be translated is divided into two types. The first type includes the proper program, or more accurately, its operational part. All other information relating to the program, kept in the form of separate tables, belongs to the second type. To some extent, the tables correspond to the descriptive part of the ALPHA-program. The whole program is stored on the drum and is read in memory piece by piece for processing. The tables needed for the operation of the next block are stored in memory and the remainder on the drum.

TABLE 1. Flow chart of the ALPHA-translator

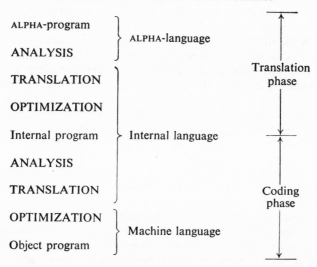

The algorithms of translation are organized in such a way that each block carries out a strictly sequential and single-stage recording and reading of the program and also enters the required information in the tables strictly by address. This procedure reduces the number the drum transactions and the address structure of memory is fully utilized.

2 The Internal Language

2.1 Requirements

The choice of internal language determines to a large extent the character of the whole translator and its structure and content will therefore be described in considerable detail.

Bearing in mind the goals of internal language, it must, in the author's opinion, satisfy the following requirements:

(1) algorithmic operations which are not explicit or which are implied must be absent;
(2) basic symbols, identifiers and variables must have a fixed form;
(3) the structure of the statements; must be free from recursiveness;
(4) it must be capable of preserving information derived from the ALPHA-program;
(5) it should be suitable for implementing optimizing transformations and the subsequent translation into machine language.†

In internal language, information about the program to be translated is divided into the program itself and the tables. The program consists of a succession of basic symbols.

2.2 The Basic Symbols

The basic symbols of internal language are in the form of a fifteen-bit binary code and are divided into identifiers, symbols and numbers.

The special feature of the *identifiers* is that the translator stores certain information for them, which is kept in tables. This information is put into the tables or extracted from them when reading the identifiers in the program. In connection with this, a tag-and-address of the identifiers is adopted in internal language, in which three or four bits of the code (*the tag part*) are set by tags which distinguishes an identifier of a given type from the other basic symbols, whilst twelve or eleven bits (the identifying part) contain the number of the identifier, which also indicates the index number of the line in the table containing the information about the given identifier.

All the information relating to the *tokens* is contained within these. The *number* also represents itself.

The identifiers are divided into those for *constants, labels, working variables, scalars* and *subscripted variables*.

Tokens are divided into operator signs and delimiters.

Operator signs in turn are divided into signs for *commutative operations, two-address operations, one-address operations, conditional branches, unconditional branches, branches with return, returns, stops, calls to standard sub-routines, calls to the administrative system and loops.*

The delimiters are divided into pairs of brackets ⟨ ⟩; *for statements* { }, *switches* ⌜ ⌝, *external blocks* B ᴎ, *subscripts* [ ], *the symbol showing the end of the call to the standard sub-routine* ▽, *the terminal symbol* * and the ALGOL 60 basic symbols "**Step**", "**To**" and "**While**".

2.3 Syntax

The syntax of the internal language is given by the following metalinguistical formulae:

⟨program⟩ := ⟨zero label⟩ ⟨line of statements⟩ *
⟨line of statements⟩ ::= ⟨statement⟩ | ⟨line of statements⟩ ⟨statement⟩

---

† It should be noted that these requirements on their own are not very clear and the reader must therefore not take them literally. They may however serve as a guide for analysing descriptions of the internal language.

⟨statement⟩ ::= ⟨unlabelled statement⟩ | ⟨label⟩ ⟨statement⟩

⟨unlabelled statement⟩ ::= ⟨assignment statement⟩ ⟨logical statement⟩ ⟨statement for call to SR⟩ | ⟨statement for call to AS⟩ | ⟨loop⟩ | ⟨external block⟩

⟨external block⟩ ::= B⟨label indicating form of external memory⟩ ⟨line of statements⟩ ꓱ

⟨loop⟩ ::= ⟨loop sign⟩ ⟨loop heading⟩ {⟨line of statements⟩}

⟨statement for call to AS⟩ ::= ⟨sign for call to administrative system⟩

⟨statement for call to SR⟩ ::= ⟨sign for call to standard sub-routine⟩ ⟨number of sub-routine⟩ ⟨list of parameters⟩ ▽

⟨list of parameters⟩ ::= ⟨blank⟩ | ⟨list of parameters⟩ ⟨label⟩ | ⟨list of parameters⟩ ⟨variable⟩

⟨logical statement⟩ ::= ⟨conditional branch⟩ | ⟨unconditional branch⟩ | ⟨switch⟩ | ⟨branch with return⟩ | ⟨return⟩ | ⟨stop⟩

⟨stop⟩ ::= ⟨stop sign⟩

⟨return⟩ ::= ⟨return label⟩ ⟨return sign⟩ ⟨return number⟩

⟨branch with return⟩ ::= ⟨sign of branch with return⟩ ⟨label showing point of return⟩ ⟨branch label⟩ ⟨return label⟩

⟨switch⟩ ::= ⟨switch label⟩ ▽ ⟨switch scalar⟩ ⟨list of labels⟩ ⌐

⟨list of labels⟩ ::= ⟨label⟩ | ⟨list of labels⟩ ⟨label⟩

⟨unconditional branch⟩ ::= ⟨sign of unconditional branch⟩ ⟨branch label⟩

⟨conditional branch⟩ ::= ⟨branch by tag⟩ | ⟨comparison branch⟩

⟨branch by tag⟩ ::= ⟨sign of conditional branch by tag⟩ ⟨Boolean variable⟩ ⟨label of branch when the Boolean variable is true⟩

⟨branch by comparison⟩ ::= ⟨sign of conditional branch by comparison⟩ ⟨sign of the relation⟩ ⟨first variable to be compared⟩ ⟨second variable to be compared⟩ ⟨label of branch when the relation is true⟩

⟨assignment statement⟩ := ⟨commutative operation⟩ ⟨binary operation⟩ | ⟨unary operation⟩

⟨unary operation⟩ ::= ⟨sign of unary operation⟩ ⟨argument variable⟩ ⟨result variable⟩

⟨binary operation⟩ ::= ⟨sign of binary operation⟩

⟨binary operation⟩ ::= ⟨sign of binary operation⟩ ⟨argument variable⟩ ⟨argument variable⟩ ⟨result variable⟩

⟨commutative operation⟩ ::= ⟨sign of commutative operation⟩ ⟨list of variables⟩ ⟨result variable⟩

⟨list of variables⟩ ::= ⟨variable⟩ | ⟨list of variables⟩ ⟨variable⟩

⟨variable⟩ ::= ⟨constant⟩ | ⟨working variable⟩ | ⟨scalar⟩ | ⟨subscripted variable⟩

⟨constant⟩ ::= ⟨identifier of constant⟩

⟨working variable⟩ ::= ⟨identifier of working variable⟩

⟨scalar⟩ ::= ⟨identifier of scalar⟩

⟨label⟩ ::= ⟨identifier of label⟩

⟨subscripted variable⟩ ::= ⟨identifier of subscripted variable⟩ [⟨subscript⟩]

⟨subscript⟩ ::= ⟨dependence on control variables⟩ ⟨variable component⟩ ⟨constant component⟩

⟨constant component⟩ ::= ⟨constant⟩

⟨variable component⟩ ::= ⟨Zerov constant⟩ | ⟨scalar⟩ ⟨working variable⟩

2*

⟨dependence on loop parameters⟩ ::= ⟨empty⟩ | ⟨dependence on loop para-
meters⟩ ⟨loop parameter⟩ ⟨step⟩
⟨loop parameter⟩ ::= ⟨scalar⟩
⟨step⟩ ::= ⟨constant⟩ | ⟨scalar⟩

For the sake of brevity, metalinguistical formulae for trivial definitions of
the type

⟨result variable⟩ ::= ⟨variable⟩

are omitted from this syntactical description.

The syntax of the loop headings practically coincides with the ALGOL
syntax of corresponding for clauses, substituting ⟨lines of the statements⟩ by
⟨expressions⟩, calculating these expressions only if the latter are not simple
variables.†

2.4 Semantics

The selection of content designations for the metalinguistic variables obviates
the need for explaining the semantics of most of the formulae. Remarks will
therefore be confined to individual constructions.

2.4.1 The separation of intermediate results, which occur when translating
expressions into a special class of working variables serves as an example of
the preservation of information about the higher level program, enabling a
more efficient economy of expressions and of memory to be achieved. This is
also the reason for classifying labels in internal language into internal and
external ones. *Internal labels* are used for transfer of controls which arise when
coding conditional expressions and componentwise operations on multi-
dimensional arrays. The branching and loops which emerge from this (the
so-called *internal loops*) have a simplified structure, as compared with the
general case and bearing this in mind, the economy of expression and of
memory can be improved. All labels which are not internal ones are *external*
ones.

2.4.2 The structure of the index variables is entirely adapted to the programming of loops. The linear dependence of the address of the index variable on the
loop parameters is treated as a special case. This makes it possible to use the
index register and the re-address system for calculating the address. In more
precise terms, if the initial address of the array m is denoted by the symbol
m_0, the variable and constant components by v and c respectively and the
loop parameters and steps which constitute the dependence on the loop
parameters by $i_1 h_1, \ldots i_n h_n$, the address A of the index variable $m[i_1 h_1 \ldots i_n h_n vc]$
is calculated from the formula

$$A = \sum_{k=1}^{n} i_k h_k + v + c + m_0$$

This representation of the index expression is called the *canonical form
of the index*. The presence of a variable component v which is not equal to

† Terms "loop", "loop heading", and "loop parameter" correspond to those of "for
statement", "for clause", and "control variable" and are introduced for better distinction
of internal language constructions from those of ALGOL 60.

zero indicates that the address A is calculated not only from the above formula but also by formation, that is to say the value of the whole variable v, calculated independently, is added to A by means of a special *statement of formation*. The statement of formation is formulated syntactically in internal language, in the form of a one-address operation σuv, where σ is the operator symbol, u is the argument and v is the function. When it is implemented, the value of the variable u is added to the address of the subscripted variable of which the variable component is v.

2.4.3   With respect to the initial address m_0 the subscripted index variables are divided into two types: arrays and blanks by means of a special sign and these in turn are divided into *dynamic arrays and formal parameters*.

The *arrays* correspond to the statistical arrays of ALGOL. For them, m_0 is determined during translation and is put into the object program beforehand, For the *blanks*, m_0 is included in the variable component v and, having been calculated during the running of the object program, it is inserted into the address of the reserved area by the statement of formation σuv.

For the dynamic arrays, u is calculated by means of the call statements to the administrative system. The blanks (formal parameters) originate from formal parameters, which can be replaced by name.

For blanks of the last kind, u is calculated with the help of special statements *storing the identifier*, syntactically also in the form of a unary operation ΨIu, where Ψ is the statement symbol, I is the argument and u is the result. When it is carried out, the address of the variable I (if I is an array the initial address is taken) is assigned to the variable u. The statements storing the identifier emerge as a result of the programming of the procedure statements and transmit to the formal parameter—"blank"—the name of the identifier which is to be put in its place (the *filler*).

2.4.4   As can be seen from the syntax, the structure of the *FOR*-statement clause is preserved in full in the loop headings of the internal language. This is also an instance of the preservation of information about the ALPHA-program in the internal language. The programming of loop headings directly in terms of the machine instructions, taking into account the information contained in the statement signs, makes it possible to bring about a substantial improvement in the quality of the *FOR*-statement programming. The information contained in the statement signs is gathered while analysing the loop headings and loop bodies and consists of binary tags which characterize the special features of the loops:

(1) presence or absence of a loop parameter;
(2) presence or absence of an exit from the loop via the **go to**-statement;
(3) presence of an assignment to the parameter other than the loop heading;
(4) whether the type of parameter is real or integral;
(5) possibility of computing the subscripts by the re-address system;
(6) whether the loop is general or internal;
(7) whether there is utilization of a parameter in the loop in addition to that entering into the subscript expressions.

2.4.5   The assignment statements occur when translating ALPHA-language expressions. Unary operations include the transfer of a number, the transformation of a type, the calculation of an absolute variable, trigonometric functions, negation and so on—31 operations in all. Binary operations include twelve noncommutative two-argument operations: shift, power, arithmetical relations and so on. The commutative operations include addition and multiplication of integers, addition and multiplication of real numbers, disjunction, conjunction and addition by mod. 2.

The special feature of the commutative operations, also called *multi-instructions*, is that they have an arbitrary number of arguments (from 2 to 8). The number of arguments is shown on a binary scale, placed in the statement sign. In addition, for the first four commutative operations it is shown in the scale whether the argument is taken with the sign of a direct operation (addition, multiplication) or of a inverse operation (subtraction or division). The arbitrary number of arguments is explained by the fact that one multi-instruction incorporates all the commutative operations of one precedence level which were contained in the initial expression in the ALPHA-language. Thus the statement

$$r := x \uparrow y - a \times \sin(b) \mid (a-b) + r - K$$

will assume the following form in the internal language:

$\uparrow$	x	y	t_1		
$\sin$	b	t_2			
$+\,01$	a	b	t_3		
$\times\,001$	a	t_2	t_3	t_4	
$+\,0101$	t_1	t_4	r	K	r

The scale of the arguments of the multi-instruction is written in the form of an index to the statement sign. The use of the multi-instructions is another example of the preservation of information about the ALPHA-program. It offers certain advantages for cleaning up the loops, processing the subscripts and in the economy of expressions.

2.4.6   The switches in the internal language fit the declarations in ALPHA-language. During branch by the switch (**go to** $S[i]$) the value of the subscript i is transferred to the switch scalar and the branch then takes place via the switch label S. The subsequent choice of the branch label—from a list of labels included in the switch brackets—is made according to the value of the switch scalar.

2.4.7   The sections of the program which have to be placed into external memory in the object program, are enclosed by the brackets of the external block. Information about the nature of external memory when converting into internal language is transferred from the declarations into the basic symbol which stands to the right of the opening bracket of the external block and is syntactically in the form of a label.

2.4.8   Tables in the internal language are divided into tables of constants, arrays, blanks and returns.

The table of constants contains the values of the scalar variables introduced by the translator to denote the constants. The constants which are the initial values of the components of the arrays (the so-called *constant arrays*) are marked in the table by means of a special scale. *The table of arrays* contains the lengths of the static arrays and references to the position in the table of the constants of the initial component of the constant arrays. *The table of blanks* shows the names of the variables which take the place of the individual reserved areas—a list of fillers of the formal parameter is given. The *table of returns* contains for each return a list of all the labels to which it is possible to revert via a given return. ·

2.5   Intermediate Language

It should be pointed out that the internal language alters progressively during the translation phase. Considered from a formal point of view it should be borne in mind that almost each of the first fourteen blocks of the ALPHA-translator has its own language in which the program to be translated is written and only the language of block 14 coincides with the above described internal language. For the blocks which carry out chiefly the optimizing transformations (8–13) this difference between the languages does not warrant a special discussion, but certain essential differences between the language which has been described here and the internal language at the level of the first seven blocks should be pointed out. These differences lie in the coding of the basic symbols rather than in the syntax of the statements.

A comparison of ALPHA-language with internal language shows that one of the characteristics of the ALPHA-language is that the significance of operations and identifiers can only be understood from the context. The meaning of an identifier is established from the declaration whilst the meaning of the operation is determined by analysing its operands (for example, the sign x in ALPHA-language can be interpreted in more than 30 different ways.) In the case of the internal language, each operator sign and to some extent each identifier carries all the information necessary for it to be understood clearly and for its subsequent implementation in the machine instructions. Thus translating into the internal language involves a transfer of information from declarations to variables and from variables into operational symbols. In order to store the transferred information, the tag part of the identifiers and of the basic symbols at the level of the first seven blocks of the translator is enlarged and comprises 10–11 digits instead of three to four out of the total length of the basic symbol in 22 digits.

In order to distinguish 15-digit coding from 22-digit coding, the last one at the level of block 7 is called the *intermediate language*. Re-coding of the intermediate language into the internal language is carried out by block 8 of the ALPHA-translator. From among the remaining differences between intermediate language and internal language we need only mention the representation of the subscripts and of the statements of formation. In the subscripts a canonical form is replaced by a whole chain of instructions for calculating the subscript expression. The operators of formation are less detailed and have the syntactical form (αM). They denote the following operation: to add the value of the variable α to all the occurrences of the address of the array M in the program, located to the right of the given statement, either to the end of the program or to the next X with the same M.

3 The Structure of the Blocks

3.1 Transit and Local Arrays: Communications

When planning the ALPHA-translator, special attention was paid to securing a uniform structure of the translator blocks and to establishing the weakest link between them. This meant that the transfer of information between the blocks could be regulated and that they could be implemented simultaneously.

The blocks are not provided with a control program and each block therefore itself introduces the next one on completion of its operation. For this purpose the program of all the blocks start from the cell 0001. The first two cells contain instructions for reading the following block from the tape. The first instruction for each block to be executed, is located in cell 0003. On completion of the work of the next block, transfer is made to 0001. The instructions in cell 0001 and 0002 read the next block in memory which immediately starts to be run from the instruction in cell 0003.

All the fundamental information about the program to be translated is transferred from block to block in so-called *transit arrays*. The number of transit arrays was kept as small as possible. The basic transit arrays are the following:

program (*master*);
table of constants with the scale;
table of arrays;
table of returns;
table of blanks;
common list.

In addition, at each phase of translation there appears a series of transit arrays specifically for these phases. However, not more than ten transit arrays are transmitted from one block to another at one time. The purpose of the common list will be explained below. Apart from the transit arrays, each block arranges *local arrays* in memory, i.e. arrays which are used within one block only.

The ALPHA-translator blocks are designed in such a way as to exclude implicit assumptions about the actual location of the transit arrays in memory. All information about the location of the program to be translated in the machine is clearly shown in the special *communicators* which occupy the last 64 cells of memory. The communicators are divided into three categories: *locators, counters* and *memorials*. The co-ordinates of the transit arrays are stored in the locators, the number of identifiers of one kind or another used at a given moment are stored in the counters. There is also a special counter which indicates the number of the next block to operate. The result of this cell, shown up on the console, makes it possible to follow the operation of the translator. The memorials store various transit information giving the mode of operation of some or other of the blocks (for example, whether the program includes procedures, whether an administrative system is necessary, and so on) or which makes possible a more careful allocation of memory.

As has been mentioned, the machine can carry out logical operations on memory comparatively quickly. To utilize this property in the translator, memory must be utilized to the full.

For this purpose the ALPHA-translator was equipped with semidynamic allocation of memory. This involves the following. If a certain block A needs to reconstruct or refill a certain array M then the block preceding A—on analysing the program to be translated—estimates beforehand, exactly or approximately, the length of the array and transmits this to the block A in a certain memorial cell. This information will allow block A to allocate a memory precisely prior to beginning its operation.

3.2 Common List

Such an *a priori* determination of the length of the new arrays is not always possible however, and the translator must deal with arrays, the exact length of which becomes known only after they have been filled. In such cases there must inevitably be a margin left in memory "for growth". The situation is complicated by the fact that there may be several indefinitely growing arrays. For storing such arrays in memory in the ALPHA-translator a common list is used. The list structure of this common list is described below by means of a hypothetical example.

Let it be required to extract from the program information of n types I_1, I_2, ... I_n. This information will be stored cell for cell in some array G. The address of the next free cell in the array G is stored in the counter r. We shall relate entrance cells i_1, ... i_n, to the informations I_1, ... I_n, in which references to the start of the information of a given type in the array G will be stored.

Let it be assumed that processing of the program provides a portion of the information I_k. If $i_k = 0$, information of the type I_k was encountered first. In this case, r is directed to i_k, and a portion of the information transmitted in G followed by an appropriate modification in r. To be specific, it will be assumed that the portions of information are divided into quanta of, say, fifteen bits each so that one cell contains three such quanta. If the portion of information contains a number of quanta which is not a multiple of three, the last cell in the array G to contain a portion will not be completely full; if the portion contains 3 million quanta another empty cell will be forcibly reserved behind the portion.

We shall now discuss the case in which $i_k \neq 0$. This signifies that G already contains some information of the type I_k. From the contents of i_k we find a reference to the start of the information I_k in G, which is scanned to the end of the first portion. If this portion concludes with a partially filled or completely empty cell the value of r will be put into the vacant position as *a continuation reference* and a portion of the information will be stored in G beginning from the position indicated by r. If the portion ends with an earlier placed continuation reference, the search for the end of the information is continued in accordance with this reference. The reference is regarded as being syntactically distinguishable from the information quanta. Table 2 shows the result of applying such a procedure for a simple example.

TABLE 2. Use of the general register

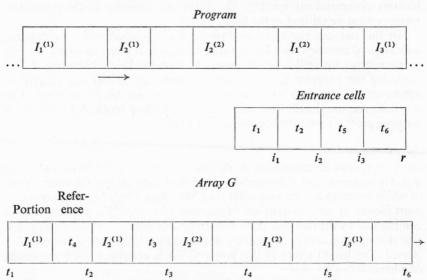

Program

Entrance cells

Array G

Thus, although the information is stored in G in separate portions, in the order in which it appears in the program, the reference system makes it possible to collect all the information of one type in one place. In the ALPHA-translator, the common list which has already been mentioned serves as the array G, one for all purposes. When operating the translator, the common list is examined from time to time and information contained in it is either discarded as useless or suitably rearranged.

An additional method for achieving economy of memory is to record on a drum at the end of the operation of the block, all transit arrays not required for the next block (the master array is always put on to the drum).

3.3   Structure of the Blocks

Each block of the translator consists usually of three parts: the forming section, the main section and the concluding section. The forming section allocates memory to local and transit arrays. Local arrays have a fixed or pre-calculated length. If necessary, a portion of memory can be reserved for expanding the common list. The remainder of the memory (sometimes a very small part) is diverted towards the *exchange array*, intended as a link with the master array (the program) (Fig. 1).

After allocation of memory the formation section adjusts the block for just made memory allocation. As a rule the area occupied by the formation program, which is usually at the end of the block, is also assigned to the

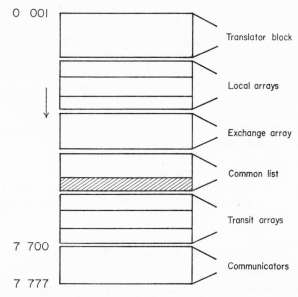

Fig. 1. A typical allocation of memory

operation of the main part. The common list is filled upward. Sometimes an upper part of memory reserved for the common list is allocated for an array for which a list structure cannot be devised.

On completion of the operation of the main section of the block the concluding section records on the drum transit arrays not needed, cleans up the common list if necessary and calls the next block.

3.4   Exchange Array

Finally, we shall discuss a few special features of the use of exchange arrays (Fig. 2). The main array is stored on the drum which can be logically treated

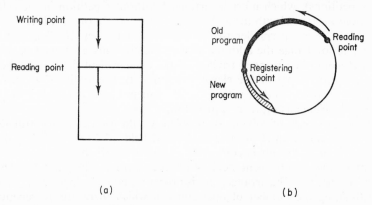

Fig. 2. Arrangement of exchange array. a = exchange array; b = master array

as loop memory. The old program is read sequentially from the drum into the bottom part of the substitute array in portions which are as large as possible (starting from the reading point). Almost all the translation blocks operate on the principle of "reading—processing—writing".

The reprocessed program is written into the top part of the substituted array, starting from the recording point. The result of this is that during operation, the recording point overtakes the reading point which is escaping it. As soon as the recording point overtakes the reading point or the reading point reaches the end of the exchange array, a section of the new program is written into the main array, starting from the end of the old program. Thus, in the main array, the reading point also overtakes the recording point. The initial interval between the recording and reading points in the exchange array is selected specifically for each block depending upon the degree to which the information in the program to be translated when operating the block, has been expanded or condensed.

4 Various Details

4.1 Hash Addressing

As has been mentioned, the translation work is organized so as to ensure linearity of scanning and local reprocessing of the program to be translated. Most of the algorithms of translation are of a local type, although in some algorithms of recoding and optimization some inventiveness had to be displayed to obtain linear scan and local reprocessing. In that case when such algorithms have resulted in a problem of identification of various elements in a certain set, the so-called method of hash addressing was applied.

The problem of identifying various elements in a set is posed in the following way. Assume that a set of elements M be given.

We shall consider the binary codes as elements of this set. The length of these codes may vary, but for the sake of simplicity we shall assume that each code is located in one memory cell.

Finally let $A = \{a_1, \ldots a_k\}$ be the sequence of the elements from M (possibly with repetitions), which must be arranged without repetition in the cells of the *arrangement field* with the addresses $L + 1, \ldots L + n \, (n \geqslant k)$. It is essential here that n is much smaller than the power of the set M. This makes it impossible to change the address code of the elements contained in M, for which A would be arranged trivially in the arrangement field. It is obvious that the reprocessing of the elements from A is essentially of a non-local character: in order to deal with the next element a_s, it is necessary to know whether the elements $a_1, \ldots a_{s-1}$ include a_s.

The simplest way of solving the problem would seem to be to arrange the elements contained in A in the arrangement field in sequence. When this is done, each new element is compared in turn with all the elements already present in the arrangement field. With this method, the total number of operations used for the arrangement is proportional to k^2 (considering a case for estimating the number of operations in which there are no repetitions in A).

By a suitable improvement of the mechanism of comparing the new element with those present in the arrangement field, a number of operations proportional to $k \cdot 1n(k)$ (cf. e.g. (1)) can be carried out.

It is found that it is possible with this problem to carry out a number of operations proportional to k, by adopting the following procedure. We shall assume that a certain integral *hash function* $f(a)$ is determined for the elements of the set M, such that $L + 1 \leqslant f(a) \leqslant L + n$. Let us further suppose that prior to the commencement of operations, the arrangement field is empty. The process of inserting the next element a_s contained in A is as follows. $f(a_s) = \mu$ is calculated. If the cell having the address μ is empty, this signifies that a_s was first encountered in A, and then directed to the cell having the address μ. If μ is occupied with an element identical with a_s, this means that a_s occurred repeatedly in A and a_s therefore is disregarded. If μ is an occupied element different from a_s, μ is increased by one (if μ equals $L + n$, then instead of adding one, μ is taken as equal to $L + 1$) and the process of comparing a_s with the contents of μ is then repeated. Since $n \geqslant k$, the process of comparison must necessarily be terminated. The validity of the assumptions made when describing the mechanism of comparison can be verified by induction through s. It is readily seen that taking $f(a) \equiv L + 1$, we arrive at the above described method of arranging the elements of A, giving a quadratic surplus.

It is clear that the efficiency of using hash addressing depends on the uniformity of the distribution of the values $f(a)$ over the interval $(L + 1, L + n)$ when calculating the elements $a_1, \ldots a_k$ and on the size of the margin n in relation to k.

Statistical experiments have shown[2] that if it is assumed that the values of $f(a)$ are distributed uniformly over the random sequences $\{a_1 \ldots a_k\}$ it is sufficient to take $n \sim 1 \cdot 5 k$, in order to arrive at not more than two comparisons with the contents of the cells of the arrangement field per element a_s. This gives a total operating time proportional to k. When $n = k$, the operating time is proportional to $k \times 1n(k)$.

By far the simplest method of calculating the hash function $f(a)$ is obviously that in which n is taken as equal to 2^m and $f(a)$ is calculated in the following way: the binary code a is divided into sections having a length of m digits, which are added by mod 2^m. Making some very general assumptions about the statistical independence of the compounded portions, this method is the best one from the probabilistic point of view and gives an almost uniform distribution even with a small number of combined portions.

In the ALPHA-translator hash addressing is used when translating the identifiers of the ALPHA-program, when economizing on coincident expressions and for economizing on constants.

4.2 Modes of Operation of the Translator

One of the applications of the "mixed programming strategy" is the analysis of the program to be translated, for absence of some syntactical units. In this case, the translator blocks responsible for programming these units can be by-passed, which further increases the translation speed. In the ALPHA-translator blocks 6 and 7 (the procedure programming) and the main parts of blocks 9 and 10 (programming of operations on polydimensional arrays) can be dispensed with in this way.

In addition, the translator can omit some optimizing algorithms when there is no need for them or when they cannot be fully implemented because of the overflowing of certain transformation arrays used for implementing the optimizing conversions, for example, the global memory economy [IX] is not carried out if the ALPHA-program does not contain any dynamic arrays and fits the operative memory without the economy, or if the tables which arise in the global economy of memory are too big to be located in the operative memory. In this case the main parts of blocks 21 and 22 are dispensed.

The economy of expressions block (No. 14) artificially shortens the size of the section within which the economy is implemented if this section is too large. The block for cleaning up the loops (No. 12) only operates on the internal loops if the volume of instructions being carried out beyond the limits of the loops exceeds the admissible dimensions.

Mention might be made of various other small details scattered throughout the whole translator and aimed at ensuring that the performance of the translator "fits" the special features—good as well as bad—of the program to be translated, as closely as possible.

4.3 Formal Control of the Program to be Translated

When constructing the ALPHA-translator, special measures were taken so as to prevent infiltration of formal mistakes from the ALPHA-program into the object program. "Formal mistakes" signifies errors in the syntax and semantic errors, the presence of which would cause looping of the translator or would make a reasonable continuation of the program or the running of the object program impossible. The universal and only method of detecting formal errors is evidently to inspect the conditions under which the error arises, followed by a signal in the form of transfer of control to the **stop** instruction (*control stop*). For a more accurate identification of the mixtake a specific control stop was devised for each condition where this was meaningful or possible.

A closure by a control stop of a chain of "HECOBMECTHAIX" logical conditions checking was a typical approach. If we assume for example that an identifier is analysed at a given moment and the given position signifies that it can only serve as an identifier for a scalar, a working cell, a constant or an array. To analyse the situation, a chain of four comparisons was designed which can transfer control to the processing of a variable of a given kind or to the continuance of the analysis. The final comparison—the fourth one— (strictly speaking a superfluous one) directs the operations either to the processing of arrays or to the control stop. These surplus control stops played an invaluable role when debugging the translator and in many cases proved to be of use during the actual operation as a signalling device for machine faults. In fact, the translator, being amply equipped with control stops (about 200 in all), acquired the unusual property of "absolute computing instability". During the programming of the first 500 problems there was only one instance of a syntactical error of the type "**if** $a := 1$ **then** B, **else** C" passing into the object program and there were no more than five instances when machine faults in the process of translation could not be pin pointed by the control stops.

The ALPHA-translator lacks a preliminary syntactical control of the ALPHA-program. However, steps were taken to ensure fullest and earliest possible indication of any formal errors in the whole program. To do this, the first block, which feeds in the ALPHA-program from the punched cards, calculates the balance of the brackets, checks their relative disposition and carries out a partial syntactical control, comparing the ALPHA-program with the so-called *compatability matrix*. The order of this logical matrix $\|m_{ij}\|$ equals the number of basic symbols of the ALPHA-language (each letter and number is considered to constitute a symbol); $m_{ij} = 1$, if the ith basic symbol can syntactically precede the jth symbol, and $m_{ij} = 0$, if this is not the case. When an incompatible pair is discovered in the ALPHA-program, the context of the program which contains this pair (10 symbols to the right and left of the pair) is printed, without the immediate stopping of the translator. In addition, Block 3 of the translator issues a list of all the nondeclared identifiers at the end of its operation.

An analysis of the errors discovered in the first 500 programs translated showed that Blocks 1 and 3 detect 93% of all formal errors. The rest of the formal errors are exposed individually by the translator. Certain types of formal semantic errors, admittedly very few (not more than 2%), are traced by the inside blocks—up to Block 12.

4.4 Quantitative Limitations

This term includes the limitations imposed on the type of program to be translated, caused by the limited capacity of memory. The difficulty lies in the fact that the information is expanded during translation. For example, if the ALPHA-translator compiles a program 3,000 machine words long, the volume of intermediate information might reach 6,000 to 7,000 words. The uncontrolled use of external memory for storing of intermediate information may lead to an unnecessary slowing down of the translation process. Therefore, when designing the ALPHA-translator, a checking device mentioned earlier was incorporated to ensure maximum utilization of operative memory. This approach entails, however, a disadvantage, namely the increase and diversity of limitations on volume. The semi-dynamic distribution of memory does not solve the problem completely, as there exist quite a few small intermediate tables or operating fields; to calculate their dimensions accurately would either be impossible in principle, or it would excessively clutter up the translator. The establishing of dimensions of such tables and operating fields creates various quantitative limitations.

The main problem in formulating the quantitative restrictions lies in balancing them against a reduction of the number of programs which, while passing through the translator from the point of view of their overall characteristics, jam at some narrow part because of failure to plan adequately the dimensions of some operating field. In addition, when analysing quantitive restrictions, it was necessary to distinguish (in order to give them preference in the sense of increasing the volume of memory to be diverted) the kind of situations to which the programmer cannot easily adapt by revising the ALPHA-program.

All this work on the analysis and the balancing of the quantitative restrictions was carried out empirically for the ALPHA-translator, mainly during the trial runs. Out of 500 programs which were translated in succession, some 30–40 led to some modifications in the translator, aimed at relaxing some or other of the quantitive restrictions.

It can now obviously be assumed that the overwhelming majority of programs with a volume of up to 3,000 instructions will pass through the translator. However, with regard to problems which have a greater volume, the quantitive limitations of the ALPHA-translator may, nevertheless, be encountered quite frequently.

4.5 Some Further Advantages of the Multiblock Structure and of the Availability of Universal Optimizing Algorithms

The obvious disadvantages of having the multiblock structure and an abundance of optimizing algorithms is that the translator becomes weighty and its speed is reduced. However, since the translator requires these features for various reasons, they result in additional advantages for organizing the operation of the translator.

The existence of several passes on the program to be translated signifies in the first place that the complex algorithms of translation can be distributed over several blocks in order to avoid excessive strain on operative memory in the main block, which is responsible for the given algorithm. A typical example of this is furnished by the programming of loops and of subscript expressions [VII]. The main blocks for programming loops and for calculating variable addresses are Blocks 16, 17 and 18. However, it was found possible to transpose a considerable part of the work on the preparation of loops and of subscript expressions for programming, to earlier blocks. The most immediate effect of such an arrangement was an increase in the operational speed of the translator, since the subsidiary and preliminary operations implemented "in passing" by the previous blocks without any marked increase in their operating time, allow the structure of the main blocks to be simplified and the speed of their operation to be increased.

Another useful property of the multiblock structure proved to be its flexibility, allowing quite drastic changes to be introduced into the blocks, during the debugging of the ALPHA-translator, without altering its general structure. In fact the disjointedness of the blocks sometimes meant that an old variant of a block could be completely changed for a new one, without changing the rest and vice versa, defects discovered in the operation of one block, and which are difficult to eliminate, could in some cases be compensated for by insertion of suitable corrections in other blocks. It should, however, be added that it was not possible to eliminate fully all the defects in the algorithms of translation, that additional small restrictions on source language needed to be formulated [II].

The specific advantage of having efficient optimizing algorithms lies in the fact that it is possible in some cases to use deliberately simplified algorithms of translation bearing in mind subsequent optimization. The use of "power reserves" for the algorithms of optimization constitutes a special feature of the ALPHA-translator. For example, the presence of algorithms for procedure analysis makes it possible to reduce the function-expressions and the function-procedures to procedures of a general type, without lowering the quality of the translation. The presence of the algorithms for economy of memory eliminates considerations of the economical introduction of designations for intermediate variables arising during translation. Orientation towards the cleaning up of loops meant that instructions for the calculation of subscript expressions and the subsequent formation and modification of the addresses could be compiled in the simplest possible way, when all these control instructions are inserted in the innermost loop, directly in front of the instructions which contains the variable address to be processed. During the cleaning up of the loops the control instructions are automatically removed as far as possible from the internal loops.

5 Organization of the ALPHA-Translator

5.1 Plan

During the planning of the ALPHA-translator, a certain ideal organization of the operation was envisaged which was to be used in due course for designing a high-efficiency translator. It was suggested that the development would involve the following stages.

1. Development of the project task and of a plan of the problem. The technical specification for the system is defined more precisely, the general outlines of the system are determined, the basic approach to the construction of the algorithms of translation and optimization are planned and the tasks for the programmers are formulated.

2. Disjointed development of the algorithms of translation and optimization. The programmers acting mostly independently of one another establish the main algorithms for the work of the translator. The work is split up more "vertically" that is to say according to the types of source language statements to be translated, rather than "horizontally" that is to say according to the phases of the work of the translator.

3. "Joining" the algorithms which have been processed and the composition of the translator. The algorithms which have been developed are linked and unified, the structure of the translator is defined and its work is assigned to different blocks.

4. Preliminary "dry" checking of the translator. A hypothetical operation of the translator is reproduced on a few simple examples, in accordance with the functions of the blocks which have been systematized. During the preliminary "dry" checking a uniform style is developed for the organization of the block as far as possible, and the structure and the content of the information to be transmitted from one block to another are defined.

5. Development of logical flow charts for the blocks. The operation is split up again, but this time horizontally instead of vertically, via the individual blocks of the translator.

6. *Careful "dry" checking of the translator.* The work of the translator is reproduced using a reasonably representative example in accordance with the contents of the logical flow charts for the blocks. The aim of desk checking is to detect the main errors in the flow charts and in particular errors in the compatability of the operation of the blocks.

7. *Programming of the blocks and the preliminary, independent debugging on simple tests.*

8. *Debugging the translator.* The individual blocks are debugged carefully and the whole translator is debugged in very great detail by a system of extensive tests, beginning with the simplest which examines only the mechanism for transmitting basic information from one block to another and ending with the first problem rich in content.

9. *Experimental operation of the translator, using for instance one hundred manufacturing problems.*

5.2 Implementation

During the development of the ALPHA-translator this organization was by no means fully implemented. It is of some interest to analyse the reasons which led to the difference between the operation as planned initially and its practical implementation.

The first stage appeared to progress quite successfully. It was rather prolonged and continued from September 1960 until February 1961, instead of the envisaged two or three months. This was due to external causes not really connected with the actual work problem. The results of the first stage (the project task and the problem plan) were well recorded and did not contain any substantial errors. The most serious miscalculation was the underestimation of the difficulties involved in programming the problems (the length of the translator turned out to be three times that estimated originally; the period of time required for its preparation turned out to be twice that estimated).

The second stage (March to October 1961) was run through with considerable success. Most technical problems connected with the development of new algorithms for translation and optimization, were successfully solved at precisely this time. The drawback in the second stage, however, was that the solution of certain problems, which appeared at first to be purely technical (for example, the programming of the expressions), was put aside to be dealt with at a later date. As a result of this, these problems emerged at later stages when they had to be solved within the rigid framework of decisions already taken in connection with other problems.

The third stage (November 1961 to January 1962) was probably the most crucial. At that time there was the maximum drop in the volume of information circulated between the programmers and it was precisely then that the greatest demands were made upon the intuition of the programmers. The biggest problem was to estimate accurately the algorithmic complexity of the implementation of a given function, to be put on the individual blocks of the translator. Analysis of the subsequent work on the translator showed that most of the decisions taken at the third stage were correct, particularly in connection with the final selection of the optimizing algorithms and with establishing the general structure of the translator. At the same time some serious errors were made in estimating the complexity of the implementation of the algorithms for the programming of the expressions and of the operations on multi-dimensional arrays and complex numbers.

The main drawback in the fourth stage (January to February 1962) was the lack of clarity and the superficiality of its execution. As a result, possibilities of visualizing more accurately the nature of the work of the individual blocks of the translator and, where necessary, adjusting the algorithms of translation even to the extent of considering their appearance in the logical plans and programs, were neglected. At the same time, it was possible at this stage to think through the transfer of information between the blocks during translation, to determine the distribution of information between memory devices of ₁the machine and to lay down a uniform method for the construction of the blocks.

The greatest shortcoming in the work on the ALPHA-translator at the subsequent stages was the impossibility of attaining a uniform construction, programming and debugging of the blocks. This lack of uniformity can be largely explained by the inexperience of the programmers and their varying degree of professional training† and also by the diversity in the volume of work which fell to the lot of the block designers. The lack of uniformity in the programming was aggravated by the need for urgency and by having to overcome, from time to time, difficulties in the implementation of the individual blocks which had not been foreseen earlier on. By far the most difficult blocks to implement proved to be the block for programming expressions, which had to be split artificially into two blocks after the preparation of the flow chart of the first variant, which had not been placed in memory, and also Block 10 for the programming of the operations on arrays, the formation and debugging of which were completed only in 1966, a full 18 months after the start on the main part of the ALPHA-translator which allowed the ALGOL programs to be translated.

The lack of uniformity in the development of the blocks meant that the dry checking of the translator could not be carried out fully. However taking those 18 blocks for which a dry check had been carried out, there was no doubt about its efficiency, at least considering the conditions under which the ALPHA-translator was created.

The separate debugging of the blocks was not carried out carefully enough. This became apparent during the trial runs. The main reason for this was the inadequacy of the tests and the fact that a great deal of labour was consumed during their preparation. The lack of uniformity in the development of the blocks meant that it was not possible to apply the best system of debugging, in which the test for the next block is automatically prepared by the preceding blocks which have already been debugged in respect of the test in question. The complex debugging of the translator went comparatively quickly (on the

† The eleven writers of the translator—all with university education, had the following experience in programming (at the end of 1961): one, 8 years; one, 6 years; one, 5 years; five, 3 years; two, 2 years; and one less than a year.

No. of the block	Name of the block	Overall length of the block in machine words†	The tables‡	The time of completion of the individual debugging	In the flow charts of the block§	In programming	Of individual debugging	Overall	Corrected during desk checking	Detected during the individual debugging	No. of runs on the machine during the individual debugging	Amount of machine time spent on the individual debugging (in minutes)	Exposed during the complex debugging	Detected during the period of the trial run	Overall, on 100 instructions	No. of the block
1	Input and control	930	210	25/9 1962	25	6	10	41	5	6	5	22	4		1·1	1
2	Processing of the declaration	1400	130	30/9 1962	40	18	15	73	17	30	26	124	10	62	3·0	2
3	Replacement of the identifiers	2560	220	11/5 1963	70	50	150	270	8	135	116	425	22	11	6·6	3
4	Expressions I	1730	130	21/3 1963	100	20	20	140		190	41	254	12	6	5·4	4
5	Expressions II	3400	200	3/5 1963	100	40	40	180		40	96	701	23	10	6·6	5
6	Analysis of procedures (old variant)	800	50	11/5 1963	15	50	25	90	15	50	42	269	15	2	7·4	6
7	Analysis of procedures (new variant)	2300	100	6/7 1964	70	15	20	105		150	17	100	2			7
7	Programming of procedures (old variant)	3130	120	28/4 1963	58	35	40	133	10	40	106	534	21	7	5·6	7
8	Programming of procedures (new variant)	2100	150	1/2 1965	50	10	25	85	63	25	20	200	15			8
9	Translation into the 15-bit code	2370	260	28/4 1963	30	35	15	80	5	100	17	194	12	8	1·9	9
9	Processing of the formations and the compositions	2120	150	30/11 1962	145	25	25	195	15	50	64	234	4			9
10	Multidimensional arrays	5600	1600	15/5 1966	400	100	100	600	4	23	60	360	50	10	4·5	10
11	Analysis of loops	770	170	23/10 1962	13	3	4	20	30	188	12	30	12	6	5·3	11
12	Cleaning of loops (start)	2800	80	29/4 1963	50	20	100	170		33	263	1353	32	22	8·6	12
13	Cleaning up of loops (finish)	550	50	11/5 1963	1	2	9	12	28	44	31	182	17	2	9·6	13
14	Economy of expressions	2400	200	5/11 1962	80	10	18	108	35	150	55	219	10	11	3·3	14
15	Formation of the machine instructions	3000	800	9/11 1962	110	35	40	185		35	88	385	23	22	6·7	15
16	Programming of the index registers	1140	60	11/11 1962	13	10	6	29	31	70	15	72	9	10	4·7	16
17	Loops (start)	1600	100	11/11 1962	30	39	31	100		27	56	226	9	16	5·9	17
18	Loops (finish)	600	100	22/11 1962	9	15	25	49	4	40	26	80	9	5	7·0	18
19	Economy of the constants	620	70	14/5 1963	15	20	20	55	63	175	58	108	6	7	8·6	19
20	Program scheme	2400	440	17/6 1963	70	40	100	210	14	85	54	182	17	25	9·0	20
21	Graph of inconsistency	1130	40	27/11 1962	30	15	95	140	23	47	52	180	8	15	9·5	21
22	Allocation of memory	850	50	26/10 1962	50	17	24	91	17	52	38	167	15	16	6·8	22
23	Cleaning up of the program	1010	100	10/12 1962	78	20	20	118		35	30	126	6	14	7·1	23
24	Composition of the program (new variant)	1300	120	25/12 1962	40	20	25	85	30	116	36	150	1			24
24	Composition of the program (old variant)	1000	100		50	40	35	125				171		11	6·5	24

† In round numbers.   ‡ Including constants and tables.   § Counting from March 1962.

tests from May to November 1963 allowing for a two months' break and on the real programs from December 1963 to January 1964) especially taking into account the unreliable working of the machine during this period. The system of expanding tests was not fully implemented, which can be first and foremost explained by the authors' impatience to get on with the programming of actual problems, once the first evidence of the viability of the translator had been obtained.

The trial run of the ALPHA-translator began in February 1964 and went on until February 1965. The criterion for the termination of the trial run was one month's intensive use of the translator which did not reveal any fresh errors. Since the trial run represented the completion of the work on the translator, it was natural that all the omissions which had been made earlier had to be eliminated. This meant that the trial run lasted more than a year and dealt with 500 problems instead of 100. The work was mainly of a trivial nature such as the correcting of numerous minor errors, although sometimes quite important decisions had to be taken, related to the improvement of the working of the blocks (particularly the economy of memory blocks) and the reduction of quantitive limitations. Very often the main difficulty during the trial run was not so much finding the error but correcting it properly. In the early stages of the trial run it often happened that the "correction" of some minor error put the translator out of order for several days. Later on a whole system of buffer tapes with the translator was worked out to avoid having to interrupt the normal passage of the programs being translated, when introducing corrections or alterations into the translator.

5.3   Quantitative Indices

The work involved in compiling the blocks of the ALPHA-translator and the path of their development are characterized by the facts shown in the table.

A few summarizing facts which characterize the ALPHA-translator as a whole are given below:

Total length of the ALPHA-translator	44,680
Including constants and tables	5,530

Work involved, in man-years (reckoning 300 man-days as 1 man-year):

Initial development period (stages 1–4)	7·0
Compilation of the flow charts	5·8
Programming of the blocks	2·3
Independent debugging	3·4
Complex debugging	6.2
Trial run	7·3
Overall work involved	32·0

Number of errors detected during:

independent debugging	2000
complex debugging	300
the trial run	220

Number of runs on the machine:
  during independent debugging   1420
  during complex debugging   105
  during the trial run   180

Machine time spent, in hours:
  on independent debugging   112
  on complex debugging   130
  on the trial run   280

Machine time spent (per error in minutes):
  during independent debugging   3·4
  during complex debugging   26·0
  during the trial run   76·4

Cost of the development of the ALPHA-translator
(150 roubles per man-month and 40 roubles per hour of machine time)
  in roubles   78,500

The figures given are fairly representative and speak for themselves. The author would like to draw attention to the fact that in the total work involved in the development of the translator, the work on the debugging stage exceeds the other stages (16·6 man-years as compared with 15·1). The comparatively high percentage of errors is a cause for some concern (see the table). The difference in the "rate" of detection of an error at the different stages of debugging is striking—3·4 minutes for one error during the independent debugging as compared with 76 minutes during the trial run.

6 Literature Survey

In the present article the use of the ALPHA-translator and its development is described post factum. Some *a priori* recommendations and opinions relating to the preparation stage of the translator projector are to be found in paper[3] and in reports [4] and [5].

By the time of writing the present article several ideas about the internal or the intermediate language were known. Thus in one of the papers devoted to FORTRAN,[6] it was shown that when programming arithmetical expressions it was an advantage to record them first in some intermediate form, analogous to three-address instructions, and only then to convert them to the single-address machine code. This idea of separating the syntactical analysis and decomposition of the complex constructions of the source language process from the process of the machine instruction formation has obviously become universally accepted. In particular, it was developed in the TA-2 translator[7] in the form of a language of the so-called "fundamental notions". The simplicity of the fundamental notions means that they can be translated into the machine language by the "tabular method", in which the rule for translating a certain basic notion is given in a constant table which contains a group of machine instructions with blank addresses, which replaces the given concept.

There is another approach to the separation of the intermediate language level in the form of a machine-orientated universal language of the UNCOL tape.[8] This way, however, to a lesser degree reflects the internal requirements of the translation process and is instead determined by technical and economic demands, for example the need for the joint development of the translators from one or several languages for a whole series of machines.

The way of using the ALPHA-translator has been dictated not only by the internal logic of the problem, but is to some extent determined also by the traditions of the Soviet school of automatic programming of the "pre-ALGOL" period[9-11] whose characteristics were taking care over the programming quality and the need to operate with a machine having a low memory capacity.

The beginnings of the mixed programming strategy based on an analysis of the source program statements can be found in a paper by Kurochkin *et al.*[12] which is devoted to the method of programming the loops in the compiler program for the STRYELA-3 machine.

In the foreign literature, the translator scheme for the KDF-9 machine, described by Hawkins and Huxtable[13] is the closest to the ALPHA-translator as regards the general approach and even certain specific ideas, particularly in the field of the analysis of procedures and *FOR*-statements.

The idea of storing and processing information on the list structure basis is so well known today that it is just impossible to point to the specific source which inspired its use in the ALPHA-translator. The only new element, at least for Soviet works on programming, is perhaps the systematic application of this method for the programming system of the translating type.

The use of hash addressing in the ALPHA-translator is taken from the papers by Yershov[2] and Ivanova.[14] However, we have recently learnt of some much earlier papers dealing with this method, in particular the work of Peterson,[15] in which a survey of the "open addressing" method was carried out which was analogous to the analysis carried out earlier.[2] In this same paper it is shown that the "open addressing" idea, which practically coincides with the mechanism of hash addressing, can be traced back to Samuel, Emdel and Boehme who used this mechanism in 1954 for looking up the tables in the assembler for the IBM-701 computer.

7 Conclusion

7.1 The development of the technique of programming from ALGOL 60 has, until very recently, gone under the guise mainly of creating universal, high-speed operating and elegant algorithms of translation stemming first and foremost from the nature of the language and its descriptive method. The stimulus for these algorithms was provided by the papers of Samuelson and Bauer[16] about sequential programming, of Dijkstra,[17] about recursive programming, of Ingerman,[18] Paul[19] and Irons[20] about syntactically directed translators.

Against this background, the approach to the development of the ALPHA-translator looks rather old fashioned and cumbersome. However, it is possible to put forward an argument for the advantage and necessity of this approach.

1. During the development of the ALPHA-translator a method for engineering construction of the system was used which aimed, first and foremost, at

satisfying prescribed operational requirements. These limits did not allow the organization of the ALPHA-translator to be subjected to some central idea which would impart internal unity and logical harmony to the translator, but on the other hand they demanded the introduction into the translator of the most diverse properties which were not linked with one another logically but which had one and the same purpose, i.e. to raise the programming quality. In this sense the complexity of the ALPHA-translator and the variety of its algorithms reflect the complexity of the actual programming process which is carried out by man.

2. Another reason for increasing the volume of the translator and for making its structure more complex is the inadequate capacity of operative memory of the machine for which the translator was built. Although it sounds paradoxical, the translator has turned out to be too big because the machine is too small! Obviously the characteristics of the machine are critical for a translator of this type. The lengthening of the translator is connected with the artificial increase in the number of blocks and the presence of a great number of functions and subroutines duplicated in the individual blocks.

3. The incorporation of the ALPHA-translator on the more modern medium size machine would mean that the translator could be relieved considerably and its speed of operation increased. It can be assumed that the translator will compile programs from the Input language for the IBM-7090 type machine with no more than ten passes and with the same programming quality as the ALPHA-translator, with a speed of not less than 1,500 single address instructions of the final program per minute of the operating time of the translator.

7.2 The development of the ALPHA-system shows that the task of creating a complex set of programs of the ALPHA-type will not present too great demands on the professional and technical standard of the programmers. Any mathematician or engineer of average ability, but possessing a definite logical type of mind and at least two years' experience of working as a programmer in a well organized computer centre, can successfully work on the staff of a group engaged in development. However, it is vital that the group contains two or three programmers of expert-class who would first and foremost act as instigators of the structural ideas, co-ordinating the separate parts of the development and having the ability to make quick, accurate decisions during the crucial period of complex elaboration of the system. As for the demands which face the supervisor of the development, it is difficult for the author to discuss the problem fully since he had to play this very role during the creation of the ALPHA-system. However, three conclusions can be drawn based on an analysis of the errors which were made during the organization of work on the ALPHA-translator.

1. The supervisor must skilfully combine the individual and the collective character of the work performed by his co-workers. To engender a spirit of co-operation and mutual understanding, a sense of responsibility for the work as a whole and to organize the actual interchange—all these are the obvious tasks which face the supervisor. However, the excessive enthusiasm for discussions at seminars or at general group meetings, and lengthy consulta-

tions with colleagues sometimes lead to shallow decisions being taken and to the loss of a liking for thorough and individual study.

2. The task of achieving the best possible tempo and rhythm of work is obviously one of the chief tasks which face the supervisor. He must be able to perceive the internal speed with which the project moves and, while maintaining the necessary tension in the tempo of the work, must not permit this to develop into rush work. The choice of the correct tempo of work is especially important during the period of the planning and programming of the system blocks, when consequences of one error or another are still not immediately apparent. In this aspect the supervisor must be able to overcome both his own natural zeal which nourishes his extreme optimism and also often the pressure of the administration which insists upon strict observance of the delivery period and of other conditions.

3. Finally, both the first and second requirements will be fulfilled when the supervisor can be completely relieved of work connected with the details of implementing the project. Using his store of experience and knowledge, he must fight the desire to correct himself the errors of his less experienced subordinates.

Acknowledgements

The author wishes to express his profound gratitude to G. I. Kozhukhin and V. I. Pottosin, who, having fulfilled admirably their functions as co-ordinators during the translation phase and the programming phase respectively, contributed a good deal to the taking of decisions concerning the ALPHA-translator.

The author also wishes to acknowledge the work of the Automatic Programming Information Centre in Brighton (A.P.I.C.) whose publications on the automation of programming are a great help in keeping abreast of the latest achievements in this field.

Finally, the author wishes to thank S. S. Lavrov for reading through the manuscript of the article and for making valuable comments.

REFERENCES

1. ADELSON-VIELSKII, G. M. and LANDIS, E. M. (1962). One algorithm for the organisation of information. Academy of Sciences of the USSR, 146, No. 2.
2. YERSHOV, A. P. (1961). The programming of arithmetical operators. Academy of Sciences of the USSR, 118, No. 3.
3. YERSHOV, A. P. (1961). Basic problems encountered when constructing a compiler program at the Institute of Mathematics of the Siberian Department of the Academy of Sciences of the USSR. Sib. mat. Zh. 2, No. 6.
4. YERSHOV, A. P. and KOZHUKHIN, G. I. (1961). A compiler program project of the Institute of Mathematics of the Siberian branch of the Academy of Sciences of the USSR. Novosibirsk. (Appendix I in this book).
5. YERSHOV, A. P. (1961). Basic problems encountered when constructing a compiler program at the Institute of Mathematics of the Siberian Department of the Academy of Sciences of the USSR. Novosibirsk. (Appendix II in this book).

6. SHERIDAN, P. B. (1959). The arithmetic translator–compiler of the IBM Fortran automatic coding system. *Communs Ass. comput. Mach.* **2**, No. 2.

7. SHURA-BURA, M. R. and LYUBIMSKII, E. Z. (1964). The ALGOL 60 translator. *J. Comput. Maths, math. Phys.* **4**, No. 1.

8. STEEL, T. B., Jr. (1961). UNCOL: the myth and the fact. *A. Rev. autom. Progrmg* **2**.

9. KAMYNIN, S. S. and LYUBIMSKII, E. Z. (1956). The automation of programming. A conference "Paths of development of Soviet mathematical machine and instrument construction." Part III. Moscow.

10. YERSHOV, A. P. (1958). A programming program for a high speed electronic computing machine. Publication of the Academy of Sciences of the USSR, Moscow.

11. TRIFONOV, N. P. and SHURA-BURA, M. R. (editors) (1961). A system for the automation of programming. Physics and Mathematics State Publishing House, Moscow.

12. VELIKANVA, T. M., YERSHOV, A. P., KIM, K. V., KUROCHKIN, V. M., OLEINIK-OVOD, Yu. A. and PODDERYUGIN, V. D. (1958). A compiler program for the computer (PPS)—The Third All-Union Conference on Computing Mathematics and the Application of Methods of Computing Techniques. 3rd–8th February, 1958. Publication Academy of Sciences of the Azerbaijan Soviet Socialist Republic, Baku.

13. HAWKINS, E. N. and HUXTABLE, D. H. R. (1961). A multi-pass translation scheme for ALGOL 60. *A. Rev. Autom. Progrmg* **3**.

14. IVANOVA, E. K. The choice of a function of the arrangement for the organization of tabular surveys—The computer centre of the Siberian branch of the Academy of Sciences of the USSR, Novosibirsk, 1961.

15. PETERSON, W. W. (1957). Addressing for randon-access storage. *IBM Jl Res. Dev.* **1**, No. 2.

16. SAMUELSON, K. and BAUER, F. L. (1959). Sequentiell Formelübersetzung. (Sequential translation of formulae). *Elektron. Rechenanl.* **4**, No. 4.

17. DIJKSTRA, E. W. (1960). Recursive programming. *Num. Math.* **2**, No. 5.

18. INGERMAN, P. (1962). A translation technique for languages whose syntax is expressible in extended Backus normal form. Proceedings of the Symposium on Symbolic Languages in Data Processing. Rome, March 26–31, 1962.

19. PAUL, M. (1962). A general processor for certain formal languages. Proceedings of the Symposium on Symbolic Languages in Data Processing. Rome, March 26–31, 1962.

20. IRONS, E. T. (1963). The structure and use of the syntax directed compiler. *A. Rev. autom. Progrmg* **3**.

IV PROGRAMMING EXPRESSIONS IN THE ALPHA-TRANSLATOR

G. I. Kozhukhin

Expressions are programmed in the ALPHA-translator by Blocks 2–5; programming constitutes a part of the phase of translation into internal language. The constituent steps in programming expressions are as follows:

(a) standardizing the identifiers and symbols of the ALPHA-program;
(b) decomposition of complex expressions and statements with a recursive structure into the simplest statements of the internal language;
(c) Determining the type and structure of formal parameters of procedures and intermediate variables which result from the decomposition.

An additional requirement during programming expressions was that as much information as possible about the structure of the ALPHA-program should be preserved. It is essential to save this information in order to ensure subsequent optimization (III.2.1). Processing of the program to be translated when programming expressions is effected by four consecutive scannings. It should be noted that the number of scannings depends not so much on the logical structure of the processing algorithms as on the capabilities of the machine (and primarily on the capacity of memory).

1 Translation of Identifiers and Standardization of Basic Symbols

1.1 Structure of Identifiers

All identifiers in the ALPHA-program are replaced by symbols of standard length (III.2.2) in order to facilitate further operation of the translator. This is accompanied by decentralization of the declaration of identifiers, i.e. the information relating to the object to be identified is incorporated in the symbol which is substituted for the identifier. Not all the information relating to the object to be identified is in fact incorporated in the symbol identifier. For example, the declaration of the procedure function involves, in addition to the declaration of the type of procedure identifier, information relating to the procedure body which will naturally not be incorporated into the translation of the original procedure identifier.

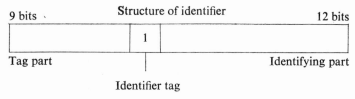

Identifier tag

Fig. 1. Structure of identifier

3

The translated identifier will have the following structure (Fig. 1). Tag bits establish the classification at intermediate language level (III.2.5) as in the diagram represented in Fig. 2. Any path in this diagram which connects the "identifier" and "information" peaks will indicate the sequence of tags which are admissible for a specific identifier.

Classification of identifiers

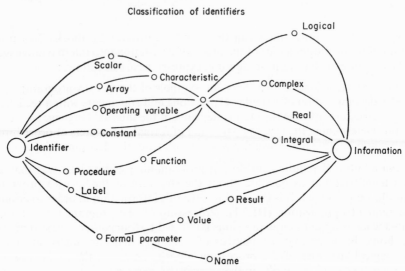

Fig. 2. Classification of identifiers

1.2 Processing of Declarations

The identifiers in the ALPHA-translator are translated in two passes. In the first of these, all declarations are analysed and a table of identifiers is drawn up. In the second scan identifiers and delimiters are substituted by standard 22-digit symbols by means of the identifier table.

1.2.1   The main work involved in the first scan of the program is that of completing a table of identifiers. Identifiers are translated with the aid of hash addressing (III.4.1) so that the table of identifiers is an arrangement field. Each class of identifier receives its own counter during translation and the current value of the counter for the respective class is used as the identifying part of the translation of an identifier I when analysing the next declaration of I.

The hash address is calculated from the expression $\sum_{i=0}^{n} a_i$ in which $\sum$ is the summation to a module 2^9 with transfer from the highest bit to the lowest one; n is the length of the identifier; a_i is a 9-bit punched card code of identifier letter or digit, a_0 is the "coordinate" of the identifier and is equal to the number of the block (obtained by calculating the opened statement brackets from left to right) in which the declaration of the identifier acts. Here, entry of labels in the program, in the form of statement labels, serves as a declaration, whilst for the case of formal parameters this role is played by their list included under the heading "procedure declaration". In order to avoid collision of formal parameters with other identifiers all the procedures (or functions) described are included during translation in supplementary statement brackets.

Each line in the table of identifiers occupies two memory cells and has the following form:

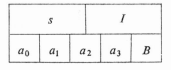

where s is the translation of the identifier (or a reference to the translation), I is supplementary information relating to the identifier (or a reference to such information); a_1 has the same significance as above; B is either an empty symbol or a reference to the continuation of the identifier if its length is greater than three.

This type of tabular structure does not occupy too much space in memory and permits practically any length of identifier in the ALPHA-program. The length of the table is constant and is 512 lines.

1.2.2   Processing of the declarations involves transferring information from the identifier declaration to the corresponding line in the table. If the program to be translated is an ALGOL-program, transfer of information does not present any difficulties and will be a direct process. The Input language will involve some difficulties due to declaration of identities; declarations of the component of the array and declarations of real and imaginary parts of a complex variable are involved.

1.2.2.1   Declaration of the components of the array having the form:

$$A[i,j] = \|b[k,l,i,j]\|$$

introduces various designations for the components of a given array. In order to avoid constantly having to follow this relationship the same symbol s is established when these two identifiers are translated. To preserve dimensionality for the whole input-identifier A, a corresponding number of empty subscripts (two in the present instance) is added. This information is entered in the table of identifiers in the following manner.

The two identifiers (b and A) are translated and introduced into the appropriate line of the table. The new symbol s is placed in the table only for the identifier b. For the identifier A, a reference to the line corresponding to the identifier b is inserted instead of the symbol s. Furthermore, supplementary information for the identifier A includes information stating that two additional empty subscripts have to be added for each occurrence.

1.2.2.2   Declaration of the real and imaginary parts of a complex variable of the form $z = x + iy$ is essentially processed in the same manner as the declaration of the components of the array. This is related to the fact that a complex variable will be treated as a relative vector of length two, and the **complex** type will only affect the understanding of the nominal operations on this array.

Thus, if the identifier z is replaced by the symbol s, the following substitutions will be performed in the entire program to be translated:

z by s [ ]   (**complex** type)
x by s [1]   (**real** type)
y by s [2]   (**real** type)

The fact that the identifier s is of one type for some entries in the program and of a different types for others will only determine the significance of operations on these entries, as stated before.

1.2.3   Translation of the identifiers when the program is examined is accompanied by some transformation of this program. These conversions are directed towards standardization of those declarations which remain in the program to be translated and are used in subsequent work of the translator. The most important of these conversions are the following:

1.2.3.1   All declarations of arrays with internal dimensions provide a standard form of the declarations of arrays without internal dimensions.

Information is fed into the table of identifiers stating that the corresponding number of entry subscripts has to be added to all the input data of the array.

For example, if the declaration of the array has the following form:

array A $[p:q]$ — **matrix** $n \times m$, then this declaration will be replaced by the **array** A $[p:q,1:n,1:m]$ and in addition to this, when the identifier A is translated its occurrence $A[i]$ will be replaced by $A[i,,]$.

Thus the internal dimension will be explicitly indicated by the number of empty subscripts.

1.2.3.2   Declarations of variables with superscript are converted into declarations of arrays. The conversion, the nature of which is explained from the example below, is effected in accordance with semantics of superscripts in the Input language:

A fragment of a program with superscripts is shown below

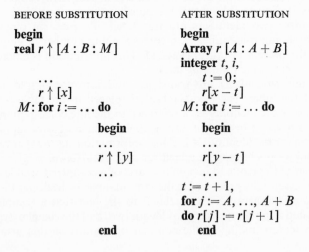

BEFORE SUBSTITUTION	AFTER SUBSTITUTION
begin	**begin**
real $r \uparrow [A : B : M]$	**Array** r $[A : A + B]$
	integer $t, i,$
$\ldots$	$t := 0;$
$r \uparrow [x]$	$r[x - t]$
M: **for** $i := \ldots$ **do**	M: **for** $i := \ldots$ **do**
begin	**begin**
$\ldots$	$\ldots$
$r \uparrow [y]$	$r[y - t]$
$\ldots$	$\ldots$
	$t := t + 1,$
	for $j := A, \ldots, A + B$
	do $r[j] := r[j + 1]$
end	**end**

$$t := 0$$

$r \uparrow [z]$	$r[z - t]$
$\cdots$	$\cdots$
$r \uparrow [\ ]$	$r[A + B]$
$\cdots$	$\cdots$
end	**end**

1.2.3.3 All the declarations of scalar variables and specifications of formal parameters are deleted from the program to be translated since all the information in these has already been entered in the table of identifiers.

1.2.3.4 Conversion of functions and function-procedures is made in such a manner as to incorporate these in the general concept of the procedure. The formal parameter which characterizes the result must also be incorporated for this purpose. During this the syntax of the procedure declaration alters slightly and this makes it possible to change automatically the assignment of the function-procedure identifier in its body to the assignment of the new formal parameter. Thus if the declaration has the form:

real procedure $\phi(x); \{\ldots \phi := \ldots\}$,

then after conversion it will have the following form:

procedure $\phi\{(x,\phi); \{\ldots \phi := \ldots\}\}$.

On the other hand, a declaration of the form:

function $F(x) = x \uparrow 2 + 1$

is replaced by

procedure $F\{(x,F); \{F := x \uparrow 2 + 1\}\}$

Introduction of an extra statement bracket in the block between the procedure identifier and the formal parameter list provides an automatic means for distinguishing the occurrences of a procedure identifier in the procedure body and after the word "**procedure**". The first occurrence of the identifier falls into the class of formal parameters while the second will fall into the class of procedure identifiers.

1.2.3.5 Declarations of initial values are converted into assignment statements by substituting the symbol := for =. Some characteristics of the assignment of the initial values to own variables are effected in subsequent scanning (see 2.3.6).

1.3 Processing the Statement Part

Substitution of identifiers and delimiters in the ALPHA-program by standard symbols is effected during subsequent scanning. The information for this substitution is in the form of a table of identifiers, on the one hand, and the program to be translated on the other.

It should be noted, however, that the main work in this scanning is not the implementation of the substitution but certain transformations of program statements, detection of semantic errors and construction of tables.

1.3.1 The semantic correctness of using identifiers is analysed on the basis of that information which is present in the table of identifiers and the context which surrounds the identifiers in the ALPHA-program. The identifier and the context are printed for all detected errors. If one single error is detected, that block begins an operation in which only semantic correctness is checked and stops on completion of the work. Three semantic features involved in the use of identifiers, which will be described below, are checked, the first of these is introduced *a priori*, and the other two on the basis of experience of operation of the translator.

1.3.1.1 Undeclared identifier. An error is detected from the absence of this identifier in the table and in the list of identifiers of standard functions.

1.3.1.2 A discrepancy between the declaration and use of the identifier in the number of subscript positions. An error is detected from extra information in the table of identifiers. The source of this error usually lies in the difficulty of distinguishing between certain small and capital letters when punching the ALPHA-program.

1.3.1.3 Checking the missing multiplication sign before opening a round bracket. The origin of these errors is evidently an undenoted multiplication in the usual mathematical writing. Experience shows that this error occurs in two situations:

(1) in contexts of the type $\ldots + 2n + \ldots$
(2) in contexts of the type $+a(\ldots$

In the first case, a syntactic error results (the identifier cannot commence with a digit) and this error is evidenced by the first block of the ALPHA-translator, while in the second case, a semantic error occurs, generally speaking, which will result in incorrect information which is blocked by subsequent blocks without indication of context.

A mistake is detected from the discrepancy between the identifier class in the table and the nature of its entry in the analysed context.

1.3.2 Conversion of program statements is controlled from their preliminary standardization. These conversions are accompanied by removal of those syntactic structures which do not require further analysis for expression. These conversions are fairly abrupt and do not obey any internal logic. Although they permit algorithms of the following blocks to be constructed in a more orderly manner (see also III.4.5).

The fundamental syntactic structures which can be processed in this scanning are listed below.

1.3.2.1 *Declarations of arrays.* As has already been mentioned, the declarations of arrays have a standard form at the commencement of the second scanning. After processing, all declarations of arrays are removed from the ALPHA-program and are replaced by statements for calculating the length of arrays, calls to the administrative system (AS) $[X]$ and statements for formation of the initial address of this array.

For example, if the declaration of the array has the form:

Array A $[1 : 10, 1 : 20]$

then it is completely removed from the object program and all data relating to the bound pairs are entered in the common list (III.3.2). The reference to the common list is placed in the special *Table of Arrays*, entry into this is effected in accordance with the number of the array.

If one of the bound pairs in the declaration of the array is not constant, i.e. has the form:

Array A $[n : q, m : p]$,

the following statements appear instead of the declarations:

$$a_1 := n; \quad a_2 := q - n + 1;$$
$$a_3 := m; \quad a_4 := p - m + 1;$$
$$S := a_2 \, x a_4; \quad AS2; \quad X(s, A),$$

where $a_1 \dots a_4$ are integral scalars; s is the standard cell in which the length of the array should be located before call to the AS; **AS 2** is the call statement for the AS which reserves for array A a section of memory and giving its commencement in s; X is the formation statement on the level of the intermediate language (III.2.5). The variables $a_1 \dots a_4$, as in the case of constant limits, are entered into the common list as information regarding the bound pairs. Thus the information relating to bounds is entered into the common list, not as lower and upper bounds, but as a lower limit and its length with respect to the dimension.

1.3.2.2 *Numbers.* All numbers are translated into machine words which correspond to their type (II.2.4) which are entered into the table of constants while constant identifiers replace these in the object program.

1.3.2.3 **Lists.** The **list** constructions used in the Input language have the form:

$\not\approx$ symbol $\not\approx$ ... $\not\approx$ symbol $\not\approx$

All such constructions are removed at this level, each one according to its sense. We introduce certain examples of such conversions.

1.3.2.3.1 A recalculation of the form ",...," in the *FOR* clause is replaced by "**step 1 to**".

1.3.2.3.2 A list of the form ",...," in operations of formation and composition is turned into the special construction in which the list index is clearly shown. The character of the construction is demonstrated by the following example:

Let a portion of the list of variables be the list

$$a[E_1], \dots, a[E_2].$$

In this case it will be replaced by the construction which is syntactically expressed as the designator of a non-declared function $\sqcap$,

$$\sqcap (i, E_1, E_2, a[i]),$$

where in the first position is placed the index by which the variables $a[i]$ are listed, the second and third contain the limits of variation of this index, while the fourth is the expression to be listed

1.3.2.3.3 List of relations of the form $< \dots <$ is removed by introducing the analogue "function" Σ. For example, the list

$$a[E_1] < \dots < a[E_2]$$

is replaced by

$$\Sigma(i, E_1, E_2 - 1, a[i] < a[i + 1])$$

where the arguments have the same sense as for function Π, and the result is equivalent to calculating the expression

$$a[E] < a[E, + 1] \& \ldots \& a[E_2 - 1] < aE_2$$

Naturally, in those cases where the listing enters a more complex chain of relations we also take into account the link between this list and neighbouring elements. A chain of relations of the form:

$$s \leqslant a[E_1] \leqslant \ldots \leqslant a[E_2] < P$$

is replaced by

$$s \leqslant a[E_1] \& \Sigma(i, E_1, E_2 - 1, a[i] < a[i + 1])$$
$$\& \, a[E_2] < P$$

1.3.2.4 *Conditional designating expressions*: This construction is removed from the program by replacing it with conditional transfers. The algorithm of this conversion is very simple and its work is initiated by the occurrence of the combination of the symbols "**go to if**" or "**go to**". The result of the application of the algorithm to the **go to** statement

go to if $a = b$ **then** (**if** $a < o$ **then** $B[i]$ **else** M)
                        else $M1$

assumes the form

if $a = b$, **then** {**if** $a < 0$ **then go to** $B[i]$ **else go to** M}
                        else go to $M1$

It should be noted that when a translation scheme had been elaborated, an error was overlooked at this point which later resulted in limiting the potential use of conditional designating expressions in the ALPHA-language (II.1.3). The history of this error is very instructive and it makes sense to discuss it at this point. The story began when it was decided to admit integers as labels in the implementation. It was clear that introduction of such labels as actual parameters in procedures led to considerable difficulties in translation, hence it was decided to use the specification of the labels for corresponding formal parameters. It seemed than that it was possible to use the above method for eliminating conditional designating expressions. The only essential condition was to place the symbol "**go to**" at the beginning of the position of the actual parameter which corresponded to the formal parameter specified as label. With these considerations, however, we overlooked the fact that if the procedure identifier itself is a formal parameter, there is at this level of translator operation no information relating to the corresponding formal parameters of the procedures which are placed at this point. The mistake from our point of view was not that we failed to consider the procedure identifiers, which are formal parameters. There were similar oversights also in other algorithms of translation. The fundamental mistake in this case was to introduce the algorithm at a level of processing at which none of the essential non-local information relating to the program translated was available as yet. A situation arose in which there was no information at a point where there was a conversion mechanism and conversely no mechanism where the necessary information was available.

If this had affected the more essential aspects of the Input language, the translator would have to be completely reconstructed. However, in so far as more than five hundred problems were solved during the period of experimental operation of the translator, no designating named expression was used as an actual parameter and we therefore placed limitations on the hardware representation.

1.3.2.5 *Switches.* In the pass described, primary conversion of switch declarations is effected which approximates their structure to the level of the internal language. The result of conversion of a declaration

switch $S := S1, S2, Q[m]$ **if** $v > -5$

Then S3 else S4

is a statement of the following form

switch S: {**go to** $S1$; **go to** $S2$; **go to** $Q[m]$; {**if** $v > -5$,

then go to $S3$ **else go to** $S4$}}

2 Programming of Expressions

2.1 Organization of the Algorithm

During the third pass further standardization of statements in the translated program is carried out and the nested structure of expressions removed.

The basis for constructing corresponding blocks in the translator is provded by known algorithms of programming of expressions, especially (1) and (2). Some special features of Input language, however, and orientation to efficient translation will make these algorithms appreciably more complex. After the first variant of the algorithm has been described, it was found for example that it could not be entered into operative memory. The algorithm had thus to be split up artificially and resolved into two parts, hence the expressions are programmed in two passes.

From the point of view of programming of expressions, the main characteristic of Input language is the fact that the meaning of the operation depends on the structures of its arguments. This means that it is impossible to program the procedure bodies without analysing the call statements to them. For example, multiplication of two formal parameters can be understood (from the point of view of structure) by 16 different means, the structure of the result depending on the meaning of the operation. In this connection, the general organization of the algorithm for programming expressions will have the following appearance.

On scanning the translated program, the stack M will be simultaneously filled. All open brackets of blocks and identifiers of declared procedures will be entered therein, with an indication of their coordinates in the program.

3*

Entering the procedure identifier in the stack is initiated on finding the beginning of the declaration of this procedure. The procedure body proper is passed by and the declarations or statements which follow this are processed. On encountering the closing bracket S of Block B, the last symbol in the stack M is analysed. If this is an opening bracket of Block B, it is deleted from the stack. On the other hand, if the last symbol in M is a procedure identifier, the procedures declared in Block B will include a procedure P for which at least one call was found in the scanning process. After this, the procedure identifier P is deleted from the stack and the bracket S is entered with its coordinates in the translated program. The procedure body P is then found from the remembered coordinates, according to a "common class' (see below) the specification, type and structure of each formal parameter are entered into the table of formal parameters. Following this, scanning of the statements of the body P commences. After programming the body of the given procedure, a return to the scanning point occurs, corresponding to the moment of finding the bracket S.

The process described is essentially recursive in so far as scanning the statements of body P may disclose any of the viewed situations.

2.2 Inductive Determination of Types and Structures

Thus, when any syntactic unit is programmed, full information will be available relating to all the variables entering into this. In order to retain this information at each step, it is essential to perform an inductive determination of the characteristics of the intermediate variables which occur. Some of the important aspects of this induction are outlined below.

2.2.1 Induction from the formal parameters is performed on the basis of information relating to the actual parameters. This information is obtained when processing calls to the procedure. A *common class* is established for each identifier, i.e. for each actual parameter of the given procedure, a specification, type and structure is allocated (label, procedure, array, etc.). This information is placed in the common list and the reference to this inserted in the procedure table. If the call to the given procedure is encountered repeatedly, the common classes will be revised. Where the common classes do not coincide, a blocking stop will operate generally speaking. One essential exception to this rule involves cases in which a lack of identity is due to a difference in types **integral** and **real**. Three cases can be distinguished: (1) a **real** type is indicated in the common class, whilst the actual parameter contains an **integral** type: the difference is disregarded and the conversion function of the factual parameter entered in the **real** type; (2) an **integral** type is indicated in the common class, while a **real** one is entered in the actual parameter, while the body of the procedure remains unprogrammed: the common class is corrected to the **real** type, the actual parameters of the **integral** type are converted to the **real** type subsequently, when programming the procedure statements (Chapter V). The case (3) differs from case (2) in that the procedure body has already been programmed: a blocking stop occurs. In so far as the Input language admits situation (3), it is evident that the algorithm described places a limitation on the use of the procedures (II.1.3.1.4). Clearing this limitation involves either a dynamic analysis of the type of variables or admission of several common classes for one procedure.

As is seen from the algorithm described, all calls to some procedure will be served by one copy of the procedure body. The absence of a mechanism of dynamic analysis of type and structure of variables in the ALPHA-translator makes it essential for all actual procedure parameters to belong to one common class. This limitation can be avoided by including in the translation a duplication mechanism for procedure bodies, so that each common class is served by its own body, constructed on the basis of a given combination of types and structures. This mechanism, however, was not realized owing to overloading of the expression programming blocks in the ALPHA-translator.

2.2.2 Induction from the compound variables is effected on the basis of analysis of each element in the list, standing under the sign for formation or composition operations. Processing of composed or formed variables (or expressions) commences in the innermost part. For example, if formation contains a list of expressions, these expressions are first programmed and extracted for the formation sign so that only the lists of variables remain to be viewed.

Conversion of the translated program during processing of the compound variables leads to the introduction of a new simple variable to replace the corresponding compound variable in the ALPHA-program, and to the introduction of a special function Φ which indicates how this new variable is constructed from component variables. After removing the internal composition (or formation) by such conversions the following level is then removed recurrently, and so on. For example, if the ALPHA-program contains a statement of the form:

$$a[,] := \|a1, a2, a3|, |b1, b2, b3\|,$$

the following statements will appear at this point after conversion:

$$\Phi(|a1, a2, a3|, T1[\ ]);$$
$$\Phi(|b1, b2, b3|, T2[\ ]);$$
$$\Phi(|T1[\ ], T2[\ ]|, T3[\ ]);$$
$$a[,] := T3[,].$$

The call statements to function Φ actually have no operational role but serve merely as a convenient method of transmitting information to the following block. They will later be taken out of the program and put into the general list to serve as information for blocks programming operations over multidimensional arrays (Chapter VI).

The structure of intermediate variables which replace formation or composition, is established from the rules of the Input language. If the order with respect to the new dimension in the case of formation, and for the singled out dimension in the case of composition is given by an expression which is made up of constants, the corresponding calculations are completed at the moment of translation. In the contrary case, these variables are regarded as dynamic arrays. Information relating to the variables is entered in the table of arrays and the bound pairs are placed in the common list. Thus, these arrays will not differ in any way from the original arrays of the ALPHA-program during subsequent operation.

The type of new variable is determined from the type of variable entering into the composition or formation. If the list of variables contains both the **integral** and the **real** types of variables then the new variable will be of the **real** type, while the conversion function will be placed before the corresponding function Φ.

2.2.3 Introduction of type and structure by arithmetic and Boolean operations is carried out in an obvious manner. In order to perform "non-component" operations depending on types, the dimension and orders with respect to the dimensions of the result of the operation are determined from the sign of the operation and from the corresponding information relating to the operands in accordance with the rules of Input language. For componentwise operations, the type and structure, is simply transferred from one of the operands.

One of the most essential characteristics which distinguishes the Input language from ALGOL, from the point of view of the algorithm for programming expressions is the presence of arrays which act as intermediate variables. This in turn makes it necessary to introduce supplementary blocks in which the intermediate arrays are located, hence localization of these arrays in the block containing the given expression is evidently too uneconomical and may result in uneconomic use of memory. At the same time the selection of the minimal sections of program which can constitute a block is rather unsatisfactory and overloads the programming algorithm with numerous checks. The ALPHA-translator has been allocated a single strategy, namely, the brackets of the block contain the basic statement of the ALPHA-program including within itself that point at which a new array appears. In those cases where the new array is dynamic the corresponding calls to the administrative system are placed in this block together with the formation of statements as was done during the second pass for the original arrays.

2.3 Decomposition of Expressions

As has been stated previously, the decomposing algorithm for expressions and statements of Input language is based on known methods of programming expressions, using a stack. The essentials of this method are as follows: The formula to be translated is rewritten symbol by symbol into the stack until an operation appears in the stack which can be programmed. An instruction is then formed to perform the operation; the store stack is contracted, i.e. at the position of the operation sign and operands, the notation of the result of the instruction is recorded. This type of processing is continued until the stack is emptied. We shall describe below only special characteristics of this algorithm in the ALPHA-translator.

2.3.1 Programming Boolean expressions. We shall consider an example:

if $x > 0$ & $y = 0$, **then** $a := b$, *else* $c := d$

Two methods of analysing Boolean expressions which enters into conditions (logical conditions) are known. The first method involves programming the calculation of the value t of the logical condition and formulating an instruction for the conditional transfer of control according to the value t. For the example considered here, this method of programming gives:

$t1 := x > 0;$ $t2 := y = 0;$ $t3 := t1 \,\&\, t2;$ $IF \neg t3,$ **then go to** M1;
$a := b;$ **go to** $M2;$ $M1 : C := d; M2 :$

The second method of programming [3] involves carrying out consecutive checks of arguments of the logical condition and constructing branches either to a further check or to the output label. The program obtained by this second means will assume the following form:

if $\neg x > 0$ **then go to** $M1;$ **if** $\neg y = 0$ **then go to** $M1;$
$a := b;$ **go to** $M2; M1 : c := d; M2;$

The first method generally gives a simpler translation algorithm while the second gives a more effective object program.

These methods are combined in the ALPHA-translator, where the last operation of the logical condition is performed by branches while the rest are calculated by logical expressions. The program for the present example is constructed by the translator in the following form:

$t1 := x > y$
$t2 := y = 0$
if $\neg t1,$ **then go to** $M1;$
if $\neg t2,$ **then go to** $M2;$
$a := b;$
go to $M2;$
$M1 : c := d; M2 :$

This type of concept will be seen to allow a good object program to be obtained in most cases without excessively complicating the algorithm for programming Boolean expressions involved in the condition. In fact, in simple conditions which are frequently encountered, such as the type "**if** $x > 0,$ **then**" or "**if** $a \leqslant x \leqslant b$ **then**", the ALPHA-translator will give results which agree with the results of the second method, and in fairly complex cases particularly if the logical condition depends, not on the relation, but on Boolean variables, the results will be almost the same as in the first method. It should be noted that in some cases (e.g. in the example used here) this method gives worse results either than the first or the second method.

2.3.2   Contraction of the stack and recording the programmed instruction are generally performed at the moment at which it first becomes possible to write out such an instruction. In this case, the stages in converting the statement

$x := a - bxc + e/f$

will be as follows:

STACK			PROGRAMMED INSTRUCTION			
$x := a - b$	x	$c +$	$\times$	b	c	$t1$
$x := a - t1 +$			$-$	a	$t1$	$t2$
$x := t2 + e/f;$			$/$	e	f	$t3$
$x := t2 + t3;$			$+$	$t2$	$t3$	x

The ALPHA-translator differs from this in that the instruction is written out only when all operations at one level of precedence have been incorporated in the stack. This makes it possible to unite all operations of a given level in one multi-instruction (III.2). In the ALPHA-translator the same example can be converted in the following manner:

STACK	PROGRAMMED INSTRUCTION
$x := a - b \quad c \quad x+$	$\times_{00} \quad b \quad c \quad t1$
$x := a - t1 + e/f;$	$\times_{01} \quad e \quad f \quad t2$
$x := a - t1 + t2;$	$+_{010} \quad a \quad t1 \quad t2 \, x$

The index of the sign of the operation indicates the actual sign of the operation (direct or reverse) with which the corresponding operand enters the multi instructions.

2.3.3 Algorithms for programming expressions have a further feature in that the nesting structure of expressions is incompletely liquidated, also affecting the subscript expressions and arguments of function designators. This is done for the sake of maximum retention of information relating to the primary structure of the ALPHA-program for subsequent optimization. For example, after operation of the expression programming blocks, a statement of the form

$$x := a[i+j] + b[f(i+j)]$$

is converted to the following statements in the intermediate language

$$+_{00}a[+_{001}ijC_1\,t1]\,b[f(+_{00}ijt2,t3) + _{01}t3C_2\,t4]\,x$$

where C_1 and C_2 are the lower bound pairs of arrays a and b, and one parameter is added to function f, to denote the result of calculating the function.

The appearance of multi-instructions with lower bounds of arrays is connected with yet another form of standardization which is introduced during programming of expressions. All subscript expressions are converted so that it is possible to make the lower bound of all arrays zero from then on.

Recording the statement as above makes it possible, for example, to explain that the choice of component of the array a in a given case is determined by the value of the variable i, and if i is a control-variable, this information allows a more nearly optimal program to be constructed. If this statement has been converted to the general form:

$$+_{001} \quad ij \quad C_1 \quad t1$$
$$+_{00} \quad ij \quad t2$$
$$f(t2,t3)$$
$$+_{01} \quad t3 \quad C_2 \quad t4$$
$$+_{00} \quad a[t1] \quad 6[t4]\,x$$

it will be much more difficult to obtain information relating to the dependence of a on i.

By analogy with the case described above, preservation of multi-instructions which calculate the actual parameter of the function designators in the position of the argument makes it possible to analyse procedure statements with a view to selecting the optimum method of programming these (Chapter V).

2.3.4   During the decomposition of expressions it is essential to perform further standardization of switches. The switch declarations are converted into lists of branch statements according to the syntax of the internal language. Thus the intermediate form of switch from para 1.3.2.5.

Switch S: {**go to** $S1$; **go to** $S2$; **go to** Q; [m];
          {**if** $v > -5$, **then go to** $S3$ **else go to** $S4$}}

will assume the form:

S: $\ulcorner$**go to** $S1$ **go to** $S2$ **go to** $M1$ **go to** $M2\urcorner$
    $M1 : r1 := m$ **go to** Q
    $M2 : $**if** $\neg$ $(v > -5)$ **then go to** $S3$ **else go to** $S4$.

where $r1$ is the standard communication cell—one for all switches which retains the number of the element of the switch list; $\ulcorner$ $\urcorner$ are brackets which bound the switch list.

2.3.5   Transfers to the compound labels of the form "**go to** $M1. M2. M3$" are also programmed during this pass. We note that the whole program counts as the scope of each identifier at the level of the intermediate language. For this reason, if branch to the compound label meant only transfer of control to said point of the program, the branch statement referred to would be well enough described in the form "**go to** $M3$". Since the branch to the compound label involves execution of all actions connected with entry into the blocks, this branch statement is programmed in the form:

      TR $P1$ $M1$ $T1$
    $P1 : $**TR** $P2$ $M2$ $T2$
    $P2 : $**to** $M3$

where **TR** ABC is the return transfer of control to B returning to A by the return statement denoted by the lavel C. The distribution of labels $M1$, $M2$, $M3$, $T1$ and $T2$ in the program is given by the following scheme:

$M1 : \{(D1) T1 : W1 \ldots M2 : \{(D2) T2 : W2 \ldots M3 \ldots\}$

where $(D1)$ and $(D2)$ are call statements to the administrative system, calculating lengths of arrays and other ancillary actions which are performed on entry into blocks $M1$ and $M2$ respectively. $W1$ and $W2$ are symbols of return statements of the self-destroying type which are automatically disappeared after their execution.

2.3.6   According to the rules of the Input language, the initial value of an own variable z must be assigned only during the first entry into the block, in which z is declared. In this connection, the statement $z := E$ constructed on processing the declarations of the initial values (1.2.3.5) is supplemented by the following statements:

$M1 : W$
TR $M3\, M2\, M1$
$M2 : z := E$
$M3 : ,$

where W is the symbol of the usual return statement. During the first passage of the program W is not changed, hence it passes control to **TR** following which it is changed there by jump of $M3$.

3 Implementation of the Algorithms in the ALPHA-Translator

As has already been stated, the algorithms described are performed by Blocks 2–5 of the ALPHA-translator. The blocks operate in complete conformity with the scannings described. Block 2 processes the declaration and fills the identifier tables. Block 3 converts identifiers and delimiters in the ALPHA-program into a 22-digit code and performs the described conversions in the ALPHA-program. Block 4 analyses expressions and conditional statements, whilst Block 5 determines the types and structure of formal parameters and intermediate variables.

Acknowledgements

Development of the blocks was carried out by the author and G. I. Babetsky, who constructed the flow-chart and the program for Block 3, while S. K. Kozhykhina wrote the program for Blocks 4 and 5.

In conclusion the author would like to express his gratitude to the colleagues at the Programming Department of the Siberian Division of the Academy of Sciences Computing Centre, who participated in discussion on the algorithm for programming expressions in the ALPHA-translator.

References

1. YERSHOV, A. P. (1958). "Programming program for high speed electronic computing machines". Academy of Sciences of the U.S.S.R., Moscow.
2. ZAIKINA, G. M. and LAVROV, S. S.(1961)."An algorithm for converting a program from ALGOL 60 into machine language". Report at the IV All-Union Mathematical Congress, Leningrad, 3–12th July.
3. KAMYNIN, S. S. LYUBIMSKII, E. Z. and SHURA-BURA, M. R. (1958). "Automation of programming with the aid of programming programs". *Problems of Cybernetics*. No. 1, Moscow Publication Fizmatgiz.

V PROGRAMMING OF PROCEDURES IN THE ALPHA-TRANSLATOR

B. A. ZAGATSKII

The task of programming procedures arises when designing translators employing ALGOL 60 and its modifications, and subsets which permit the utilization of procedures. The commonest method for programming procedures is described in an article by Ingerman.[1] The essential features of this method are as follows. The procedure statements and the procedure declarations are programmed independently of one another. For each actual parameter the program "*thunk*"† is formed which "carries out" the actual parameter and issues the name of the result. A call to the subprogram into which the procedure body is converted is formed in the place of each procedure statement. A call to the corresponding "thunk" is inserted before each entry of the formal parameter and the name issued by this "thunk" is used in various ways, depending on the character of the formal parameter.

The main value of this method lies in its comparative simplicity of implementation. Its drawback is the poor quality of the program obtained. An analysis of some actual programs shows that in many cases the form of the actual parameters and the way in which they are used means that their substitution could be carried out in a far simpler way. The universality of the "thunk" method compels one to proceed in all situations by the most common method.

During the development of the ALPHA-translator the author was faced with the problem of finding algorithms for programming the procedures which would take into account the substantial complexity of the use of the procedures in the program to be translated while at the same time preserving the universality of the method. For this purpose, a mixed strategy for programming procedures was included in the ALPHA-translator, whereby the universal method just described was supplemented by a series of simpler rules for the programming of the procedures. A suitable programming method is selected for the ALPHA-translator on the basis of an analysis and classification of the actual parameters in the procedure statements and of the nature of their usage in the procedure bodies.

† A *thunk* is a piece of coding which provides an address. When executed, it leaves in some standard location (memory, accumulator, N index register, for example) the address of the variable with which it is associated. There is precisely one thunk associated with each parameter in each specific procedure statement. (The handling of arrays requires a slightly extended definition.) If an actual parameter is an expression, the associated thunk (each time it is used) evaluates the expression, stores the value in some temporary location, and delivers the address of the temporary location. If an actual parameter is a subscripted variable, the thunk (each time it is used) delivers the address of the specified element of the array. If an actual parameter is a conditional expression the thunk selects from alternatives and delivers the appropriate address. Copyright © 1961, Association for Computing Machinery, Inc.

In this way programming procedure is broken down into two tasks: classifying the actual parameters and finding ways of programming the substitution of the actual parameters of a given class, and analysing the statements and the procedure bodies to obtain the information needed to classify them.

The algorithm for programming procedures is described in connection with the general structure of the ALPHA-translator, that is with a few assumptions about the form of the program to be translated both before and after programming procedures. During the translation process, statements and procedure bodies are converted into the statements of the internal language (III.2). The description of the programming algorithm is given mainly in Algol terminology and therefore the form of the program to be translated before programming the procedures has no particular significance. The only essential condition is that information about the kind, type and dimension of all formal parameters of the procedures (IV.2) is gathered before commencing the operation of the algorithm described.

The algorithm for programming procedures in the ALPHA-translator operates with some limitations on the utilization of the procedure in the ALPHA-program (II.1). Out of these only the absence of the recursive procedures and the recursive calls is used in the algorithms just described. The rest of the limitations are only connected with the mechanism for gathering the above mentioned information about the formal parameters.

1   Classification of the Actual Parameters and Ways of Programming their Substitution

As a result of the work of the algorithm for programming the procedures, each statement S of the procedure P is replaced by a word of the kind: ABC, where A and C are programs in the internal language which carry out the substitution of the actual parameters of the statement S in the procedure body P (A and C may be empty) and B is the program which implements the call to the procedure body P.

After this body has been executed there is a return to the word C.

We shall now set forth the ways of programming the substitution of the actual parameters for the formal ones.

1.1   Actual Parameters—Calculated Expressions

In order to simplify this account we shall introduce some concepts.

1.1.1   The calculating expression which contains† at least one operational sign or function designator outside the subscript brackets will be referred to as the calculating expression *in the strict sense*.

The composed variables, the formed variables and the subscripted variables with subscripts where an empty position is situated to the left of an occupied one in the subscript positions will be referred to as *composite variables*.

We shall state that a given variable is recalculated when the procedure

† "X contains Y" means that Y enters X graphically as a constituent.

statement is being carried out, if it is recalculated in the procedure body or (and) constitutes the actual parameter of this statement which is to be recalculated in the procedure body.

The special cell which connects the formal parameter with its corresponding actual parameter during the running of the final program, will be referred to as the *connection cell*. Every formal parameter has its own connection cell. The nature of the information stored in it will become evident further on.

When programming the substitution of an actual parameter, it is sometimes necessary to introduce a new variable, of the same kind and structure as the corresponding formal parameter and localized in the block. In future this will always be referred to as the *T-variable*.

We shall refer to the program which assigns the value of the actual parameter of the *T*-variable as the *"Thunk" without address*.

We shall refer to the program which assigns to the *T*-variable the value of the actual parameter with conversion of its type to the type of the *T*-variable, as the "thunk" *without address with a type conversion*.

We shall refer to the program which, in the case of the actual parameter of a subscripted variable or of a simple variable, supplies the connection cell with the address of the actual parameter as the *"thunk" with address*; in the case of the actual parameter—the calculating expression in the narrow sense or of the composite variable, it assigns the value of the actual parameter of the *T*-variable and supplies the connection cell with the address of the *T*-variable.

We shall refer to the program which assigns to the *T*-variable the value of the actual parameter by converting its type to the type of the *T*-variable and which supplies the connection cell with the address of the *T*-variable, as the *"thunk" with address with type conversion*.

If the variable is an array its address is taken to be the address of its first component. The address is given in the internal language by means of the statement (III.2.4).

The actual parameters will be called *related* if they correspond to a given formal parameter of some procedure.

1.1.2 All the actual parameters which are calculating expressions will be classified.

1st class. The actual parameter of any structure and of any type which coincides graphically with all the actual parameters related to it; it does not contain the function designators nor any formal parameters; it is not a composite variable.

2nd class. An actual parameter of any type and structure which possesses properties such that neither itself not any variable which enters it graphically is recalculated while executing the procedure statement which contains the actual parameter in question.

3rd class. An actual parameter of any type and structure which is a calculating expression in the narrow sense, where at least one variable which enters the actual parameter graphically, is recalculated during the execution of the procedure statement which contains the actual parameter in question.

4th class. An actual parameter of any type and structure which is the variable to be recalculated in the procedure body.

5th class. An actual parameter of any type and structure which is a subscripted variable where at least one variable which enters the subscript positions graphically, is recalculated during execution of the procedure statement which contains the actual parameter in question.

6th class. An actual parameter of the 5th class called by name and substituted for the formal parameter to be recalculated in the procedure body.

7th class. An actual parameter of any type and structure which is a subscripted variable called by name and substituted for the formal parameter, to be recalculated in the procedure body.

8th class. An actual parameter of any type which is a simple scalar variable called by name and substituted for the formal parameter to be recalculated in the procedure body.

We shall now give the different methods of programming the substitution of the actual parameter, the calculating expression, for the formal one. The following points should be noted beforehand. During the programming of the procedure body the type and structure of the formal parameter are taken from the corresponding actual parameters (see Chapter IV). If at least one of them is a **real** number the formal parameter will be taken as of the **real** type. Thus the only possible difference between the types of actual and formal parameters is that the actual parameter is an **integer** whilst the corresponding formal parameter is **real**.

Some of the programming methods will have variations—(a) (b) and (c). In that case, variation (a) will be used for an actual parameter which is not a composite variable and which is of the same type as the formal parameter; variation (b) will be used for an actual parameter whose type does not coincide with the type of the formal parameter; variation (c) will be used for an actual parameter which is a composite variable.

If the actual parameter is a composite variable and its type does not coincide with the type of the formal parameter, a combination of variations (b) and (c) will be used.

1.1.3 The various methods of programming actual parameters are enumerated below.

Method 1. In the procedure body all formal parameter entries are changed to the corresponding actual parameter.

Method 2. At the start of the procedure body a program, which assigns the value of the actual parameter to the *T*-variable, is compiled. In the procedure body all the formal parameter entries are changed to the *T*-variable.

Method 3. At the end of the procedure body a program, which assigns the value of the *T*-variable to the actual parameter, is compiled. In the procedure body all formal parameter entries are changed to the *T*-variable.

Method 4. A program is compiled in the procedure statement position at the word A:

(a) assigning the value of the actual parameter to the *T*-variable;

(b) assigning the value of the actual parameter, converted from an integer into a real number, to the T-variable.

In the procedure body all the formal parameter entries are changed to the T-variable.

Method 4. A program is compiled in the procedure statement position at the word A:

(a) supplying the connection cell or the address of the actual parameter;
(b) assigning the value of the actual parameter, converted from an integer into a real number, to the T-variable and placing the address of the variable into the connection cell;
(c) assigning the value of the actual parameter to the T-variable and placing the address of the variable into the connection cell.

At the start of the procedure a program is compiled substituting all formal parameter entries of the procedure body by the contents of the connection cell. The substitution of the formal parameters by the contents of the connection cell is indicated in the internal language by means of special formation statements (see III.2.5).

Method 6. Equivalent to Method 4. It is listed as a separate method so that if need be it is given priority over the 5th method.

Method 7. During procedure statement programming the following are compiled:

(a) "thunk" without address;
(b) "thunk" without address with type conversion.

A program, which carries out the call to the necessary "thunk" is compiled in the procedure body before each formal parameter entry. All formal parameter entries into the procedure body are replaced by the T-variable.

Method 8. During the procedure statement programming the following are compiled:

(a) "thunk" with address;
(b) "thunk" with address with type conversion;
(c) "thunk" with address.

A program, which carries out the call to the necessary "thunk" and which replaces the formal parameter entry to be processed, by the contents of the connection cell, is compiled in the procedure body before each formal parameter entry.

Method 9. A program is compiled in the procedure statement position, in the word C:

(a) assigning the value of the T-variable to the actual parameter;
(b) assigning the value of the T-variable, converted from a real number into an integer, to the actual parameter.

In the procedure body all formal parameter entries are substituted by the T-variable.

Method 10. When programming the procedure statement two "thunks" are compiled:

(a) the first one is a "thunk" without address; the second one is a program which assigns the value of the T-variable to the actual parameter;
(b) the first one is a "thunk" without address with type conversion;

the second one is a program which assigns the value of the T-variable, converted from a real number to an integer, to the actual parameter.

In the procedure body, a program for the call to the requisite first "thunk" is compiled before each formal parameter entry; after each formal parameter entry as a result, a program is compiled for call to the requisite second "thunk". All the formal parameter entries into the procedure body are substituted by the T-variable.

Method 11. When programming the procedure statement two "thunks" are compiled;

(a) the first one is a "thunk" with address; the second one is an empty program;
(b) the first one is a "thunk" with address type conversion;

the second one is a program which assigns the value of the T-variable converted from a real number to an integer, to the actual parameter;

(c) the first one is "thunk" with address;

the second one is a program which assigns the value of the T-variable to the actual parameter.

A program is compiled in the procedure body before each formal parameter entry, for the call to the requisite first "thunk" and for the substitution of this formal parameter entry by the contents of the connection cell; after each formal parameter entry as a result a program is compiled for the call to the requisite second "thunk".

It should be pointed out that the numbering of the methods was chosen so that the higher the number the greater is the generality of the substitution mechanism.

For each actual parameter the number of the method for the programming of its substitution is a function of the class number of this actual parameter, of the method of substitution (by name, value and result, value and result together), of the correlation between the types of the actual and formal parameters, of the structure of the actual parameter and—for arrays—of whether the actual parameter is a composite variable or not.

A table is given below making it possible to select a method of programming the substitution for each actual parameter.

It may happen that some actual parameter falls simultaneously into more than one class. Several methods of programming will then be required. The method with the greatest number will be chosen.

Several actual parameters, to which the various methods of programming have been prescribed, may correspond to one formal parameter P. The method

Number of the programming method

	Type of the actual parameter coincides with the form of the formal parameter				Type of the actual parameter conflicts with the form of the formal parameter			
Class no.	By name	By value	By result	By value and result	By name	By value	By result	By value and result
An actual parameter which has a zero dimension (a scalar)								
1	1	2	3	2 & 3	—	—	—	—
2	4	4	9	4 & 9	4	4	9	4 & 9
3	7	4	9	4 & 9	7	4	9	4 & 9
4	5	4	9	4 & 9	7	4	9	4 & 9
5	7	4	9	4 & 9	7	4	9	4 & 9
6	8	4	9	4 & 9	11	4	9	4 & 9
7	5	4	9	4 & 9	11	4	9	4 & 9
8	5	4	9	4 & 9	10	4	9	4 & 9
An actual parameter which has a positive dimension (an array) and which is not a composite variable								
1	1	2	3	2 & 3	—	—	—	—
2	5	5	9	6 & 9	5	5	9	6 & 9
3	8	4	9	6 & 9	8	4	9	6 & 9
4	5	6	9	6 & 9	8	6	9	6 & 9
5	8	5	9	6 & 9	8	6	9	6 & 9
6	—	—	—	—	—	—	—	—
7	5	6	9	6 & 9	11	6	9	6 & 9
8	—	—	—	—	—	—	—	—
An actual parameter which is a composite variable								
1	—	—	—	—	—	—	—	—
2	5	5	9	5 & 9	5	5	9	5 & 9
3	—	—	—	—	—	—	—	—
4	8	4	9	4 & 9	8	4	9	4 & 9
5	8	4	9	4 & 9	8	4	9	4 & 9
6	—	—	—	—	—	—	—	—
7	11	4	9	4 & 9	11	4	9	4 & 9
8	—	—	—	—	—	—	—	—

A dash in a line of the table indicates that the given kind of actual parameter cannot be related to the corresponding class.

with the greatest number is chosen. The substitutions of all actual parameters corresponding to the formal parameter are also programmed by this method.

If the actual parameter is called simultaneously by value and result, its substitution is programmed using two different methods at the same time, indicated as follows in the table:

$n \& m$

where n and m are the numbers of the methods.

1.2　The Actual Parameter—The Designational Expression

There are two methods used for programming the substitution of the actual parameter for the formal one.

(1) If the actual parameter corresponds graphically to all the actual parameters related to it and does not contain any formal parameters and (or) any function designators, all the entries of the corresponding formal parameter in the procedure body are substituted by this actual parameter.

(2) In all other cases, when processing the procedure statement, a *"thunk" with transfer of control* is set up—a program which calculates the value of the actual parameter and carries out the transfer of control by this value.

In the procedure body all the go to statements to the corresponding formal parameter are replaced by transfers to the requisite "thunk".

1.3　The Actual Parameter—The Identifier of the Array

When the subscript brackets with empty subscript positions have been added to the identifier of the array, the actual parameter thus obtained becomes a calculating expression, ways of programming the substitution of which were examined in Section 1.1.

1.4　The Actual Parameter—The Switch Identifier

The subscript brackets with the subscript expression which is the integral scalar d are added to the actual parameter, so that the actual parameter is converted to the designational expression. In the procedure body a program is compiled before each go to statement to the switch designator which assigns to the variable d the value of the subscript expression of this switch designator while the subscript brackets together with their contents are discarded from the program. The net result is that we arrive at case 1.2 (the actual parameter —the designational expression).

1.5　The Actual Parameter—The Identifier of the Procedure

Let the actual parameter F be substituted for the formal parameter f. In this case it is considered that there is a *list of substitutes* for f—a list of relative actual parameters which will replace it.

If all the elements in the list of substitutes coincide graphically, that is, are identical to F, all f entries in the procedure body are substituted by F ones.

Otherwise, when processing the procedure statement, a program is compiled in the word A which transfers the ordinal number of F in the list of substitutes to the connection cell. In the procedure body the *formal procedure statement*, that is the procedure statement whose identifier is f, is replaced by a group of *actual statements* each of which is obtained from the formal one by replacing f by the corresponding element in the list of substitutes. Prior to this group of statements a program is compiled which carries out the control of transfer to the requisite statement in the group, according to the value of the connection cell. Each statement in the group is processed using the normal algorithm.

1.6　Programming of Function-Procedures and Function-Expressions

It is considered that by introducing supplementary formal and corresponding actual parameters which denote the result of the calculation of the functions, the function designators and declarations of the functions can first be converted into procedures statements and declarations so that the normal algorithm for procedure programming can be applied to them with the one difference that all actual parameters of the statements of the functions *a priori* are not recalculable. The last supposition is valid because side effects are disregarded (II.1).

2   The Algorithm for Defining the Class and Method of Programming an Actual Parameter

From what has been said above it follows that in order that a method of programming an actual parameter could be found, the following must be known:

(a) the kind of the actual parameter (calculating expression, designational expression, procedure identifier)†
(b) whether or not all the actual parameters corresponding to a given formal parameter are identical.

In addition, for the actual parameter—the calculating expression—the following must also be known:

(c) the structure of the actual parameter;
(d) whether the actual parameter is a composite variable;
(e) whether the types of actual parameter and the corresponding formal parameter correlate;
(f) the method of substituting the actual parameter (by name, value, result, value and result together);
(g) the number of the class to which the actual parameter belongs.

For the formal parameter—the procedure identifier there must be a list of substitutes and a list of the actual parameters which correspond to it. Obtaining the information of the type (a), (b), (c), (d), (e) and (f) does not present any great problem. It is sufficient to scan the program to be translated once, and during this the necessary analysis of the actual and formal parameters is carried out. But to ascertain the class number of the actual parameter—the calculating expression—it must be known which variables can be recalculated when executing each procedure statement and in each procedure body, as follows from Section 1.1. This requires a special method for processing the program to be translated which will be described below.

Since one method of programming is chosen for all the related actual parameters which comprise the programming methods for the individual actual parameters, it would appear to be convenient to collect and store the information about the series of related actual parameters in a special *table of formal parameters*, into which entries are made according to the number of the formal parameter.

---

† There is no need to consider the actual parameters—the array and switch identifiers in view of what has been stated in Sections 1.3 and 1.4.

Information about the *procedure bodies* is collected and stored in a *table of procedures* into which entries are made according to the number of the procedure.

The algorithm for the selection of the method of programming the actual parameter which is described here consists of three parts which operate consecutively.

2.1   The First Part

An examination of the program to be translated is made, during which the following steps are implemented.

(a) All the procedure statements are copied out into the subsidiary file with a list structure, called the *common list* (III.3.2).

The number of the line in the common list is then inserted into the procedure table for each procedure, beginning with the one in which the first statement of this procedure is located. At the end of each statement, excluding the last one, the number of the line in the common list in which the next procedure statement starts, is inserted. The last statement of this procedure is indicated by the end tag.

In the case of the formal procedure statement, all the actual statements which arise as a result of replacing the parameter—procedure identifier by corresponding actual parameters are copied out into the common list.

If the procedure statement P is located in another procedure body the name of the next procedure within which P is located is indicated in the common list at the end of statement P.

(b) For each procedure body lists of the variables to be recalculated in this procedure are compiled. In that case, when—as happens in the ALPHA-translator—at the beginning of the translation the initial identifiers are replaced by symbols which are numbered consecutively, it is convenient to use the logical scales. For each procedure a scale is allotted, the length of which is equal to the number of variables in the program to be translated. For the variables which are to be recalculated in the corresponding scale positions the **true** values are set down. The scales are placed into the common list. Their starting point in this is shown in the procedure table.

During the operation of the first part, only those variables for which there is an explicit assignment in the body appear in the lists of the variables to be recalculated.

(c) A *procedure graph* is constructed which shows, for any given procedures, which procedures we are able to call from its body. It takes the form of a Boolean square matrix whose dimension is equal to the number of procedures in the program. If the jth procedure statement is encountered in the ith procedure body, the **true** value occurs where the ith line and the jth column intersect in this matrix. A similar matrix, but for other purposes, is described in a paper by Hawkins and Huxtable.[2]

2.2   The Second Part

As a result of the operation of the second part of the algorithm, complete lists of the variables to be recalculated, for each procedure body and each procedure statement, are compiled. Lists for the procedure statements in the form of scales, are placed into the common list, and at the end of each statement the beginning of the corresponding scale in the common list is indicated. Assuming that the initial identifiers of the ALPHA-program are replaced by symbols that have consecutive numbering, the second part is carried out by a block written below in a language which is "almost" Input language. To avoid confusion in the details of arithmetic of the basic symbols of the program to be translated, two text variables are introduced, for which the basic symbols serve as the values. The significance of the non-declared procedures is clear either from the choice of the identifiers and of the parameters delimiters or from the comments.

> **begin**
> **integer** n, m;
> **comment** n *is the number of procedures in the program,*
> *m is the number of variables;*
> > **begin**
> > **Boolean matrices** $A[1:n, 1:n]$, $S[1:n, 1:m]$;
> > **comment** *The matrix $A[,]$ represents the procedure graph and is discussed below. The matrix $S[,]$ is the array of the scales of the variables to be recalculated in the procedure bodies. The ith row of this matrix is the scale of the variables to be recalculated in the ith procedure body;*
> > **integers** i, j, k, p;
> > **procedure** *The formation of the scales for the $(i)^{th}$ procedure statements with modification of the scales of procedures which include them;* **value** i; **integer** i;
> > > **begin**
> > > **Boolean vectors** $S1, S2, S3$ $[1:m]$;
> > > **text variables** ACP, FRP; **integers** $1, F$;
> > > **comment** *In the procedure body the statements of non-declared procedures are used. The result of their operation is described informally in the headings;*
> > > *The preparation for the analysis of the first statement of the ith procedure;*
> > > $S1[\ ] := S[i]$;
> > > *The analysis of the next statement:*
> > > $FRP :=$ *the first formal parameter of the ith procedure;*
> > > $S2[\ ] := S2[\ ] := false$
> > > **if** *the ith procedure is with parameters* **then**
> > > **for** $l := 1, l + 1$ **until** *the procedure statement is completed* **do**
> > > *Analysis of the actual parameter:*
> > > $ACP :=$ *The first symbol of the $(i)^{th}$ the actual parameter of the procedure statement;*
> > > **if** ACP *is a variable and* $\neg FKP$ *is called by value* & $S1$ [*The number* (FRP)] **then**
> > > $S2$ [*The number* (ACP)] $:= S3$ [*The number* (ACP)] $:=$ **true**;
> > > $FPR :=$ *next formal parameter*
> > > **end**;

$S2[\ ] := S2[\ ] \vee (S1[\ ] \oplus S3[\ ])$;
The insertion of $S2[\ ]$ *into the common list with an indication at the end of the statement of the reference to* $S2[\ ]$;
$F :=$ *the number of the procedure in whose body the statement is located*;
if $F \neq 0$ **then** $S[F,] := S[F,] \vee S2[\ ]$;
if *the statement is not the last one* **then**
{*Transfer to the next statement*;
go to *Analysis of the next statement*}
end *of the procedure for the formation of the scales*;
$p := 0$; **while** $p < n$ **do**
for i := 1 ..., n **do**
begin
for $j := 1, \ldots, n$ **do** {**if** $A[i,j]$ **then go to** M};
The formation of the scales for the $(i)^{\text{th}}$ *procedure statements with modification of the scales of procedures which include them*;
for $k := 1, \ldots, n$ **do** $A[k,j] =$ **false**;
$p := p + 1$; **if** $p = n$ **then go to** N;
M; **end**;
N; **end**
End *of second part*;

2.3 The Third Part

The procedure statements which are located in the common list are again analysed. All the information necessary for finding a method of programming the actual parameter from the table, is collected in a table of formal parameters. It is convenient to obtain the final number of the method for programming the actual parameter—calculating expression by enumerating the methods in the order of increasing universality, as was done in Section 1. The number of the method is inserted into the table of formal parameters. During the analysis of the next actual parameter, the method of programming is defined and the number of this method is put down on the table of formal parameters, if it exceeds the earlier number in the table.

Thus, when the work of the algorithm which defines the method of programming the actual parameter is complete, the number of the programming method for the actual parameters corresponding to every formal parameter can be found in the table of formal parameters. Lists of the variables to be recalculated when carrying out each procedure statement are located in the common list.

3 Algorithm for Procedure Programming

This algorithm is a library of individual algorithms, each of which carries out one of the programming methods described in Section 1, and a switch which selects the appropriate algorithm. The algorithm for programming procedures is applied during one pass of the program to be translated.

In Section 1, when discussing the programming methods, it was said that when programming procedures, it is necessary, for each formal parameter, to introduce a connection cell and in some cases the T-variable which has the type and structure of the formal parameter. It is convenient to keep the names of these variables in the table of formal parameters.

All the methods of programming the substitution of the actual parameter for the formal one which use the thunk device demand a method of procedure which allows—when the object program is being run—to call from the procedure body to the "requisite" thunk, that is to the thunk of that actual parameter which enters the procedure statement being executed at that moment. This is done in the following way. Each thunk is marked with a particular label. A switch is formed, the switch list of which consists of the labels of the thunk of the actual parameters corresponding to one formal parameter and taken in the order in which these actual parameters occur in the program. A certain integral scalar α is introduced. All the statements of one procedure are numbered in the order in which they occur in the program. When programming in the position of the procedure statement, in the word B, a program which assigns to the variable α the number of the procedure statement to be processed is compiled in front of the call to the procedure body. In the procedure body the call to the "requisite" thunk is carried out via the call to the switch designator, in whose subscript position the variable α is located.

4   Implementation of the Described Method in the ALPHA-Translator

The described method for programming procedures is implemented by the two Blocks 6 and 7 which operate one after the other, each carrying out one pass of the program to be translated.

We shall describe the initial information for these blocks and the main stages of their operation.

4.1   Initial Information

After the operation of the first five blocks of the ALPHA-translator the program to be translated is written in the intermediate language with 22-bit coding of the basic symbols (III.2.5). Since we are not describing the language as a whole we are limited to such data as is necessary for the account which is given below.

Each identifier in this language consists of two parts. The first part—the tag part—shows to which class the identifier belongs. In the case of variables, there is also at this point some information derived from their declarations. The second part of the identifier is the symbol number within the class.

In particular, all the formal parameters in the ALPHA-program are separated out into an individual class and numbered in succession so that each procedure has its own range (possibly empty) of numbers of the formal parameters which belong to it.

The statement part of the program to be translated (the master file) has already been processed by the blocks for programming expressions. As a result each assignment statement is replaced by a series of "multi-instructions" each of which consists of the operation sign, the variable-arguments and the variable-result. The actual parameters of the procedure statements and the subscript expressions, which are the calculating expressions in the strict sense, are replaced by such multi-instructions.

All the designational expressions which are the actual parameters of the procedure statements or (and) which enter the switch lists, are converted into the statements for branch to the values of this designational expression.

All actual parameters—array identifiers are converted into actual parameters—variables with empty subscript positions.

All actual parameters—switch identifiers—are converted into programs which cause the branch to the requisite term in the switch list of this switch (the number of the term is calculated in the procedure body before each entry of the corresponding formal parameter).

In the lists of actual (formal) parameters following each actual (formal) parameter which is an array (name of an array) new actual (formal) parameters are inserted which impose bound pairs of the array. The new actual parameters are called by value for the new formal parameters.

The declarations and statements of all the functions are converted into procedures and declarations statements. For this purpose one more parameter is added to the list of actual parameters for each function designator, which has the type and structure of the value of the function. In the declaration of the function a new formal parameter is accordingly added to the list of formal parameters which has the type and structure of the value of the function. In the function body all the entries of its identifier are replaced by the new formal parameter. The new actual parameter is therefore called by result for the new formal parameter. The function designators are taken out of the calculating expressions which contain them and are put in front of them. The entries of these designators in the calculating expressions are replaced by the corresponding new actual parameters.

The rest of the information is kept in the form of additional transit arrays.

Information of a very different kind is kept in the common list (III.3.2). Entry into the common list is carried out by references located in the other master tables.

In the table of the arrays certain information is stored for each array, which includes a reference to the common list and to the location of the bound pairs of this array. Entry into the table of the arrays is according to the number of the array.

The numerical value of each constant is stored in the table of constants. Entry into the table of constants is according to the number of the constant.

In the table of the procedures, information for each procedure is stored containing, in particular, data about the number of calls to this procedure, the range of numbers of its formal parameters and as to whether this procedure is a function. Entry into the table is according to the number of the procedure.

The method of substituting each formal parameter is kept in the table of formal parameters (by name, value, result, value and result); the kind it takes (calculating expression, designational expression, procedure identifier); its type (real, integer, Boolean or complex); the number of subscripts; reference to the common list where the bound pairs are stored if this formal parameter is an array; if the formal parameter is a procedure identifier, a reference is kept to the common list where the list of procedure identifiers is located—the actual parameters which correspond to this formal parameter (the list of the substitutes).

4.2 Analysis of the Procedures

The operation of Block 6 which analyses the procedures consists of the following stages.

4.2.1 The master file is scanned and

(a) all the procedure statements are copied out into the common list with the indication, for each statement, of the procedure body in which it is located;

(b) a list of the variables is compiled for each procedure for which there is an explicit assignment in the procedure body (which are the results of the multi-instructions entering the body);

(c) a graph of the procedures is constructed which shows, for any procedure, to which of the procedures contained in its body, calls may be made.

4.2.2 For each procedure statement a list of variables is compiled which are recalculated upon its execution. When doing this the list of variables to be recalculated in the procedure body and the list of actual parameters of this procedure statement is used.

If a certain statement enters the procedure body F, the list of variables to be recalculated in the body F is supplemented by the list of variables to be recalculated on the execution of this statement.

The order in which the processing is carried out is determined by the procedure graph. At each stage statements of those procedures are processed whose bodies do not contain not yet processed statements. (Because of the absence of recursive calls and recursive procedures at least one statement from which there is no call to any other procedure will always be found. The process starts with this statement.)

Information about the position of the lists of variables to be recalculated when the procedure statements are executed is put into the table of the procedures.

4.2.3 The actual parameters of the procedure statements are classified and methods of programming their substitution chosen in accordance with the rules given in Section 1. The number of the method which is selected and various other informations are put into the table of the formal parameters.

4.3 Programming the Procedures

4.3.1 Block 7 scans the master file and, on the basis of the information obtained by Block 6, programs the procedure statements and bodies according to the rules in Section 1. The program ABC, which arises in the position of the procedure statement, is then enclosed within special brackets which separate it from the rest of the instructions of the master file. The procedure body remains in the statement brackets and the procedure identifier is put in front of it. The word B is programmed formally as a statement of the *go to* statement to the procedure identifier. A reference to the list of variables to be recalculated as a result of the execution of this statement is put in front of the closing bracket of the procedure statement.

When programming the procedures, the table of arrays can be supplemented (when establishing new variables—arrays) as can the table of constants (when establishing new constants—numbers of the procedure statements).

4.3.2 Some of the closing stages in the programming of the procedures are carried out by the intermediate Block 8 of the ALPHA-translator, whose chief task is to recode the main 22-bit symbols into 15-bit ones. Block 8 carries out the following functions which are connected with the programming of the procedures.

4.3.2.1 The procedure identifiers are extracted from the program because they are changed into labels. Branch to the procedure identifier is substituted by the return transfer of the control to the corresponding label. A return statement is placed at the end of procedure body. A list of labels (which mark the words C in the related procedure statements) to which it is possible to return from the given statement, is compiled.

4.3.2.2 The final lists of labels of the relative thunks are also copied from the common list at the end of the procedure body before the return operator (see Section 5.3).

4.3.2.3 At the end of the procedure statement program a list of the identifiers of the variables for which assignments are made when executing a given statement is copied out. This list, which is enclosed in a special kind of delimiters, is used when cleaning up the loops (VII.1).

4.3.2.4 The formal parameters are withdrawn from the program by being changed into identifiers of a corresponding nature (scalars, labels or index variables). The formal parameters called by name are changed into subscripted variables—"blanks" (III.2.4). By analysing the statements of the formation and the removal statements of the identifiers connected with the given formal parameter, a list of "fillers" which replace the given parameter of the identifiers is compiled, for each blank. These lists form a new transit array—the table of blanks.

The algorithms for programming procedures were worked out and implemented in the Department of the Theory of Algorithms and Programming, at the Computer Department of the Siberian Branch of the Academy of Sciences of the USSR. At every stage the work was discussed at departmental seminars. The author would like to express his thanks to all who took part in these seminars and especially to G. I. Kozhukhin and A. P. Yershov for their valuable advice and constant attention to the work.

REFERENCES

1. INGERMAN, P. A. (1961). Thunks. *Comms Ass. comput. Mach.* **4**, 1.
2. HAWKINS, E. N. and HUXTABLE, D. H. R. (1963). A multi-pass translation scheme for ALGOL 60. *In* "Annual review in automatic programming", Vol. 3. Pergamon Press, Oxford.

VI PROGRAMMING OPERATIONS OVER MULTIPLE ARRAYS AND COMPLEX VARIABLES IN THE ALPHA-TRANSLATOR

Yu. M. Voloshin

1 Posing the Problem

1.1 Analysis of Expansion of ALGOL *60 in the Input language*

We shall analyse the specific peculiarities of Input language as compared with ALGOL 60, which make it necessary to program operations over multiple dimensional variables, in accordance with the scheme shown in Fig. 1.

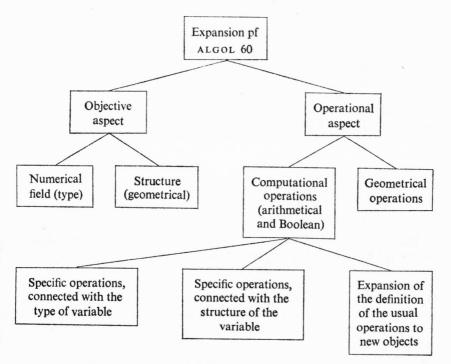

Fig. 1. Scheme of analysis of expansions of ALGOL 60

1.1.1 The most important difference between Input language, and ALGOL 60 is that the former makes it possible to introduce and apply multi-dimensional arrays wholly and (or) in terms of their non-scalar components rather than in terms of their scalar components. This feature is provided by the declaration of the array structures and by determination of operations over arrays (computational and geometrical) and allows operations with objects such as

4

a matrix which consists of vectors, etc. to be carried out. For example, a matrix C obtained as the result of the product of matrices A and B, can be expressed in the form:

real A, B, C-**matrices** $n \times n$; $C := A \times B$

1.1.2 We shall note some characteristic features of complex variables in Input language. One peculiarity is due to the fact that a transition from the region of real values to the complex ones and vice-versa must be checked by the human being who will write down the program in Input language, unlike the automatic insertion of conversion functions for transitions **integral** $\rightarrow$ **real** and **real** $\rightarrow$ **integral**.

For example, although the values of the expression con $(z) + z$, where con (z) is conjugate z, are real numbers for any given complex values of the variable z, the text

> **real** a;
> **complex** z;
> $a := z + con$ (z)

contains an error since the semantics of Input language are such that the declaration of the variable a requires the **complex** type. The real value of the indicated expression may be obtained by using the function Re (a).

Another characteristic consists of the fact that Input language does not contain any formal means for introducing complex numbers. Actually, complex numbers can be introduced into the text of the problem by using certain syntactic language constructions. For example, the calculation $z = \sin(\frac{1}{2} + \frac{3}{2}i)$ can be described in the following form:

> **complex** z, i; **real** a, b;
> $i = a + ib$; $a = 0$; $b = 1$;
> $z := \sin (0 \cdot 5 + i \times 1 \cdot 5)$.

The actual use of variables which assume complex values in Input language is ensured by introducing into the language functions such as *mod*, *Re*, *Im*, *arg*, *con* and by giving supplementary definitions for the usual arithmetic operations over complex variables.

1.1.3 The whole resources of linear algebra are applied directly to the language by means of such standard operations of linear algebra as matrix and scalar multiplication, calculation of a determinant (*det*), the degree of a matrix, etc. Apart from this, all the usual operations are defined as componentwise for objects of higher dimensions than matrices.

1.1.4 On the other hand, linear algebra contains operations over vectors and matrices which often have a geometric (non-computational) character. Such operations include for instance the formation of conjoined matrices in solving a linear system of equations, various methods of bounding, constructions with block matrices, etc. The construction of a conjoined matrix for a system $AX = B$ where A is a matrix of coefficients, X a vector of unknowns and B a vector of free terms, involves attaching to the matrix A an additiona¹ i.e. the vector B.

In computational practice, the tasks encountered involve homogeneous processing of variables which are not components of an array. In such cases, it is sometimes better to regard these values as components of a certain array with clearly determined structure, i.e. to carry out the actual geometrical operation of constructing an array and during further processing (especially when interchanging with external memory, input, output) denote this array by a single symbol. Forming and composing are operations of constructing arrays in Input language. The operation of formation makes it possible to form an array from arrays of lesser dimension (or from scalars); the operation of composition enables some arrays of identical dimensionality to be along one of the dimensions to form a larger array of the same dimensionality. These operations can be expressed in a clear way by using Hockney's good example[3] (p. 7, Fig. 2). It should be noted that geometric operations enable both variables

Formation   Composition

Fig. 2. Scheme of geometrical operations

and expressions to be composed. The variables and expressions thus obtained will be referred to as "*compound* ones". One important property of these operations is the preservation of linear ordering of scalar components of the compound array. If scalar compounds of some sub-array A in the compound array B are arranged in memory in consecutive cells, it will always be possible, after actually carrying out the operations of constructing the array B and arranging its scalar components in consecutive cells of memory, to indicate for the resulting array B a dimension which is such that projection of the sub-array A in any direction parallel to the given dimension will be a vector, the components of which are allocated in consecutive cells of memory.

1.2   The Problems of Programming and Optimizing Operations Over Arrays
The following two lists may provide some idea of these problems.
Programming
   (1) The operations of constructing arrays of variables and expressions;
   (2) the operations of linear algebra;
   (3) componentwise operations;
   (4) complex arithmetic;
   (5) operations over Boolean arrays.

Optimization
   (1) Reducing the number of selections and transfers during the actual performance of the operations of constructing arrays in the object program;
   (2) flexible programming of the operations of linear algebra (open or closed sub-routines);

(3) combining the loops of componentwise operations with replacement of intermediate operating arrays by scalar working variables;

(4) reducing the nesting of loops of componentwise operations;

(5) full consideration of all individual cases of complex arithmetic.

1.2.1 The problem of programming operations over arrays may be briefly formulated as follows: complete removal of the specificity of Input language and .conversion of all non-ALGOL constructions of the language (both for operations and for objects) to pure ALGOL constructions. Let us now examine these problems starting with the operation of constructing arrays. We shall analyse a simple example:

```
begin
arrays A, B, C [1 : 3], D [1 : 3, 1 : 3]
real Sp; integer k;
D [,] := |A [  ], B [  ], C [  ]|; Sp := 0;
for k := 1, ..., 3, do Sp := Sp + D [k,k];
A [1] := 0; B [2] := 1; C [3] := −1
end
```

Firstly, the statement $D [,] := |A [B], B [ ], C [ ]|$ which forms the matrix D from the vectors A, B, and C may be expressed in the form of a loop of explicit transfers of components of vectors A, B and C into the matrix D. The program will then assume the following form:

```
begin
array A, B, C [1 : 3], D [1 : 3, 1 : 3];
real Sp; integer k, t1, t2;
for t1 := 1, ..., 3 do
for t2 := 1, ..., 3 do
D [t1, t2] := if t1 = 1 ← then A [t2]
else if t1 = 2 ← then B [t2] ← else C [t2];
    Sp := 0;
for k := 1, ... 3 do Sp := Sp + D [k,k];
    A [1[ := 0; B [2] := 1; C [3] := −1
end
```

Secondly, if it is found possible to form the matrix D prior to executing the program of the actual allocation of the components of vectors A, B and C in memory in such a way that they form the matrix D, the program will have the form:

```
begin
array D [1 : 3, 1 : 3];
real Sp, integer k;
    Sp := 0;
for k := 1, ... 3 do Sp := Sp + D [k,k];
D [1,1] := 0; D [2,2] := 1; D [3,3] := −1
end
```

since A [1], B [2] and C [3] will have become components of the matrix D : D [1,1], D [2,2] and D [3,3], respectively.

These two variants reflect two possible methods of programming the operation of constructing arrays. The second method is preferable since this does not involve having to select elements of the compound array in a rather complicated organization. Unfortunately, this advantage cannot always be exploited; for example, the presence of a variable bound pair in one of the sub-arrays of the compound array requires the first method of programming. The second method necessitates substitutions of all the components entries of sub-arrays which enter into the compound array and denotation of these in terms of the resulting compound array. The essential difference in performing the operations of constructing arrays by these two methods, from the point of view of executing a program should be stressed. The first method is thus a purely dynamic one, since the instructions for selecting and referring components of the compound array are contained in the object program, whereas the second method is purely static since the actual compound array is established during translation. Choice between these two methods of programming will be made in the A L P H A-translator by analysing the situations encountered, as outlined below.

1.2.2 When operations of linear algebra are programmed (matrix and scalar multiplication, degree of matrix, calculation of inverse matrices, etc.) we encounter the following alternative which will be analysed for the case of the example in 1.1.1. The statement of Input language $C := A \times B$ where A, B and C are matrices can be represented at the level of A L G O L 60 by the following two methods:

(1) **integer** i, j, k; **real** t, s;
   for $i :=$ **step** 1 **until** n **do**
   begin
   for $j := 1$ **step** 1 **until** n **do**
   begin $s := 0$
   for $k := 1$ **step** 1 **until** n **do**
   begin $t := A$ $[i,k]$ x B $[k,j]$; $s = s + t$;
   end; C $[i,j] = s$
   end
   end

(2) *Multiplication of matrices* (A, B, C)

In this manner the statement of Input language, $C := A \times B$, can be programmed either by an explicit representation of the algorithms of the matricial multiplication (first method) or by including a call to a standard undeclared procedure (second method). The first method is termed the open insertion of a sub-routine, the second is described as application of a closed sub-routine. Each method has its own advantages and drawbacks. The advantage of the first method is that statements for the open form of the inserted program appear at the place of the Input language statement (similar to what has been stated above) and are accessible to all subsequent optimizing means of the translator such as economy of expressions, global economy of memory, etc. The drawback of this method of programming lies in the fact that the length of the program may be considerably extended. The second method extends the program to a lesser degree, but in this case implementing the object program entails extra time in operating the system which organizes the calls to corresponding standard sub-routines. Either of these methods is thus selected for statements of Input language which are operations of linear algebra and which require a fairly large number of calculations in order to restrict the volume of the object program as well as its running time. Operations such as multiplication of matrices, multiplication of matrices by vectors, addition and subtraction of matrices, etc. are performed by an open insertion of corresponding algorithms of their calculation. More complex operations such as calculating inverse matrices, determinants and others are thus performed by calls to the corresponding standard sub-routines.

1.2.3   The implementation of componentwise operations over arrays leads to the representation of loops of these operations over their components. In many cases, where the program in Input language containing operations over arrays imposes certain relationships in the dimensions of the arrays entering into it, it has been proved possible to combine several loops of component operations into one loop and thus reduce the number of instructions in the object program, which enter into the organization and control of the loop. For example, a fragment of the program in Input language

> **real numbers** A, B, C-**matrices** $n \times n$;
> $C := A + 2 \times B; \ldots$

will assume a form equivalent to the following piece of a program in Input language when using the method for programming expressions adopted in the ALPHA-translator (IV.2)

> $\ldots$ **real** A, B, C, T-**matrices** $n \times n$:
> $T : 2 \times B$
> $C := A + T; \ldots$

where the matrix T is the working array.

In accordance with what has been stated, this same fragment after representation of the loops of componentwise actions in ALGOL statements will assume the following form:

> $\ldots$ **arrays** A, B, C, T $[1 : n, 1 : n]$;
> **integer** i, j;
> **for** $i := 1$ **step** 1 **until** n **do**
> **for** $j := 1$ **step** 1 **until** n **do** $T[i,j] := 2 \times B[i,j]$;
> **for** $i := 1$ **step** 1 **until** n **do**
> **for** $j := 1$ **step** 1 **until** n **do** $C[i,j] := A[i,j] + T[i,j]; \ldots$

It will be readily seen that in the present case, the above fragment is functionally equivalent to the fragment

```
... arrays A, B, C, T [1 : n, 1 : n];
integer i, j;
for i := 1 step 1 until n do
for j := 1 step 1 until n do
begin T [i,j] := 2 × B [i,j];
      C [i,j] := A [i,j] + T [i,j]
end ...
```

where the loops of the componentwise operations are combined. We should also note that this fragment does not require the intermediate working array T since its components are used immediately after their calculation; This is why only one scalar working variable is required here and the fragment will consequently assume the following form:

```
... arrays A, B, C [1 : n, 1 : n];
integer i, j;
real t;
for i := 1 step 1 until n do
for j := 1 step 1 until n do
begin t := 2 × B [i,j]
C [i,j] := A [i,j] + t
end ...
```

A full analysis of possible cases of loop combinations of component actions is given below.

1.2.4 Returning to the text of the example examined, we notice that componentwise processing of the array is performed completely, i.e. the loops cover all values of subscripts of arrays from the lower bounds in bound pairs to the upper in corresponding declarations.

If it is taken into account that the components of matrices A, B and C are allocated in memory in lexicographical sequence, forming vectors of linear allocation of the matrices A, B and C, the example in question can be described in the form:

```
arrays A, B, C [1 : 1, 1 : n ↑ 2];
integer j; real t;
for j := 1 step 1 until n ↑ 2 do
begin t := 2 × B [1,j]; C [1,j] = A[1,j] + t end ...
```

This fragment is functionally equivalent to the preceding one since the *FOR* clause **for** $j := 1$ **step** 1 **until** $n \uparrow 2$ **do** provides a complete search of all component arrays, the structure of which will be immaterial during their processing by componentwise loops.

The relevance of the conversion carried out is evident as two nested *FOR* statements give one. Such a conversion will be termed *reduced nesting* of componentwise loops.

This conversion can be more generally used in many cases for reducing the nesting of loops of componentwise operations and also when only some group of subscripts runs through all values.

Let us examine the following fragment:

... **arrays** $A1, A2, A3 [H_1 : B_1, H_2 : B_2, ..., H_s : B_s]$
$A1 [...] := A2 [...] + A3 [..] ...$

We shall assume that the list of subscripts in $A1$ comprises sequence l_1 of occupied positions, then m_1 positions will be empty, next n_1 are occupied, then p_1 empty, and finally q_1 at occupied positions; thus $l_1 + m_1 + n_1 + p_1 + q_1 = s$

The variables l_2, m_2, n_2, p_2, q_2 and l_3, m_3, n_3, p_3, q_3 will have the same significance for $A2$ and $A3$ respectively. We note that if the fragment is to be semantically correct, it is essential that the total number of empty subscript positions in the arguments and in the result be the same

$$m_1 + p_1 = m_2 + p_2 = m_3 + p_3 = N$$

and also that the ith empty position in all lists of subscripts (in $A1, A2, A3$) should correspond to the dimensions of these arrays with the same bound pairs.

We note that the direct reduction of this assignment statement to ALGOL constructions requires N nested FOR statements. It follows from the conditions of the example that the entries of arrays $A1, A2$ and $A3$ into the statement involves two sets each of empty subscript positions. Thus if the further condition

$$l < m_1 = m_2 = m_3 \quad (*)$$

is fulfilled, the whole of the first set of empty subscript positions can be actually replaced by one empty "subscript", having compelled the loop parameter at this position to run through the values of the subscript from the value equal to the lower bound in the bounding pair of the last subscript of the first set up to a value equal to the product of the lengths of this set with respect to the dimensions of empty positions. This can be done in the second set of empty positions as well. The result of these conversions is to provide two loops (from the number of sets) instead of N loops. In the general case, the number of such sets may be more than two. For example, if $m_1 \neq m_2$, it is evidently no longer possible to operate with two componentwise loops instead of N. For this reason it becomes necessary to decompose the sets of empty subscript positions of the arguments and of results, with the result that conditions of this type $(*)$ must be observed for such sub-sets in order to reduce their number to a minimum, whilst the length of each is at a maximum. Each of these sets will correspond only to one loop of componentwise operations. The description of the algorithm of such a decomposition is described below.

1.2.5   The programming of complex arithmetics involves reducing operations over complex variables to operations over their scalar real components, since variables which are considered as **complex** are treated as ordered pairs of variables of the **real** type (a relative vector of length 2). The same alternative is available here as when programming the operations of linear algebra: open or closed utilization of standard algorithms, implementing operations of complex arithmetic.

Analysis shows that it is not rational in this case to use the interpretation method since open insertion gives better object programs in most cases. To optimize the implementation of complex arithmetic, all specific cases corresponding to all possible combinations of types of arguments of arithmetic operations over arrays are taken into consideration. For example, each of the following combinations of the types:

real × **complex**
complex × **real**
complex × **complex**

is implemented by insertion of special sub-routines.

1.2.6 The specificity of programming of operations over Boolean arrays in Input language is ensured by the specific representation of the Boolean variables in the memory cells (II.2.4). The components of Boolean arrays are arranged in series in 45-digit memory cells in such a way that all processing of logical arrays is performed by machine instructions which operate with complete cells. We shall use the simple example of carrying out operations over Boolean arrays (the relevant comments are entered in the example in the form of labels):

Boolean arrays A, B, C $[1 : n, 1 : n]$;
integer i, j, k;
$C[i,j] := A[i,k]$ & $B[k,j]$

In terms of bit operations, this text, recorded in Input language, is equivalent to the following:

begin
Boolean array A, B, C $[1 : (n \uparrow 2 + 44)/45]$;
integer $i, j, k, N1, N2, N3, K1, K2, K3$;
Boolean $t1, t2, t3, t4, t5$-**vectors** 45;
Boolean $C5 -$ **Vector** 45;

Comment: *Vector C5 is the machine representation of the Boolean value* **true** *in the form of a one in the first digit*; *calculating the number of the cell in the array A containing the first argument*:
$N1 := entier\ (((i - 1) \times n + k - 1)/45 + 1$;
calculating the number of the digit containing the first argument:
$K1 := (i - 1) \times n + k - 45 \times entier\ (((i - 1) \times n + k)/45)$;
calculating the number of the cell in the array B containing the second argument:
$N2 := entier\ (((k - 1) \times n + j - 1)/45) + 1$;
calculating the number of the digit containing the second argument:
$K2 := (k - 1) \times n + j - 45 \times entier\ (((k - 1) \times n + j)/45)$;
calculating the number of the cell in the array C where the result should be placed:
$N3 := entier\ (((i - 1) \times n + j - 1)/45) + 1$;
calculating the number of the digit to which the result of the operation should be sent:
$K3 := (i - 1) \times n + j - 45 \times entier\ (((i - 1) \times n + j)/45)$;
4*

*shifting the cell containing the first argument by K*1 *digits to the left*:

$t1 := shift\ (A[N1], K1);$

*shifting the cell containing the second argument by K*2 *digits to the left*:

$t2 := shift\ (B\ [N2], K2);$

calculating the conjunction:

$t3 := t1\ \&\ t2;$

separating the digit containing the result of the operation:

$t3 := t3\ \&\ C5;$

shifting to the right the cell containing the result in the first digit by a number of digits equal to the ordinal number of the digit of the result in the cell of array C:

$t3 := shift\ (t3, -K3);$

shifting one of the first digit into the same position:

$t4 := shift\ (C5, -K3);$

clearing the digit into which the result should be placed:

$t5 := C\ [N3] \lor t4;$

$t5 := t5 \oplus t4;$

storing the result:

$C\ [N3] := t5 \lor t3$

end of example.

The content of this example shows the method of programming operations over Boolean arrays in essential outline. In so far as this type is concerned, the programming of Boolean operations assumes bit representation of Boolean information. In the case of constant Boolean arrays, bitwise **packing of the components** of these arrays into the cells must be carried out during translation. Thus, the processing of the text

 Boolean A—vector 3;

 $A := |\textbf{true, false, true}|;$

results in the following. Constants (Boolean values) **true, false,** and **true** are transferred from the scheme (ALPHA-program) to the table of constants with marks in a special scale of constants saying that these extracted constants are components of a compound constant array.

The number of the first constant of the compound array is placed into the the table of arrays, in the information on the array, introduced in order to denote the formation of the vector |**true, false, true**| (III.2.4.8). Let these constants be C_i, C_{i+1} and C_{i+2}; the packing of the components C_i, C_{i+1} and C_{i+2} involves the creation of a new constant C_j, representing the Boolean values of C_i, C_{i+1}, C_{i+2} in the first three digits.

The rather cumbersome implementation of digital operations over separate components is to some extent compensated by the considerable reduction of the volume of memory required for Boolean arrays.

It should be noted that this awkwardness arises only when expressing the Boolean operations over the arrays in the form of operations over scalar components in the program in Input language. If, however, the Boolean operations are carried out over the arrays as a whole (by the introduction of an internal dimension or the use of empty subscript positions), a proper selection of lengths consistent with the dimension of the memory cells of the machine, will demonstrate the advantages of digital packing of the components of the arrays not only from the point of view of memory capacity but also from the point of view of economy of operations. For example, the fragment

> ... **Boolean arrays** A, B, C [1 : 90]
> $C [\quad] := A [\quad] \& B [\quad]; ...$

will in fact be implemented in the form of the fragment

> ... **Boolean arrays** A, B, C [1 : 2] - **vector** 45; **integer** i;
> **For** $i := 1$ **step** 1 **until** 2 **do** $C [i] := A [i] \& B [i]; ...$

providing the componentwise operations over the least (internal) dimension will be executed by the machine instructions simultaneously for all components.

2 Implementation of Operations over Arrays in the ALPHA-Translator

2.1 General Organization

In the ALPHA-translator the operations over arrays are programmed by two Blocks 9 and 10, and require one scanning of the compiled program. Block 9 implements geometrical operations over arrays, which up to the instant of working of this block are taken from the program into the common list by Block 8, and the work of the block involves only processing the operations taken out, so that the program is not processed by Block 9. The registration of actual entries of operations involved in constructing arrays into the program is performed by Block 10. It processes the computational operations over arrays, including the processing of complex arithmetic and operations over Boolean arrays, which are further jointly named *special* operations.

Blocks 9 and 10 complete the translation stage in the transfer phase to the internal language (III.1.2). In the absence of operations on the construction of arrays and special operations, the preceding block issues a signal, causing Block 9 to activate Block 11 immediately.

2.2 Block Analysing Geometrical Operations Over Arrays

2.2.1 When Block 9 comes into operation, the language and presentation of information in the tables are already extremely close to the internal language (III.2). The specific characteristic of the internal language at the level of Blocks 9 and 10 lies in the so-called β-symbols—numbered empty subscript positions.

Thus, in processing the variable $A[,]$ β-symbols will be introduced for the empty subscripts, such that the variable will generally be used in the form $A[\beta 1, \beta 2]$.

It should be noted that the preceding blocks expand nested geometrical operations, so that by the time Block 9 operates, for example, the compound variable $|A[\quad], |x,y\||$ (where $A[\quad]$ is a vector of length 2, x and y are scalars), appearing as matrix 2×2, will be substituted by the intermediate variable $T2[,]$ in the program, and in the common list, the right-hand parts of the following identities will be written down:

$$T1 [\quad] \sim |x,y|,$$
$$T2 [,] \sim |A [\quad], T1[\quad]|,$$

where $T1 [\quad]$ is the intermediate variable, representing the formation of vector $|x,y|$, and $\sim$ is the sign of correspondence. Entry into the common list (CL) is carried out by reference to the row of the table of arrays (TA), as given in the first address, that row corresponding to the compound variable. Block 9 uses the following transit arrays:

(1) common list (CL);
(2) table of constants (TC);
(3) table of arrays (TA);
(4) table of blanks (TB).

Reprocessing the first three tables, two new ones are obtained:

(1) informational table $(TL4)$;
(2) operational table of scalar identities $(L3)$.†

2.2.2 Description of the Flow-chart of Block 9 (Fig. 3).

2.2.2.1 Before examining operations implemented by the statements of the flow-chart, we shall examine the structure of the TA. Entry to the TA is according to the name of the array. The structure of the row of information in the TA, occupying one memory cell, is as follows:

where the first 9 digits are informational, out of which from the 6th to the 9th are filled up by the previous Blocks of the translator and carry the following information about the array:

6th digit—Boolean array;
7th digit—own array;
8th digit—dynamic array;
9th digit—working array.

The first 12 digit group is used for storing the reference in the CL for the right-hand part of the identity (in the case of a compound array); the set of second 12 digits are for reference in the CL on lengths with respect to dimen-

† The meaninglessness of these symbols is not associated with the nature of the case.

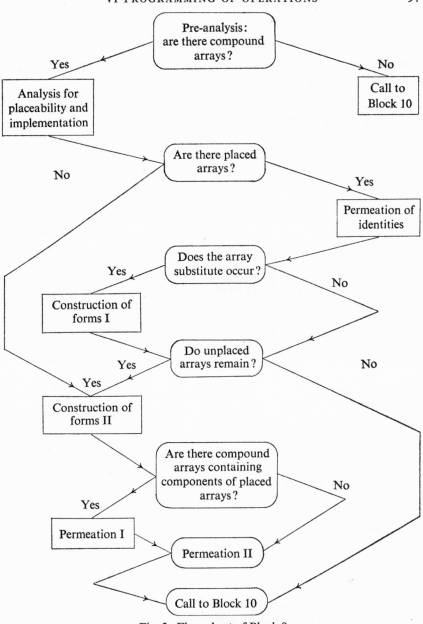

Fig. 3. Flow-chart of Block 9

sions;† the last group of digits denotes a drum array (all 12 digits are ones), or—in the case of constant arrays—for storing the number of the first constant

† It may be recalled here that all lower bounds in the bound pairs from the array declarations are reduced to zero by the blocks of programming of expressions (4.2.3.3).

from this array. The structure of the *TB* is similar to that of the *TA*, with the only difference that in the third address of the row of the *TB* a reference to the "contents" of a given blank formal parameter may be included, occurring at the level of Blocks 9 and 10 in a separate *table of blank fillers* (*TF*). The first 5 digits are used by Block 9, for the following tags:

$\alpha1$—compound array is processed by the statement "Analysis for placability and implementation",

$\alpha2$—the array is "placed" (see below),

$\alpha3$—the array appears as a component of some placed compound array,

$\alpha4$—the array contains the component q of some placed array,

$\alpha5$—(provided that $\alpha4 = 1$) component q is an array.

2.2.2.2 *Preanalysis.* In the absence of compound arrays, Block 9 calls Block 10. Otherwise the necessary reallocation of the memory is performed, the lengths of the working fields and some other numerical characteristics of information are calculated.

2.2.2.3 *Analysis for placeability and implementation.* As was indicated in 1.2.1, the actual creation of compound arrays at the moment of translation is an optimal implementation of geometrical operations. Therefore all specific situations in which such an implementation is possible must be made as fully as possible. According to the syntax of Input language, the formation and composing of lists of variables (or expressions) the elements of which may be variables and (or) enumerations of variables (or, in the case of expressions —expressions and (or) enumerations of expressions) comprise geometrical operations both on variables and on expressions. At the moment of operation of Block 9, the lists are collected into a special π-form (IV.1.3.2.3). Thus, the list of variables

$$x[m], \ldots, x[n]$$

assumes the form

$$\pi(i, m, n, x\,[i], x\,[i]),$$

and the list of expressions

$$x[m] \times y\,[m], \ldots, x[n] \times y[n],$$

accordingly:

$$\pi\,(i, m, n \times x\,[i]\,y\,[i]\,t, t),$$

where i is an index, according to which the list passes from m to n; $\times x\,[i]\,y\,[i]\,t$ —multi-instruction (III.2.4.5), realizing multiplication giving the result t, the result being placed after the last comma.

It should be noted that formation and composition of expressions for implementation in the ALPHA-translator does not in any way differ from the formation and composition of the variables with the exception of one case. Let us, therefore, examine the following example:

real A - **vector** 3; **real array** x [1 : 3];
$A := |x[1] \uparrow 2, x[2] \uparrow 2, x[3] \uparrow 2|$.

Calculation of the squares of variables $x[1]$, $x[2]$ and $x[3]$ can be taken out of the formation (which is in fact dealt with by the block for programming expressions (IV.2.2.2), insofar as the above fragment is functionally equivalent to the following:

real A - **vector** 3; **real array** x [1 : 3];
real $t1, t2, t3$;
$\quad t1 := x[1] \uparrow 2;$
$\quad t2 := x[2] \uparrow 2;$
$\quad t3 := x[3] \uparrow 2;$
$\quad A := |t1, t2, t3|$.

Thus, the formation of an expression is reduced to the formation of a variable. On the other hand, in the case of the text

real A - **vector** n; **real array**
x [1 : n]; $A := |x[1] \uparrow 2, \ldots, x$ [n] $\uparrow 2|$,

which, for $n = 3$, is functionally equivalent to the example examined above the removal of calculations from the formation would demand the organizing of a loop of calculations and the introduction of an intermediate array of variables. Therefore, when enumerating expressions, the calculations remain in the π-form.

We shall designate a compound array as *placeable* if the operation of constructing this array is carried out at the time of translation.

We shall designate an element of a list as *floating* if it represents one of the following objects:

(1) a list;
(2) a blank—formal parameter;
(3) a dynamic array;
(4) a sub-array of a static array (i.e., an array with constant limiting pairs, but the given entry of which contains some occupied subscript positions).

Thus, a floating element of a list reflects two dynamic aspects:

(1) a variable position in memory (list, formal parameter and dynamic array);
(2) a variable position within the array, of which the floating element (sub-array of a static array) is a component.

We shall designate an element of a list as *fixed*, if it represents one of the following objects:

(1) a constant array;
(2) a sub-array of a placeable compound array.

The second of these objects (sub-array of a placed array) is connected with the process of programming operations for the construction of arrays.

Drawing a parallel with the above-mentioned floating elements of a list, one may state that the idea of the fixed element of the list, in its turn, reflects two static aspects:

(1) a fixed position in memory (constant array);
(2) a fixed position of a sub-array in an array (sub-array of a placeable array).

We shall now formulate the necessary and sufficient condition for placeability a compound array: a compound array is placeable if, and only if, none of the elements of its list is either floating or fixed and, moreover, if among the elements of its list, no two are identical and (for composition) the number of the dimension along which the composition is carried out equals unity. In other words, the different scalars and operating variables or the different arrays with constant bound pairs and with all empty subscript positions can serve as elements of the list of the placeable array. The condition of the diversity of all elements of the list is necessary, since the placing of arrays with identical elements of the list results in unjustifiable use of memory, to say nothing of the complexity of substituting entries of elements of this list into the program in terms of the resulting array.† The arrays to be composed are placed in only in the case of composition along the first dimension, since the placing of arrays, composed along a non-first dimension, is of dubious advantage on account of the infringement of linear allocation of components in the resulting array.

The analysis for placeability is carried out by a loop which scans the table of arrays. The results of the analysis are recorded in digits $\alpha 1$, $\alpha 2$, $\alpha 3$, $\alpha 4$ and $\alpha 5$, of the corresponding lines of the TA, and also in the corresponding lines of the informational table $TL4$, each line of which has the following structure:

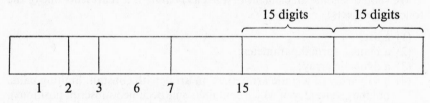

where

$$\text{digit } 1 = \begin{cases} \text{W1, for formation } (F); \\ \text{W0, for composition } (C); \end{cases}$$

digit 2 = 1, if the number of element in the register equals 1 and this element is a list (L);

digits 3–6—number of dimension along which the composing proceeds (for C);

digits 7–15—number of elements in the list;

first 15-digit group—scalar, according to which the enumeration is carried out (for L);

---

† Input language clearly does not prohibit the writing of constructions with the use of identical list elements, similar to the following:

begin integer x; $|x,x| := |1,2|$; output (x) **end.**

second 15-digit group—constant, operating variable or scalar, showing the start of the list (the initial value of the index, from which the list proceeds according to the given subscript position).

On fulfilment of conditions of placeability for a given compound array (next in the scanning loop), the identities are constructed, expressing each element in the list in terms of the resulting compound array. Thus, elements of lists of the following three compound arrays:†

$$A34 \ [\quad] \sim |a31, a32, t6|,$$
$$A35 \ [,] \sim |A34 \ [\quad], A33 \ [\quad]|,$$
$$A36 \ [,] \sim |[1] \ A35 \ [,], A3[,]|,$$

which will appear as the result of decomposition of the compound array

$$A36 \ [,] \sim |[1]||a31, a32, t6|, A33 \ [\quad]|, A3 \ [,]|,$$

which is a matrix 4×3, are expressed by resultants in the following manner:

$$a31 \sim A34 \ [C2];$$
$$a32 \sim A34 \ [C1];$$
$$t6 \sim A34 \ [C12];$$
$$A34 \ [\quad] \sim A35 \ [C2];$$
$$A33 \ [\quad] \sim A35 \ [C1,];$$
$$A35 \ [,] \sim |A36 \ [C2], \ldots, A36 \ [C1]|;$$
$$A3 \ [,] \sim |A36 \ [C12,], \ldots, A36 \ [C13,]|,$$

where $C2$, $C1$, $C12$ and $C13$ are constants equal to 0, 1, 2, 3 respectively. The right-hand side of these identities after their inclusion in parentheses (to facilitate their subsequent separation from the common list) and contracting the lists in the L-form (without the position of the result, which is superfluous for listing the variables) are entered in the CL.

For elements of a list appearing as arrays, the references to these right-hand sides in the CL are placed into the first address of the corresponding line of the TA, for elements of the list—scalars and operating variables—they are placed into the control table of scalar identities $L3$, in each line of which 12 digits of the second address serve to accommodate the reference in the CL, and the left-hand side of the identity (scalar or operating variable) is entered in the first 15 digits of the line.

For each of the elements of the list of a given placed array, the remaining compound arrays are analysed to obtain information, accumulated in $\alpha3$, $\alpha4$ and $\alpha5$ of the corresponding lines of the TA.

The work of this flow-chart statement is completed by exhausting all the lines of the TA. For constructing the identities the control signals *REPL A*, *REPL* α and *REPL t* are developed, which characterize the presence of identities for arrays, scalars and operating variables respectively.

2.2.2.4 *Permeation of identities.* This flow-chart statement serves to carry out substitutions and interchanges of identities in the case of a nested structure

† In this example, taken from an actual ALPHA-program, the original numeration of program variables is preserved.

of placed arrays, so as to express the elements of lists of these arrays through a resultant one. Thus, for the last example of para. 2.2.2.3, the fulfilment of this permeation gives the following identities:

$$a31 \sim (A36 \, [C2, C2]);$$
$$a32 \sim (A36 \, [C2, C1]);$$
$$t6 \sim (A36 \, [C2, C12]);$$
$$A34 \, [\quad] \sim (A36 \, [C2]);$$
$$A33 \, [,] \sim (A36 \, [C1,]);$$
$$A35 \, [,] \sim (|\pi(a73, C2, C1, A36 \, [a73,])|);$$
$$A3 \, [,] \sim (|\pi(a74, C12, C13, A36 \, [a74,])|).$$

These identities express elements of lists of the placed arrays $A34$, $A35$ in terms of the resulting placed array $A36$. The right-hand sides of the new identities (where these appear) are entered into CL, and references to them substitute references to the old identities in TA and $L3$.

The identities, expressing elements of registers of formation (F) and of composition (C) operations in terms of the resulting compound array, will be designated as identities, inverse as regards the initial identities, giving the direct form of the operations of F and C.

The process of obtaining inverse identities directly when there is no nesting of operations F and C, is evident. Let there be a direct identity for operation F (the dots in the subscript brackets represent some series of empty subscript positions)

$$T \, [\ldots] \sim |\ldots, A \, [\ldots], \ldots|,$$

in which $A \, [\ldots]$ is i^{th} element of the list of operation F. Then the inverse identity for $A \, [\ldots]$ has the form:

$$A \, [\ldots] \sim T \, [i, \ldots].$$

If the direct identity for the operation C has the form

$$T \, [\ldots] \sim |[1] \ldots, A \, [\ldots], \ldots|,$$

in which components of array A occupy positions from the nth to m^{th} inclusive along the combined first dimension, the inverse identity for $A \, [\ldots]$ will assume the form:

$$A \, [\ldots] \sim |T \, [n, \ldots], \ldots, T \, [m, \ldots]|.$$

If the operations F and C are nested these basic rules are supplemented by four inductive rules, corresponding to four possible combinations of the nesting of operations F and C.

(1) $F \, (F)$:
　　Initial inverse identities:
$$A \, [\ldots] \sim T1 \, [i, \ldots],$$
$$T1 \, [\ldots] \sim T2 \, [j, \ldots].$$
　　The resultant identity:
$$A \, [\ldots] \sim T2 \, [i, j, \ldots].$$

(2) $F(C)$:

Initial inverse identities:

$$A [\ldots] \sim T1 [i, \ldots],$$
$$T1 [\ldots] \sim |T2 [n, \ldots], \ldots, T2 [m, \ldots]|.$$

The resultant identity:

$$A [\ldots] \sim T2 [n + i - 1, \ldots].$$

(3) $C(F)$:

Initial inverse identities:

$$A [\ldots] \sim |T1 [n, \ldots], \ldots, T1 [m, \ldots]|,$$
$$T1 [\ldots] \sim T2 [i, \ldots].$$

The resultant identity:

$$A [\ldots] \sim |T2 [i, n, \ldots], \ldots, T2 [i, m, \ldots]|.$$

(4) $C(C)$:

Initial inverse identities:

$$A [\ldots] \sim |T1 [n, \ldots], \ldots, T1 [m, \ldots]|,$$
$$T1 [\ldots] \sim |T2 [p, \ldots], \ldots, T2 [q, \ldots]|.$$

The resultant identity:

$$A [\ldots] \sim |T2 [n + p - 1, \ldots], \ldots, T2 [m + p - 1, \ldots]|$$

The permeation of identities is carried out by a iterative loop, which is broken if it is found impossible to apply any one of the rules.

2.2.2.5 *Construction of forms I.* Since the identities for elements of lists, which are arrays, contain empty subscript positions, it is convenient for the further simplification of these identities to introduce β-symbols in place of the empty positions. On substituting entries in the program of list elements of placed compound arrays with occupied positions of subscripts by Block 10 these formal positions (β-symbols) are replaced by the corresponding subscript expressions. A given flow-chart statement simplifies the identities, containing empty subscript positions, by introducing β-symbols. The example of para. 2.2.2.4 will assume the form:

$$A34 [\beta 1] \sim (A36 [C2, \beta 1]),$$
$$A33 [\beta 1] \sim (A36 [C1, \beta 1]),$$
$$A35 [\beta 1, \beta 2] \sim (A36 [\beta 1, \beta 2]),$$
$$A3 [\beta 1, \beta 2] \sim (A36 [+\beta 1 \, C12 \, a101, \beta 2),$$

where $+\beta 1 \, C12 \, a101$ denotes the multi-instruction of the addition with the result $a101$, which allows for the deviation, equal to 2, with respect to the first dimension.

The identities into which β-symbols have been introduced, are entered in CL, and references to them replace the old ones in TA.

2.2.2.6 *Construction of forms II.* Statements of the flow-chart, other than those analysed above, process those compound arrays, which were found not to have been placed during examination of arrays for placeability. As indicated (para. 1.2.1), in this case it is necessary to construct formulae in the form of conditional calculating expressions for selecting and despatching components of the compound arrays not placed. By way of illustration, we shall quote an example of such a formula in common mathematical notation.

Let

$$T\,[,] \sim |[2]\;|\;[2]\;A\,[1, 1, ,], \ldots, A\,[1, 2, ,], B\,[1, ,] \ldots, B\,[2, ,], \ldots,$$
$$|[2]\;A\,[2, 1, ,], \ldots, A\,[2, 2, ,], B\,[1, ,], \ldots, B\,[2, ,]||$$

be the composition of matrix T with dimension 2×16 having bound pairs for the dimensions $0:1$ and $0:15$ respectively. In order to clarify the formula presented below we depict the structure of the matrix T

$$T = \begin{pmatrix} A_{1100}\,A_{1101}\,A_{1200}\,A_{1201}\,B_{100}\,B_{101}\,B_{200}\,B_{201} \\ A_{1110}\,A_{1111}\,A_{1210}\,A_{1211}\,B_{110}\,B_{111}\,B_{210}\,B_{211} \end{pmatrix}$$

$$\begin{pmatrix} A_{2100}\,A_{2101}\,A_{2200}\,A_{2201}\,B_{100}\,B_{101}\,B_{200}\,B_{201} \\ A_{2110}\,A_{2111}\,A_{2210}\,A_{2211}\,B_{110}\,B_{111}\,B_{220}\,B_{221} \end{pmatrix}$$

Then

$$T_{ij} \begin{cases} A \\ \quad 1+\left[\dfrac{j}{8}\right], 1+\left[\dfrac{j-8\left[\frac{j}{8}\right]}{2}\right], i, j-8\left[\dfrac{j}{8}\right]-2\left[\dfrac{j-8\left[\frac{j}{8}\right]}{2}\right], \\ \qquad\qquad\qquad\qquad\qquad\qquad\qquad \text{if } j-8\left[\dfrac{j}{8}\right] < 4; \\ B \\ \quad 1+\left[\dfrac{j-8\left[\frac{j}{8}\right]-4}{2}\right], i, j-8\left[\dfrac{j}{8}\right]-2\left[\dfrac{j-8\left[\frac{j}{8}\right]-4}{2}\right]-4, \\ \qquad\qquad\qquad\qquad\qquad\qquad\qquad \text{if } j-8\left[\dfrac{j}{8}\right] \geqslant 4, \end{cases}$$

where $[x] = entier\,(x)$; $i = 0, 1$; $j = 0, \ldots, 15$.

The formulae, employed for selecting components of compound arrays, are formed by a given flow-chart statement in the internal language making use of β-symbols. In this syntax the formula for selecting components of the compound array which has not been placed

$$T\,[,] \sim |A\,[C2,]\,B\,[\quad]|$$

will assume the form ($M_b 1$ and $M_b 2$—internal labels (III.2.3.1); $C2$—zero constant):

    if $= \beta_1\,C2\,M_b 1$
        $\Rightarrow A\,[C2, \beta 2]\,T\,[\beta 1, \beta 2]$
            go to $M_b 2$
    $M_b 1 \Rightarrow B\,[\beta 2]\,T\,[\beta 1, \beta 2]$
    $M_b 2$.

Actually, on the basis of technical considerations, and also on account of the fact that, at this level, it is still not known in which direction the transfers should be made (from the compound to sub-arrays or the other way round), the formula for selecting components of the compound non-placed array is also written in the form of an "identity", linking the compound array with elements of lists of operations F or C:

$$T [\beta 1, \beta 2] \sim \text{if } \neg = \beta 1 \; C2 \; M_b 1$$
$$(A \; [C2, \beta 2]) \text{ go to } M_b 2$$
$$M_b 1 \qquad (B \; [\beta 2]) \; M_b 2$$

The right-hand sides of these identities are also contained in round brackets and are placed in CL.

In the general case, the construction of these formulae involves the construction of conditions and of *displacements* in the subscript positions. In these constructions, lengths with respect to dimensions of the relevant arrays and blanks, and also information from Table $LT4$, are used. The analysis is conducted by means of a loop according to the number of elements of the list. The quantities from conditions, with which β-symbols are equated, are called *boundaries*. These boundaries show values of β-symbols, corresponding to a given subscript position, at which the transfer from one list element to another takes place.

We shall note the characteristics of processing list enumerations (L). If the lists have a nested structure the programming blocks eliminate it, introducing intermediate arrays. Thus, after eliminating the nesting of the lists, the example of the composition of matrix T takes the form ($C1$ and $C12$—constants, equal to 1 and 2 respectively, $a1$, $a2$ and $a3$-scalars):

$$T1 [,] \sim |[2] \; \pi \; (a2, C1, C12, A \; [a1, a2, ,], A \; [a1, a2, ,]),$$
$$L \; (a3, C1, C12, B \; [a3, ,], B \; [a3, ,])|;$$
$$T [,] \sim |[2] \; L \; (a1, C1, C12, T1 \; [,], T1 \; [,])$$

In this way, the enumeration for the resultant array T is carried out by parameter $a1$, which is not contained explicitly in the subscript positions of $T1$, and enters only in the list for $T1$. Therefore, when constructing formulae for selecting the component, it is necessary in this case to take into account the fact that to obtain the final formula for T, $a1$ must be replaced by $1 = \left[\dfrac{\beta 2}{8}\right]$, where the square brackets denote taking the integral part. The rule governing such substitutions is placed in CL by reference, occupying the third address in the line in the TA, of the corresponding T.

The rules for analysing lists of expressions differ somewhat from the rules for analysing lists of variables. At Internal language level these constructions differ in syntax and have the following form:

(1) *List of variables*:
$$L \; (a, a, b, A \; [\ldots], A \; [\ldots]);$$

(2) *List of expressions*:
$$L \; (a, a, b, \langle \text{program} \rangle, \langle \text{result} \rangle).$$

The rules for analysing lists of variables and of expressions in formations and in compositions are given below.

I. *In formations (F)*

   (i) *List of variables*

All empty positions are occupied by β-symbols, starting from $\beta2$.

The parameter (scalar), according to which the list is carried out, is substituted by $\beta1 + \langle\text{displacement}\rangle$, where $\langle\text{displacement}\rangle$ is equal to start of list $\rangle - \langle\text{preceding boundary}\rangle - 1$.

   (ii) *List of expressions*

In the $\langle\text{program}\rangle$ all empty positions (if there are any) remain; the parameter is processed as in (i);

in the $\langle\text{result}\rangle$ all empty positions are processed as in (i).

II. *In compositions (C)*

   (i) *List of variables*

The list parameter is substituted by

$$\left[\frac{\beta N - \langle\text{former boundary}\rangle}{m}\right] + \langle\text{start of list}\rangle,$$

where N is the number of dimensions (of the empty position), with respect to which the list proceeds;

m is the length with respect to the dimensions in A [...], along which the composition proceeds.

The empty position N is occupied by the expression

$$\beta N - \langle\text{preceding boundary}\rangle - m\left[\frac{\beta N - \langle\text{preceding boundary}\rangle}{m}\right];$$

all remaining empty positions are occupied by β-symbols with numbers, corresponding to empty position;

   (ii) *List of expressions*

In the $\langle\text{program}\rangle$—all empty positions remain.

The parameter is processed as in (i), only in this case the length with respect to the dimension in the $\langle\text{result}\rangle$ is taken for m. The empty position N (position along which the composition proceeds) in the $\langle\text{result}\rangle$ is processed as in (i), where m is the length with respect the dimension in the $\langle\text{result}\rangle$; all remaining empty positions are processed as in (i).

The application of these rules to the example in question—composition of matrix T—gives the following identities (for the sake of clarity formulae in which **ent** indicates an integral part are written instead of multi-instructions).

$T1\ [\beta1, \beta2] \sim \textbf{if}\ \neg < \beta24\ M_b2\ (A\ [\alpha1,\ 1 + \text{ent}\ (\beta2/2),$
$$\beta1,\ \beta2 - 2 \times \text{ent}\ (\beta2/2))$$

   go to M_b1
   $M_b2\quad (\beta\ [1 + \text{ent}\ ((\beta2 - 4)/2)],\ \beta1,$
   $$\beta2 - 4 - 2 \times \text{ent}\ ((\beta2 - 4)/2)])$$
   $M_b1;$

$T\ [\beta1, \beta2] \sim T1\ [\beta1,\ \beta2 - 8 \times \text{ent}\ (\beta2/8)];$

and the rule of substitution is $a1 \sim 1 + \text{ent}\ (\beta2/8)$.

The empty positions in programs, calculating expressions to be listed, are occupied by β-symbols in Block 10 taking into consideration characteristics of multi-instructions, the variables of which contain empty subscript positions.

2.2.2.7 *Permeation I.* This flow-chart statement processes the entries of components of placed arrays into elements of lists of unplaced arrays, performing substitutions and replacements analogous to those made by the flow-chart statement of "Permeation of identities". The processing is carried out also by an iterative loop.

2.2.2.8 *Permeation II.* This flow-chart statement takes into account the nested structure of operations involved in the construction of compound arrays which have not been placed. As a result of processing formulae for selecting components of unplaced arrays by this flow-chart statement, the formulae obtained do not contain the entries of compound arrays, other than of placed ones. In this case, we consider (in the permeation of enumeration) the information about substitution of parameters previously taken out from *CR*. The analysis is carried out by an iterative loop.

2.2.2.9 As a result of the work of Block 9 inverse identities are constructed for elements of lists, expressing them (the elements) in terms of the resultant placed array; for arrays which have not been placed, formulae are constructed in the form of conditional calculating expressions for selecting components of list elements. All this information is preserved in *CL*.

2.2.2.10 Some technical characteristics of implementation may be noted. As is readily seen when Block 9 is operating *CL* may expand rapidly. In order to secure this possibility, sub-routines implementing flow-chart statements, are situated in memory, in the opposite sequence to that represented on the flow-chart (see Fig. 3), so that after completion of the work of the next statement the place occupied by it in memory may be freed in the growing common list. The initial formulae of formations and compositions are discarded from *CL*. If it is found that any of the expressions constructed by this block contains as arguments only constants, then all the actions under them are carried out in the process of translation by a special sub-routine, "OPERA".

2.3 Block of Processing Calculating Operations Over Arrays

2.3.1 Block 10 analyses the program to be translated, programming specific operations and considering the information about compound arrays, obtained by Block 9. We may note some characteristics of the internal language at the level of Block 10, concerning the specific operations. The specific operations are classified into

unary (*sin. arg,* $\neg \Rightarrow$ etc.);
binary (x, $\uparrow$, *shift,* $\leqslant$ etc.);
with scales ($+$, &, $\vee$, $\oplus$).†

Information about the types and structures of the operands is found in the statement symbol. The standard operation $\sum$ (summation) is provisionally

† In contrast to the multiplication of scalar variables, the arrays being multiplied are not completed in multi-instructions (IV.2.3.2), so that the special multiplication is converted into a class of binary operations.

added to the class of unary operations. In the operation of Block 10, we use in addition to the tables enumerated in para. 2.2.1 a table of fillers for blanks (*TF*), a scale of constants (*SC*) and the special constant tables (*TAB*) of Block 10, representing, in the internal language, standard algorithms of calculation of functions such as the sine of a complex argument, matrix operations, etc. Furthermore, the block employs rather a large quantity of local working and and informational arrays.

Before processing the program in Block 10, constant logical arrays are condensed if necessary (see para. 1.1.5) and entries of list elements of placed compound arrays are replaced in some tables, in accordance with identities, constructed in Block 9.

2.3.2 We shall now examine, in basic outline, the operations performed by the flow chart statements shown (Fig. 4).

2.3.2.1 The main leading sub-routine reads the program to be translated, by symbols, and on discovering the sign of the assignment statement the flow-chart statement "main analysis" transcribes the statement into the operating field (*OF*), in this way making its analysis, the results of which are entered in the informational tables *COD*, *ARG* and *RES*. Table *COD* stores information about the operation and occupies two cells COD_1 and COD_2, having the following structure:

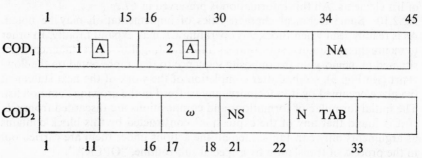

where the first eleven digits in the line COD_2 represent the following items:

  1   special operation;
  2   Boolean operation;
  3   componentwise operation;
  4   implementation must be carried out by means of a table;
  5   all variables are complex scalars;
  6   the analysis on the matching of arguments and of result is required (see below);
  7   arguments and result are matched.
  8   implementation must be carried out by means of a standard subroutine
  9   at least one of the variables is of a **complex** type
 10   direct expansion is necessary;
 11   at least one of the variables is a compound one.
 NA number of arguments;

$NTAB$ number of table TAB being required;

$$\omega = \begin{cases} 1 & \text{for operation vector} \times \text{matrix,} \\ 2 & \text{for operation matrix} \times \text{vector,} \\ 3 & \text{for operation matrix} \times \text{matrix,} \\ 0 & \text{for remaining operations,} \end{cases}$$

NS maximum number of β-symbol (maximum number of empty positions in the variables);

2 $\boxed{A}$ and (or) 1 $\boxed{A}$ —statement sign (one or two 15-digit words).

Tables ARG and RES store the information about variables (ARG—for arguments and RES—for the result). The number of positions in ARG is equal to the number of arguments. Each position of the tables occupies two storage cells ARG_1 and ARG_2 (RES_1 and RES_2):

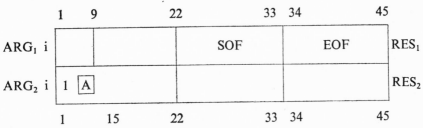

where the first nine digits in ARG_1 represent the following items:

1 compound unplaced array;
2 array;
3 blank;
4 scalar;
5 operating variable;
6 logic;
7 complex;
8 presence of an empty position;
9 operating array or operating blank;†
SOF start on OF (serial number of symbol);
EOF end on OF (serial number of symbol);
1 $\boxed{A}$ identifier of variable.

The 3rd and 2nd addresses of ARG_2 are used to store scales of subscript positions (see below) and reference to CL for compound arrays respectively.

More precisely speaking, not only assignment statements but also all the remaining statements of the internal language capable of containing multidimensional arrays or special operations are copied into the operational field (OF).

Tables COD, ARG and RES are the main informational tables, controlling all algorithms of Block 10. The bulk of the information recorded is worked out by the "main analysis" statement, the remainder by the subsequent

† Intermediate arrays, introduced when programming multidimensional expressions.

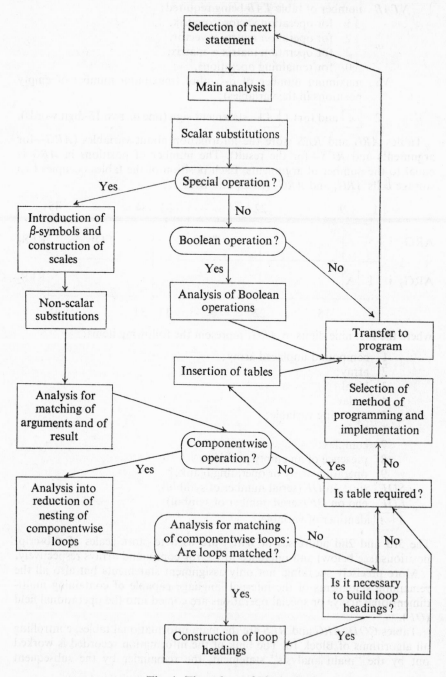

Fig. 4. Flow-chart of Block 10

analysing statements of the flow-chart. The significance and value of the information obtained will be explained in the course of presentation.

2.3.2.2   After obtaining information about operation, *scalar substitutions* of all entries of scalars, which are found in lists of formations and compositions of arrays are produced if necessary. For this purpose, use is made of control table of the scalar identities $L3$. Thus, for the multiplication multi-instruction

$$\times\ aA\ [+bctl]\ t2$$

where the following identity applies

$$a \sim (B\ [C1,\ C1])$$

we obtain by substitution the multi-instruction

$$\times\ B\ [C1,\ C1]\ A\ [+\ bctl]\ t2$$

The argument processed in this way is entered into OF with the coordinates of this argument in OF modified in the corresponding line in ARG_1. In the case of an entry of a substituted scalar into a subscript expression, an instruction for transferring the right-hand side of the identity to the left is issued, which is entered into a special operating field (LOF). During writing into the program the contents of the LOF are also incorporated. The analysis of non-specific operations is thus completed, and they are incorporated into the program. Exceptions comprise Boolean operations over scalars, which are programmed in accordance with the rules, stated in para. 1.2.6.

2.3.2.3   For special operations, scales of subscript positions of arguments and of results are also constructed in which the empty subscript positions are marked with units; β-symbols are introduced into arguments and results in place of the empty positions, in which the number of the β-symbol corresponds to the number of the empty position, with the exception of multiplication operations of the type "vector × matrix", "matrix × vector" and "matrix × matrix", information about which is given in ω of COD_2.

In these cases β-symbols are introduced in the following manner:

(1) $\omega = 1$ (vector × matrix):
$\times\ A1\ [\quad]\ A2\ [,]\ A0\ [\quad]$
$\times\ A1\ [\beta1]\ A2\ [\beta1,\ \beta2]\ A0\ [\beta2];$

(2) $\omega = 2$ (matrix × vector):
$\times\ A1\ [,]\ A2\ [\quad]\ A0\ [\quad]$
$\times\ A1\ [\beta1,\ \beta2]\ A2\ [\beta2]\ A0\ [\beta1];$

(3) $\omega = 3$ (matrix × matrix):
$\times\ A1\ [,]\ \times\ A2\ [,]\ A0\ [,]$
$\times\ A1\ [\beta1,\ \beta2]\ A2\ [\beta2,\ \beta3]\ A0\ [\beta1,\ \beta3]$

This introduction of β-symbols corresponds exactly to the construction of the necessary loops when implementing these matrix operations. In this way, Table $B2$ is constructed, in which lengths are entered with respect to the dimensions of the empty subscript positions. This information is employed for the construction of loop headings.

2.3.2.4 After this the necessary substitutions of all entries of subscript variables, the components of which have been entered into the lists of placed compound arrays are completed, taking into consideration the identities devised for them.

2.3.2.5 Analysis is carried out on the *matching of arguments and of results*. By this we mean the consideration of situations of which the following may serve as examples:

(1) Operation of the matrix product of the form
$$\times A \,[,] \, B \,[,] \, A \,[,].$$

It is clear that when multiplying matrices A and B (see example in 1.2.2) components of matrix A, appearing as the result, will be filled up by the calculated values before use of their initial values by the loops has ceased. Therefore it is necessary to establish the intermediate matrix T as the result and to construct a loop for transferring components of the matrix T to matrix A.

(2) Operation of transferring a vector to a vector
$$\Rightarrow A \,[,n] \, A \,[m,]$$

which represent the nth column and the mth row of matrix A (respectively) when expanding the loop of transfers in the form:

for $i := 0$ **step** 1 **until** p **do** $\Rightarrow A \,[i,n] \, A \,[m,i]$

may lead to the blocking of a component that has not been yet used. In this case it is also required to introduce an intermediate vector for the result. In such situations, which require the introduction of an intermediate variable for the result, we shall say that the arguments are matched with the result. The analysis of such situations is complicated where the variables include compound unplaced arrays and empty positions so that, in general, the elements of lists of compound variables may be empty positions, the fillers of which in their turn can appear as composites containing empty positions, etc. Therefore, the analysis matching the arguments with the result is essentially recursive, and the program implementing this flow-chart statement is also recursive. In this analysis, the componentwise character of the analysed operation is taken into account, since for such operations the equality of the numbers of subscript positions, having an empty subscript even in the case of coincidence of names of arrays (or blanks) in arguments and in the result, does not lead to matching (compare the example $\Rightarrow A \,[n,] \, A \,[m,]$ with that quoted above).

In some cases, as a result of the analysis when matching arguments and result it may be necessary to introduce an intermediate variable for the result, although the anticipated blocking fails to materialize during the actual operation. These cases are associated with blanks—the formal procedure parameters. Let $p1, p2, p3$ be formal parameters of some procedure F, which contains in its body the assignment statement

$$p1 := p2 \times p3$$

If this procedure has two calls $F(A, B, C)$ and $F(B, C, A)$ where the actual parameters A, B and C are matrices, then having called by name the actual parameters the corresponding assignment statements for the specified calls will have the form:

$$A := B \times C,$$
$$B := C \times A.$$

It is obvious that in the multiplication operation of matrices

$$\times D2 \ [,] \ D3 \ [,] \ D1 \ [,]$$

where $D1$, $D2$ and $D3$ are blanks corresponding to the formal parameters $p1$, $p2$ and $p3$, there is actually no matching, but when analysing the matching of arguments and results, we find there is matching all the same, because in filling the table of fillers for blanks by the preceding blocks of the translator, loss of information about individual correspondence of fillers to actual calls occurs. In our example, A and B will serve as fillers for the blank $D1$, corresponding to parameter $p1$, B and C for the blank $D2$, and C and A for the blank $D3$. When carrying out the analysis we find in the list of fillers for the result $D1$ a matrix, for example A, which is contained in the list of fillers for the second argument—the blank $D3$.

2.3.2.6   As previously shown (1.2.3), the programming of componentwise operations over arrays involves the construction of loops of these operations over their components. We note that all loops introduced by Block 10—loops of componentwise actions and loops of matrix actions—have a simple structure of headings, and the bodies of these loops have no exits. They are called *internal* and in constructing them the appropriate information is provided which facilitates the general analysis of loops when organizing loop control in the subsequent blocks of the ALPHA-translator. In the construction of loops of componentwise operations optimizations are carried out, as examined in 1.2.3 and 1.2.4.

2.3.2.7   Before constructing headings of loops of componentwise operations, an analysis is carried out on the reduction of nesting of the loops. This analysis is based on information about contents of subscript positions, stored in the corresponding scales. The essence of the algorithms implementing this analysis briefly comprises the following. The scales of all the variables of a given operation includes a scale which contains the shortest of all first sets of empty subscript positions. Following this in all scales all the first sets of empty subscript positions split (if this is possible) according to the shortest one found into two sub-sets, the first of which consists of subscript positions, comparable with the shortest, and the second consists of the remaining ones. The first sub-sets, formed in this way, are marked as a single "empty subscript" in the corresponding rows of table $B2$, so as to ensure the calculation of the number of repetitions of the loop through the lengths with respect to the dimension for those positions which have appeared coupled in the given "empty subscript" when constructing loop headings corresponding to a given "empty subscript". All second sub-sets are declared as the new sets and the shortest of all the scales of the remaining sets is then found; the remainder are split if necessary, etc. This process terminates on exhaustion of the last of the sets of empty subscripts, which represent the original ones and (or) can arise by such a chain process of splitting.

We shall now examine the example:

$$
\begin{array}{ccccccccc}
 & I & & I & 0 & I & I & \cdot I & 0 & |I| \\
0 & I & 0 & I & & I & I & I & & |I| \\
0 & I & & I & & I & I & I & 0 & |I| \\
 & I & & II & & & III & & & IV
\end{array}
$$

Here we have three scales (we may recall that I in the scale denotes an empty subscript position). Applying the algorithm described, in place of the six original ones, we obtain four new "empty positions" of subscripts I, II, III, IV. In this way, only four nested loops need be constructed instead of six.

2.3.2.8 Before proceeding to construct loop headings for componentwise operations, implementing the special operation R, an analysis is carried out to obtain information about the possibility of utilizing previously constructed headings of loops of componentwise operations where these exist and appear as a result of expanding the componentwise operation immediately preceding R and not separated from R by labels. We shall say that regions of actions of the two componental loops, corresponding to two componental operations, are matched (more briefly—*loops are matched*), if there are matched arguments and results for some hypothetical componentwise operation, the arguments of which represent the union of the arguments of the two given operations, and the results, the union of the results. Thus, as a result of the analysis on the matching of loops, carrying out the following two successive operations of summating vectors

$$A [\ \ ] := B [\ \ ] + C [,1] + D [\ \ ]; \ C [2,] := B [\ \ ] + E [\ \ ] + F [\ \ ],$$

we obtain, by combining the arguments of these operations:

$$\{B, C_{10}, D\} \cup \{B, E, F\} = \{B, C_{10}, D, E, F\}$$

and the results

$$\{A\} \cup \{C_{01}\} = \{A, C_{01}\}$$

where 10 and 01 are scales of subscript positions (2.3.2.7), giving the hypothetical componentwise operation

$$\theta \{B, C_{10}, D, E, F\}\{A, C_{01}\},$$

where θ is the symbol of the operation, in which the arguments were found to be matched with the result, since they have a common element C with different scales of 10 and 01. This shows that the summation of vectors examined cannot be united in one componental loop.

A given analysis is carried out on the basis of information, gathered in a special table AIL and left by the flow-chart statement "Analysis on the matching of arguments and of the result" for componentwise operations. The information contains the names of scalar variables, names and scales of subscript positions of arrays (or blanks) of arguments and of results of operations.

In the case of non-matching of loops the analysis is carried out on the coincidence of constructed loop headings with those anticipated, with the help of tables $B1$ (for constructed loops) and $B2$ (for anticipated loops), and in the case of coincidence renaming of tables $B2 \rightarrow B1$ does not occur and new headings are not constructed. If the joined loops are associated with a common intermediate operating array (or blank) it is substituted by two (for the **complex** type) or by one (in all other cases) scalar operating variables.

2.3.2.9 If necessary, componentwise loop headings are constructed, taking into account the results of the analysis on the reduction of loop nesting. Headings have a simple structure, being in the form of an arithmetic progression, having an initial term 0, an interval 1 and a final term equal to $(n-1)$, where n is either the length, with respect to the dimension of the corresponding empty subscript position, or the length, with respect to the dimension of the joined series of empty subscript positions equal to the product of the corresponding lengths.

2.3.2.10 After the construction of loop headings for componentwise operations—and for non-componentwise ones, having skipped the corresponding flow-chart statement—a particular strategy for programming the operation is selected. The selection is made in conformity with the information, worked out by the "basic analysis" block.

Basic types of analysis of special operations:

(1) implementation by means of a standard sub-routine (this requires the operations *det*, *shift*, the integral power of the matrix);
(2) direct expansion (this requires operations *mod*, relations, branches according to the flag, branches by comparison);
(3) implementation by means of tables from TAB;
(4) processing call statements to standard sub-routines (SR);
(5) processing statements of summation $(\sum)$;
(6) processing operations on complex scalar variables without tables $(+, -, \Rightarrow)$.

We shall consider some characteristics of these methods of implementation. The tables are used to program the non-componentwise operations over complex variables, matrix multiplications and elementary functions over complex arguments. The complete account of the types and structures of arguments requires 50 such tables, associated in the composite table TAB. This number is not very large, if one considers that the single operational sign $\times$ at the level of Input language may designate any one of the 58 (according to types and structures) cases of operations of multiplication differentiated by Block 10.

When implementing operations containing complex operating scalars, these scalars are substituted by two scalars of the **real** type (one is for the real part, the other for the imaginary part). This is done in order to relieve the table of arrays, since even the complex scalars for programming expressions by the blocks are substituted by vectors of length 2 (IV.1.2.2.2). This approach is connected with the fact that variables of the **complex** type were introduced into Input language after the acceptance of basic decisions about the structure and functions of blocks of the ALPHA-translator, concerning the phase of translation into the internal language. Therefore, the whole analysis of complex variables by blocks of the translator displays a certain adaptability to the main mechanisms of translation, developed in the main outline without considering complex variables.

The file *TAB* contains tables in which the implementation of corresponding complex special operations is described in terms of the internal language. Since *TAB* is stored on a drum, a control mechanism is used in the block (to reduce the number of calls to the drum) whether the table required at the given instant has not previously been taken out of *TAB*. Substitution of special operations in the program by tables is entirely analogous to the mechanism of executing the procedure statements in ALGOL 60, if one considers the special operation as the procedure statement, and the table as the body of the procedure.

In the case of compound variables which have not been placed, formulae constructed in Block 9 are considered for selecting or despatching components with substitution of β-symbols by the corresponding loop parameters.

For the operations, implemented by the statements of calls to the *SR*, in the case of the compound operands which have not been placed, intermediate arrays (which may be dynamic ones) are introduced.

The characteristics of entries of operating variables into the program (two entries: the first—assigning the value, the second utilizing it (III.2.4.1) in many cases make it necessary to substitute them by scalars.

2.3.2.11   After completing the processing of the next operation, the results of programming from fields are written into the program to be translated.

2.3.2.12   In the program implementation of algorithms of translation of Block 10 great difficulties are encountered which are explained by the small size of memory. In order to provide the necessary size of the operating fields, part of the analysing sub-routines has to be held on the drum, their recall for work in memory having been arranged by the special transfer mechanism.

3   Conclusion

3.1   The algorithm of formation of placed compound arrays, described above, in the general case does not constitute an optimum solution since the decisions about placing are taken on the basis of local information, gathered within the range of a list of operations *F* or *C*, and depend, moreover, essentially on the order of the scan of lists in the processing loop. For optimum completion of the operations of construction of arrays at the time of translation all connections through elements of lists for all compound arrays must be made.

3.2   Independent utilization of all possibilities of Input language, concerning multi-dimensional arrays, is limited in practice by technical possibilities of the machine, principally by the size of memory. This results in the fact that many optimizing algorithms of Blocks 9 and 10 possess an excessively large reserve capacity. Thus, the algorithms of the analysis on placeability can give significant optimization of the operating program in large numbers of operations of construction of arrays out of a large number of the initial ones. The algorithm for reducing the nesting of componental loops also gives appreciable economy in the case of large numbers of empty subscript positions. From this point of view, the use of these algorithms in ALPHA-translator bears an experimental character.

3.3 The term "geometrical operations" for operations of construction of arrays is introduced in ref. 1, containing the analysis of such kinds of operations. For a comparison of methods for carrying out matrix operations in an ALPHA-translator with matrix compilers ref. 2 may be recommended. Different suggestions regarding the introduction into ALGOL 60 of complex variables and of multi-dimensional arrays and operations on them have been published in the ALGOL bulletin [4].

In conclusion, the author wishes to express his thanks to R. Mishkovich, for having programmed a large part of the algorithms of Block 10.

REFERENCES

1. BULAVSKII, V. A. (1958). The symbolism of recording calculating schemes in programming automation. *Izv. vuzov. Matematika*, **5**, No. 5.
2. McGINN, L. C. (1957). A matrix compiler for Univac. Automatic Coding. *J. Franklin Institute, Monograph*, No. 3.
3. HOCKNEY, R. W. (1963). "Input language for automatic programming systems" (A. P. Yershov, G. I. Kozhukhin, Yu. M. Voloshin, eds.). Academic Press, New York and London.
4. *ALGOL Bulletin*, 1960–1962, No. 10–15.

VII PROGRAMMING LOOPS AND INDEX EXPRESSIONS IN THE ALPHA-TRANSLATOR

M. M. Bezhanova and I. V. Pottosin

The problem of programming the *FOR*-statements, or as we shall call them simply, the *loops*, is first of all a question of ensuring that the number of instructions generated in the program which implement the *FOR*-statements of the source program is as small as possible. Programming of subscript expressions depends on whether the subscripted variable is located outside the loops or in the body of a certain loop and also on whether the value of the subscript expression is connected with the loop parameter or not. On the strength of this, programming of loops and subscript expressions in the ALPHA-translator have many common features.

The following operations provide an economy in the programming of the loops in the ALPHA-translator:

Cleaning up of the loops;
Classification of the loops and the selection of the simpler methods of programming them;
An analysis of the relationship between the subscript expression and the loop parameters.

The task of *cleaning up* the loops, i.e. of eliminating calculations from the loop body, the result of which does not vary when the loop is repeated, and which can be implemented outside the loop, was outlined in an article by Yershov and Kurochkin[1] in 1958; however until now it has not been put into practice in any translator known to us. As a result of the cleaning up of the loops, the source program is reduced by means of equivalent conversions to a program in which the number of operations in the loop body is smaller than that in the original program. In view of the fact that the loops are parts of the program which are repeated many times over, such a conversion leads to a lessening of the calculation time for the object program.

An ALGOL 60 *FOR*-statement may be very complex both on account of the *FOR*-clause and its body. Applying the universal method for programming instructions for implementing a loop may therefore prove to be very awkward in the case of ordinary loops. In the ALPHA-translator simple cases are set aside on the basis of an investigation of the *FOR*-clause and an analysis of the loop body, and are programmed separately. For all other cases the universal procedure is applied. A similar approach to the programming of loops is described in an article by Hawkins and Huxtable.[2]

In languages for translators which were designed in the Soviet Union during the "pre-ALGOL" period, the dependence of subscript expressions on a loop parameter was stated explicitly. Provided this dependence is known, it is possible to compile readdress and rerun instructions quite economically. The papers of Kurochkin and Frolov[3, 4] with which the authors are familiar, on the programming of loops in compilers for STRYELA machines, may serve as an example of this. However, for a program written in ALGOL, the actual determination of the nature of this dependence constitutes a separate task. In the ALPHA-translator there is linear dependence of subscripts expressions on the parameters of the enveloping loops (where this exists). When determining this dependence, the nature of the incrementing of the the loop parameter when executing the *FOR*-statement, is also taken into account.

It should be noted first of all that the ALPHA-translator was developed for a specific machine. The features of the machine which influenced the idea of programming the loops and subscript expressions are as follows: the presence of a very limited number of index registers (only one in the case in question); the comparative simplicity of modification the instructions by addition (it is possible to indicate in one instruction both the address of the modified instruction and the address of the increment to be added).

Therefore, the question of the suitability of similar methods of programming loops and subscript expressions, and also of analysing the loops connected with them and of converting the subscript expressions on machines of a different type, is not discussed in this article but obviously the algorithms described will be suitable for other machines without having to make any substantial alterations.

1   Cleaning Up the Loops

1.1 Definitions

If the opening bracket of a certain loop comes before a certain statement S whilst enclosing bracket follows S, this loop is said to *envelop* the statement S, which is said to be *nested* in this loop.

We shall refer to an enveloping loop, which does not contain in its body a loop enveloping S, as a loop of the *first level* with respect to the statement S. A loop which is of the first level with respect to some loop of the kth level referred to S, is called a loop of the $(k + 1)^{th}$ *level*, with respect to the statement S. The statement itself is considered conventionally as the enveloping loop of zero level with respect to the given statement. An enveloping loop which is not enveloped itself by another loop is called the maximum level loop or the *maximum* loop.

For each statement there exists a series of enveloping loops, up to the Nth level, where N denotes the level of the maximum loop. We shall refer to such a series as a system of loops of the Nth *order*.

A variable is said to depend directly on a loop if this loop envelops a certain statement which assigns a value to this variable. A simple variable *depends* on a loop if it depends on this loop directly. An array *depends* on loop C if any one of its components depends directly on C. A subscripted variable *depends* on the loop C if it is a component of the array depending on C or if it contains, in its subscripts, variables which depend on C. The statement *depends* on the loop C if it contains at least one variable which depends on C. It is assumed that there are no variables which depend on a zero level loop.

We shall number the loops in the order in which their *FOR* clauses enter the program from left to right (for a zero level loop the statement itself is taken as the *FOR* clause.) Let $r_i < \ldots < r_{N+1}$ be the number of the system of loops which envelope a given statement S to be considered (r_i is the number of the loop of the $(N - i + 1)^{\text{th}}$ level with respect to S). For each variable α which occurs in S we shall determine the function $r(\alpha)$, called the *weight* of the variable and equal to the number r_k, from the series $r_1 \ldots r_{N+1}$, such that,

(1) α does not depend on the loop r_k;
(2) either $r_k = r_1$ or α depends on the loop r_{k-1}.

We shall reiterate some definitions from the theory of graphs.[5]

It is presumed that the concept of an oriented graph consisting of vertices and arrows (arcs) linking them, is familiar as is the notion of a sub-graph, a tree, the connection of a graph and of a path in a graph. A vertex of a tree is said to be *suspended* if no arrow enters it; and *terminal* if no arrow comes from it.

1.2 The Algorithm for Cleaning Up the Loops

In the ALPHA-translator cleaning up the loops is carried out at internal language level (III.2). It implies that each statement in the ALPHA-program is already programmed as a series of assignment statements using commutative and non-commutative operations (multi-instructions). Since the main specific character both of the cleaning up of the loops and the processing of superscripts is connected with the presence of the multi-instructions, we shall for the sake of simplicity, refer to any assignment statement of the internal language as a multi-instruction.

We shall first examine only expressions whose program in the internal language is in the form of a series of multi-instructions R involving only addition and multiplication of one type.

Cleaning up of the loops entails reconstructing a series of multi-instructions R which occurs in the system of enveloping loops $r_1, \ldots r_{N+1}$, generally speaking, into some other series of multi-instructions R^*, where to every multi-instruction from R^* a distance will be given, i.e. the number of that loop in front of which it can be placed.

Let us bring a certain graph G into line with the series of multi-instructions R. The set of suspended vertices in the graph corresponds to the set of argument occurrences in the original expression. The set of non-suspended vertices is defined by the set of multi-instructions or, what amounts to the same thing, by the set of intermediate (working) variables which are the results of these multi-instructions. The adjacency relation and its orientation is determined in the following way. An arrow leads from vertex α to vertex β, if the variable corresponding to the vertex α is an argument of the multi-instruction which corresponds to the vertex β. It is then said that α precedes β and that β follows α. It is easy to see that graph G is a tree. We shall refer to a non-suspended vertex of graph G as a $\ll + \gg$ type vertex, if it corresponds to the addition multi-instruction and as a $\ll \times \gg$ type vertex otherwise.

The algorithm for cleaning up the loops will be described in the form of rules for the conversion of graph G to a certain graph G^* corresponding to the series

R^*, where the distances of the multi-instructions from R^* will be determined during the conversion.

Graph G^* is constructed in stages. The number of stages does not exceed $N + 1$, each ith step corresponding to cleaning up the loop r_i; as initial data for the first step, we shall assume that $G_0 = G$ and $G_0^* = \wedge$ where $\wedge$ is an empty graph. Let the graphs G_{i-1} and G^*_{i-1} be obtained as the result of implementing the $(i-1)^{th}$ step. We shall make a few inductive suppositions which are obviously correct for $i = 1$:

(a) For the general case, graph G^*_{i-1} is disconnected and represents a set of trees;

(b) There exists a one-to-one mapping of T_{i-1} between the terminal vertices of G^*_{i-1} and some suspended vertices of G_{i-1};

(c) A weight is assigned to each suspended vertex of G_{i-1}. For $i = 1$, the weight which is assigned to the vertex V equals $r(x)$, where x is the variable which relates to V in graph G.

We shall point out three elementary conversions which can be applied to each suspended vertex W of graph G_{i-1} and by means of which graph G_{i-1} can be converted into graph G_i.

1. *Joining together the suspended vertices.* In this conversion, suspended vertices of weight $r \leqslant r_i$ (if there is more than one of these preceding W), are replaced by a single suspended vertex to which is assigned the weight r_i and which is joined to W by an arrow.

2. *Filtering the suspended vertices.* Let a non-suspended peak W' of the same type as W precede the vertex W and let more than one vertex precede the vertex W'. Then, if there is a suspended vertex V of weight $r \leqslant r_i$ amongst the latter, V is "dissociated" from W' and joined by an arrow directly to W.

3. *Reducing the non-suspended vertices.* Let only one vertex V precede the vertex W, V being a suspended vertex of weight $r \leqslant r_i$. In this case the vertices W and V are replaced by one vertex V, whilst preserving its weight, and the arrow from W (if there was one) will now come from V.

We shall now describe the step involved in converting G_{i-1} into G_i and G^*_{i-1} into G_i^*. We shall again number all the non-suspended vertices in the graph G_{i-1} such that if W' precedes W, then $N(W') < N(W)$, where $N(W)$ is the number of the vertex W.

We shall examine the next vertex W in a numerical order which has been fixed. We shall apply the second conversion to it followed by the first, and the third (if the conditions of a conversion for W are not fulfilled, then the conversion will leave G_{i-1} unchanged; the second conversion can be applied to W repeatedly.) We shall examine the first conversion in more detail. Let $V_1 \ldots, V_k$ be the suspended vertices which are to be joined together, and let the terminal peaks $Z_1 \ldots Z_m$ of the trees which form the graph G^*_{i-1} relate to some of these vertices $V_{i1} \ldots V_{im}$ in accordance with T_{i-1}. The sub-tree of the graph G_{i-1} consisting of the terminal vertex W and the suspended vertices $V_1 \ldots V_k$ is then added to the graph G_{i-1} by joining the vertices $V_{i1} \ldots V_{im}$ to the vertices $Z_1 \ldots Z_m$ respectively. Let Z be the terminal vertex of the tree obtained in the graph G_{i-1}. The mapping of T_{i-1} between the vertices of the graphs G_{i-1} and G_{i-1}^* is supplemented by establishing the correspondence between W and Z.

The graphs G_i and G_i^* are obtained after applying the second, first and third conversions to all the numbered vertices of the graph. The mapping of T_i between the vertices of the graphs G_i and G_i^* is obtained from T_{i-1} by discarding the relations of correspondence for the vertices, which have disappeared from G_{i-1}, from T_{i-1}, and by adding to T_{i-1} the above mentioned correspondence between the vertices W and Z. It is easy to see that the inductive propositions (a), (b) and (c) apply when passing from $i-1$ to i. It is also easy to see that for a certain s^{th} step ($s \leqslant N+1$), G_s will consist of one vertex.

The graph $G^* = G_s^*$ will be the goal, whereas each set of trees, added to the graph G_{i-1}^* at the ith stage, will correspond to the group of multi-instructions which were carried out from the loop r_i.

The algorithm for cleaning up the loops, described above, can be applied to its full extent only to those subscript expressions which at the time of operation of the appropriate block of the ALPHA-translator, satisfy exactly the above mentioned requirement with regard to the presence of multi-instructions for addition and multiplication of one type only.

In all other cases the algorithm is applied to the sequences R which consist of only one multi-instruction which is not a multi-instruction—the transfer operation, the minus operation, the negation operation and the identifier transfer. In this case the second conversion does not operate and all that happens is a possible dismembering of the multi-instruction and the carrying out of the separated sub-multi-instructions to the highest possible level.

The application of the algorithm in the general case has the following features:

(1) The arguments of the multi-instruction may be operating variables for which the concept of weight in the sense of the elementary definition given in para. 1.1 has not been established. The weight of operating variables is determined in the following way. Let the operating variable t be the result of the multi-instruction $\theta x_1 \ldots x_k t$. Then $r(t) = \max(r(x_1), \ldots r(x_k))$. Since, in a series of multi-instructions for calculating a certain expression, there always occurs at the beginning one in which all the arguments are non-operating variables, the definition is correct.

(2) Let us examine an instance when all the arguments of the multi-instruction have a weight of less than r_{N+1}. This means that all the calculations can be carried out at least from the first level loop. This does not mean, however, that the whole of the original statement $\theta x_1 \ldots x_{k_y}$ can be carried out from the loop. This is due to the fact that the execution of the statement involves not only calculating the expression but also assigning the value calculated to the result y. If y is an operating variable, this statement may be carried out from the loop, at least, of the first level. In this case, the original multi-instruction completely disappears in the internal loop whilst the result is renamed—the scalar z instead of an operating variable (but still keeping record of the fact that this scalar had been an operating variable (cf. VIII.1.4)). But if y is a non-operating variable, the net result is as before, the multi-instruction

$\theta x_1 \ldots x_k y$ being substituted by two multi-instructions, $\theta x_1 \ldots x_k t$ and $\Rightarrow ty$, where t is the operating variable.

1.3   Executing Operations on the Constants

Since the constants cannot depend on any loop, as there is no assignment to them, they are grouped into arguments of the multi-instructions which are to be carried out from the maximum loop when cleaning up the loops.

An additional optimizing conversion is implemented in the ALPHA-translator, which consists of executing, during translation, certain multi-instructions of which the only arguments are constants (all commutative operations are executed whilst of the non-commutative operations only the **integer** to **real** number type conversions are executed).

1.4   An Example

We shall now examine a fragment of the program to be translated, in the internal language before cleaning up the loops. The series of multi-instructions which is of interest to us, calculates the subscript expression

$$((a + b) + c) + d \times e$$
$$\ldots \textbf{for } i := \ldots \{\textbf{for } j := \{\ldots [+abt_1 + t_1 ct_2$$
$$\times det_3 + t_2 t_3 t_4] \ldots \} \ldots \} \ldots$$

Let the variable b be dependent on the first loop and not on the second one whilst the variables a, c and e are not dependent on either of these loops. The cleaning up of the loops will take place in two stages. The initial situation is shown in Fig. 1. The Arabic numerals next to the suspended vertices indicate their weight, the Roman numerals number the non-suspended vertices.

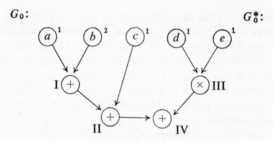

Fig. 1. Original graphs of G_0 and $G_0{}^*$

At the first stage the following conversions, chosen from the first, second and third conversions, are applied to each of the vertices I–IV.

    I—none of the conversions;
    II—the first and second conversions;
    III—the first and third conversions;
    IV—the second and first conversions.

The result of the first stage is shown in Fig. 2 (a dotted line joins the peaks which correspond to one another in accordance with mapping T_1).

G_1: G_1^*:

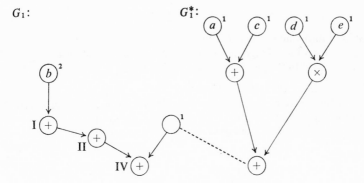

Fig. 2. Graphs G_1 and G_1^*

The following conversions are applied to the vertices I, II, and IV of graph G_1 at the second stage:

    I—the third conversion;
    II—the third conversion;
    IV—the first and third conversions.

The result of the second and final stage is shown in Fig. 3.

G_2: G_2^*:

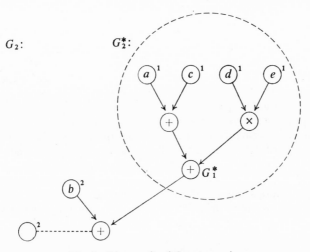

Fig. 3. The result of the conversion

Thus, after cleaning up the loops, the fragment of the program which was examined will assume the following form:

$$\ldots + ac\alpha_1 \times de\alpha_2 + \alpha_1 \alpha_2 \alpha_3 \textbf{ for } i := \ldots \{+b\alpha_3 \alpha_1$$
$$\textbf{for } j := \ldots\{\ldots[a_1]\ldots\}\ldots\} \ldots$$

5*

2 Analysis and Classification of the Loops

Classification of the loops is based both on a syntactical analysis of the *FOR*-clause and on a knowledge of which variables are dependent on a given loop. The loops are sub-divided into the following types:

loops which have a special parameter;
loops which have a standard parameter which, in turn, are sub-divided into
loops which have a regular parameter incrementation;
loops which have an irregular parameter incrementation;

The following types are included within the category of loops which have a *special* parameter or special loops; loops with a **real** number type of parameter and also loops with an **integer** type of parameter such that the loop parameter is a subscripted variable,† or loops whose bodies contain assignments to the loop parameter, i.e. the value of the loop parameter can be changed other than just by the operation of the *FOR*-clause. All remaining loops which have the **integer** type parameter are regarded as loops which have a standard parameter, or *standard* loops.

Standard loops having headings of the type:

for $i := E_1$ **step** D **to** E_2 **do**

or of the type:

for $i := E_1$, $i + D$ **while** G **do**

are regarded as loops with regular parameter incrementation or regular loops, where i is the loop parameter, E_1 and E_2 are arithmetical terms, G is a logical expression and D is a constant or variable which does not depend on the loop.‡

Both these types of loops are characterized by the fact that the values of the parameter correspond to the consecutive elements of the arithmetic progression, with step D which does not vary when the loop is executed.

All other standard loops are regarded as loops with an irregular parameter incrementation, or as *irregular* loops.

Some further information is necessary about the standard loops which make possible the use of various methods of programming. The existence of an exit inside the loop, i.e. **go to** a label situated outside the body of the loop, is determined for all standard loops. In addition to this, it is determined in the case of regular loops whether the value of the loop parameter is used in the loop body in some multi-instruction, besides being used in the subscripts (assuming that the latter have already been reduced to a canonical form—see below).

In order to avoid complicating the analysis of the operations involved in calls to procedures when executing the loop body, the presence of the procedure

† A loop parameter which is a formal parameter, and which is to be replaced by a name, becomes a subscripted variable by the time analysis of the loops takes place (III.2.4).

‡ It should be mentioned that the initial program may contain, instead of D, an arithmetical expression, the calculation of which had been carried out completely when cleaning up the loop. The analysis of the loops deals with the program which has already been altered by the cleaning up of the loops.

statement or the call to the procedure-function in the body of the loop is considered equivalent to using the loop parameter outside the subscripts, in the body of the loop. When the procedure statement is present in the body of the loop, the given loop is also considered to be a loop with an exit.

A more detailed account of methods of programming the loops, depending on their type, which can be used in the translator will be given later on. A few general comments may, however, be suitably put forward at this stage.

When programming a loop, the following must be established:

How to program the successive assignments to the parameter, which are set by the *FOR* clause and where the instructions for these assignment statements must be placed with respect to the instructions which implement the statements of the loop body.

How to alter the subscript expressions which depend on the loop parameter, in connection with changing its values.

The universal method for programming the assignment to the loop parameter consists of the following.

Instructions are compiled for each element of the *FOR* clause according to the syntactical form of the element, which carry out the assignment to the loop parameter and which check the condition "element exhausted". For each element these programs are arranged one after the other according to the order of the element in the *FOR* clause. The instructions for the statements of the loop body follow them. Call to execution of the loop body is made with the aid of the return transfer of control instructions. The return statement is put after the loop body. The last element in the *FOR* clause implements the branch to the statement following the *FOR* statement, according to the condition "element exhausted".

This universal programming method is applied to special and irregular loops. Applying it to regular loops would complicate considerably the organization of the loops in straightforward cases and therefore the regular loops are programmed in a different way. In the regular loops the check on the exit from the loop is performed either by checking the contents of an index-register or by checking the value of a counter.

In the regular loops the parameter only occurs in the subscripts in most cases. It is sufficient therefore to alter the subscripts. The need to recalculate the actual parameter itself may not arise. Therefore, in regular loops, the parameter need only be recalculated when a loop parameter beyond the subscripts is used, or when the loop has an exit: then the value of the loop parameter may prove to be necessary outside the loop.

Subscripts which depend on the loop parameter are altered depending on whether or not the corresponding subscript expression is a linear function of the loop parameter. The linearity of the dependence of the subscript expression on the loop parameter is examined only for standard loop parameters, as it is only in these loops, as a rule, that this linearity can be used to simplify the alteration of the subscript.

To alter a subscript in the event of its non-linear dependence on the loop parameter or dependence on the parameter of a special loop, this subscript is calculated and its address is formed in the corresponding instruction. To alter a subscript in the event of its linear dependence on the standard loop parameter, either the value of the loop parameter, multiplied by the coefficient when the loop parameter is in this linear form, can be sent into the index-register or the re-address method can be applied, i.e. incrementing the corresponding instruction by a value which corresponds to the step of the loop parameter multiplied by the coefficient for the loop parameter. For irregular loops only the first method can be used, but for regular loops both the first and the second can be used.

All that has been said above, demonstrates, in our opinion, some flexibility in the choice of a loop programming method, based on an analysis of the loops, which leads to a more economical programming of the loops.

3   Converting the Subscript to a Canonical Form

3.1   Stating the Problem

Let us consider the subscripted variable

$$a[E_1, \ldots E_n],$$

contained in the statement, which has a system of enveloping loops with the numbers $t_1 < \ldots < t_{N+1}$. Let us isolate from this system the series of loops $r_1, \ldots r_m$ such that the loops with numbers $r_1, \ldots r_{m-1}$ are regular whilst the loop r_m is standard.

Providing the components of the array are arranged lexicographically in memory, the ordinal number A of the component $a[E_1, \ldots E_n]$ is represented by the formula

$$A = \sum_{i=1}^{n-1} E_i \times \prod_{j=i+1}^{n} L_j + E_n, \tag{1}$$

where L_j is the length with respect to the jth dimension of the array a. We shall refer to the *expanded* subscript of the variable $a[E_1, \ldots E_n]$ as expression A. Subsequently, the term "(subscript) expression" will signify only the expanded subscript. Assuming that E_i contains only operations of integral addition and multiplication, then it can be taken that the expression A is implemented in the internal language by a series of addition and multiplication multi-instructions.

The method of calculating the subscript expressions which was chosen for the ALPHA-translator demands that the dependence of the expression A on the parameters of the considered loops $r_1, \ldots r_m$ be clearly indicated. This dependence is given as a canonical form of the subscript (III.2.4.2), thus

$a[i_1 h_1 \ldots i_s h_s v c],$

where $i_1, \ldots i_s$ are the parameters of some of the loops $r_i, \ldots r_m$;
$h_i, \ldots h_s$ are the coefficients (constants or scalars) of the linear dependence of the index on the loop parameters, called the steps for the parameters;
v is a variable (a zero constant, scalar or working variable)
c is a (constant) fixed component of the canonical form.

The expression A is calculated according to the canonical form in the following way:

$$A = \sum_{k=1}^{s} i_k h_k + v + c \tag{2}$$

Thus, the task of reducing the subscript expressions to a canonical form consists of carrying out an analytical conversion of formula (1) to the form (2), which involves picking out from (1) the linear dependence on the loop parameters (where these exist), formulating multi-instructions which calculate the steps h_k and the variable v, and determining the constant c. In addition, it is required that if h_k can be calculated during translation, the calculation should be done.

The steps for the parameters and the variable component must satisfy certain additional demands connected with the nature of their dependence on the picked out loops. With the satisfaction of these additional demands the canonical form is determined by induction in the following way.

Let i_m, i_{m-1}, ..., i_1 be the parameters of the picked out loops r_1, r_2, ..., r_m respectively. Let us define the notion of the factorization of the subscript A with regard to a certain segment $\{i_j, ..., i_k\}$ of the sequence of parameters of the picked out loops.

I. The representation of A in its initial form (1) is the factorization of A with regard to the empty sequence of the parameters.

II. Let us assume that the factorization relating to the sequence of parameters $\{i_1, ..., i_k\}$ has the form

$$A = H_1 i_1 + ... + H_k i_k + A_k,$$

(if $k = 0$, the linear terms are absent and $A_0 = A$ in accordance with (1)) and has already been determined. Then, if A_k can be represented in the form

$$A_k = H_{k+1} i_{k+1} + A_{k+1},$$

where H_{k+1} (which may be equal to zero) and A_{k+1} do not contain i_{k+1} as a constituent and do not depend on the loop r_{m-k}, then the representation of A in the form

$$A = H_1 i_1 + ... + H_k i_k + H_{k+1} i_{k+1} + A_{k+1}$$

is the factorization of A with regard to the sequence $\{i_1, ..., i_{k+1}\}$. Otherwise, it is considered that the factorization of A with regard to the sequence $\{i_1, ..., i_{k+1}\}$ does not exist.

Let n be the maximum length ($m \geqslant n \geqslant 0$) of the sequence $\{i_1, ..., i_n\}$, with regard to which the factorization of A exists. This means that A will be represented in the form

$$A = H_1 i_1 + ... + H_n i_n + A_n,$$

where H_i, ... H_n and A_n are constants (possibly equal to zero) or expressions containing operations of integral addition and multiplication.

On the basis of the derived factorization the canonical form is constructed simply. The zero values of the steps and the corresponding parameters are withdrawn from the linear form. For the non-constant H_k multi-instructions are compiled which calculate them and the scalar h_k which is the result of the last multi-instruction, is taken as a step in the parameter. The decomposition of A_n into variable and fixed components will be described below.

3.1 The Algorithm for Obtaining the Canonical Form

The algorithm for obtaining the multi-instructions which calculate $H_1, \ldots, H_n$ and A_n by a sequence of multi-instructions which calculate A from the formula (1) will be described in the form of a system of conversions of graph G, which relates to A according to the rules in para. 1.

We shall in addition introduce a few definitions which concern the trees.

The path which joins a given suspended vertex with the terminal vertex in tree D is considered to be the *route* in tree D.

The path in D from the suspended vertex which is related to a given occurrence of a into E, is referred to as the *route of the variable a* in the tree D, related to a given term $E(a)$.

The *sub-tree* which is obtained by joining all the routes of a in tree D is referred to as the *a-sub-tree*.

The *complement* $\bar{T}$ to the sub-tree T in the tree D is the sub-tree formed from the routes of all the suspended vertices not belonging to T.

An a-sub-tree T such that any vertex of the type "$\times$" which belongs to T belongs only to one path in T, is referred to as the *linear a-sub-tree*.

Since, with reference to the sequence $\{i_1, \ldots, i_n\}$ the factorization of A for each i is made in the same way, only the process for obtaining H_1 and A_1 can be described. We shall refer to graph G which is constructed for A as the A-tree (according to the rules of para. 1).

Let us examine the i_1-sub-tree in the A-tree. If the i_1-sub-tree is empty, this means that $H_1 = 0$ and $A_1 = A$. Assume that the i_1-sub-tree is not empty and not linear. Then A is certainly the non-linear function of i_1 and the factorization of A for i_1 does not exist, so that the factorization in this case is terminated.

We shall assume that the i_1-sub-tree is linear. Before setting about the separation of the sub-trees in the tree A which corresponds to the terms H_1 and A_1, we must be certain that their arguments are not dependent upon the loop with the parameter i_1. To make sure of this, the weights of all the suspended vertices which are added to the i_1-sub-tree should be less than or equal to r_m (it may be recalled here that r_m is the number of the loop with parameter i_1). If a vertex whose weight is greater than r_m is found amongst these vertices, then factorization with respect to i_1 will not take place.

We shall now assume that the condition laid down for the weights is fulfilled, and that in conjunction with the linear dependence of A on i_1 factorization of A by i_1 is guaranteed. We note that if A, considered as a function of i_1, assumes the form

$$A(i_1) = H_1 i_1 + A_1$$

then $A_1 = A(0)$ and $H_1 = A(1) - A(0)$. The algorithm for the determination of A_1 and H_1 will be based on the utilization of these relations. We shall first establish a method of separating in the A-tree the so called H_1 and A_1-sub-trees and, from which the H_1- and A_1-trees will subsequently be formed, giving the terms H_1 and A_1 respectively.

Let us examine the i_1-sub-tree in the A-tree and mark all the "×"-type vertices. The H_1-sub-tree is then obtained from the i_1-sub-tree by joining to it all the paths which lead from the suspended vertices, in the A-tree, to the marked vertices.

We note that the sub-tree so obtained indicates all the operations needed to calculate $H_1 i_1$. If there are no vertices of the ×-type, the H_1-sub-tree coincides with the i_1-sub-tree.

We shall now establish the conversion of a tree, called the *reduction* of the tree. The reduction is carried out in three stages:

(a) *Executing the operations on the constants.* Let W be a non-suspended vertex in the tree which is the final one in the sub-tree D whose only suspended vertices are those which are related to the constants. Then the sub-tree D is cancelled out so that W becomes a suspended peak related to a constant which is equal in value to the term corresponding to the sub-tree D.

(b) *Reduction of non-essential vertices.* A suspended vertex is said to be non-essential if it comes before a vertex of the "+" type (the "×" type) and is related to a constant which has the value zero (one). A non-suspended vertex of the type "×" is non-essential if amongst its predecessors there is a suspended vertex related to a zero constant. Any vertex is non-essential if its successor is a non-essential one. Cutting down on non-essential vertices consists of elimination from the tree of all non-essential vertices and arrows which come from them.

(c) *Reduction of non-suspended vertices.* A non-suspended vertex is said to be eliminated if it is preceded only by one other one.

Cutting down on the non-suspended vertices in the tree involves eliminating from the tree every reduced vertex W and then joining with an arrow the only vertex preceding W to the one following it. If W is a final vertex, it is simply eliminated from the tree together with the arrow which goes into it.

Let us examine the H_1-sub-tree. We shall relabel all the suspended vertices of the i_1-sub-tree contained in H_1 by means of a symbol for the constant which is equal to unity. In the resulting sub-tree (considered as a separate graph) we apply the reduction conversion to as many vertices as possible. The resulting graph is the H_1-tree.

The A_1-sub-tree is obtained directly from the A-tree by relabelling by means of a symbol for the constant which is equal to zero, all the suspended vertices in it which correspond to i_1. The A_1-tree is obtained by applying the reduction conversion to the A_1-sub-tree. If the A_1-tree is empty, the factorization for A is discontinued.

The above described algorithm is applied to A_1 to find the factorization by i_2 in the way it was applied to A. At each kth step we obtain trees which give the terms H_k and A_k, the latter being the initial term for the next step. When there has been a discontinuation at a certain n^{th} step, a division of A into variable and fixed components is made.

We shall refer to the path of a variable-constant in the A_n-tree as a *constant path*. Of all the constant paths in the A_n-tree the only ones examined are those for which a non-constant path, which crosses the given path in a vertex of the "$\times$" type does not exist. Let us examine the C-sub-tree which is made up of all such constant paths. If it is empty, the fixed component equals zero. If it is not empty then the reduction conversion is applied to the C-sub-tree. The resulting C-tree (consisting of one vertex) gives the value to the fixed component.

The V-tree, i.e. the formula for calculating the variable component v, is obtained by applying the abbreviation conversion to the complement of the C-sub-tree in the A_n-tree.

Note. The above described algorithm in the ALPHA-translator has an additional conversion connected with adjusting the regular loop parameters to the initial value which is equal to zero. In other words, factorization of the index A by the regular loop parameter is obtained not in the form

$$A = H_1 i_1 + A_1$$

but in the form

$$A = H_1 i_1' + A_1'$$

where $i_1' = i_1 - i_1$ (init) and $A_1' = A_1 + H_1 i_1$ (init). Such an adjustment of the parameter of the regular loop (which is made only in subscripts) simplifies the construction of the initial form of the variable instructions (see Section 4.4).

The required modification of the algorithm is obtained by replacing an occurrence of i_1 in the tree A by the symbol! (or value) $< i_1$ (init) instead of zero, to obtain A_1' instead of A_1.

3.3 Example

When considering the example it must be borne in mind that the canonical form of the subscripts is constructed together with cleaning up the loops and carrying out operations on constant arguments. The preceding translator blocks reduce the subscripts to a form which contains only multi-instructions of integral multiplication and addition (see para. 5.1). The loops with the parameters i, j and k are regular ones:

array $a[1 : 10, 1 : 10]$;

...

for $i := b, \dots \{$
for $j := 0, \dots \{$
for $k := 1, \dots \{$
$\quad a[k + i \times (i + j - 1), j + k + 5]$
$\quad a[k + 5, \sin(j)] \dots$

After programming the expressions the subscripts have the form

$a[+ _{001}ij \text{ "1" } t_1$
$\times _{00}it_1 t_2$
$+ _{001}k t_2 \text{ "1" } t_3$
$+ _{0001}jk \text{ "5" "1" } t_4]$
$a[+ _{001}k \text{ "5" "1" } t_5.$
$\sin jt_6$
$+ 01 t_6 \text{ "1" } t_7]$

After eliminating from the subscripts all operations except integral multiplication and addition, the second subscript will have the form

$$\sin j t_6$$
$$+_{01} t_6 \text{ "1" } t_7$$
$$a[+_{001} k \text{ "5" "1" } t_5, t_7]$$

(the first subscript will remain unchanged):

The conversion of the tree of the first subscript is shown in Fig. 4.

This conversion corresponds to the factorization of the subscript by the parameters k and j, which has the form:

$$A' = k \times 11 + j \times (i \times 10 + 1) + (i - 1) \times i \times 10 + 5$$

The conversion for the trees of the second subscript is shown in Fig. 5. The factorization of this subscript has the form:

$$A'' = k \times 10 + \alpha_7 + 50$$

The result of the conversions carried out on the portion of the program to be examined is shown below:

for $i := b, \ldots \{$
$\times_{00} i \text{ "10" } \alpha_1$
$+_{00} \alpha_1 \text{ "1" } \alpha_2$

The A-tree of the expanded index

$+_{01} i \text{ "1" } \alpha_3$
$\times_{00} \alpha_3 \ i \alpha_4$
$\times_{00} \alpha_4 \text{ "10" } \alpha_5$
for $j := 0, \ldots \{$
$\sin j \ \alpha_6$
$+_{01} \alpha_6 \text{ "1" } \alpha_7$
for $k := 1, \ldots \{ \ldots$
$\quad a[\text{"11" } k \alpha_2 \ j \alpha_5 \text{ "5"}]$
$\quad a[\text{"10" } k \alpha_7 \text{ "50"}]$

4   Generation of Instructions for Calculating Subscripts

4.1   The General Approach

When the instructions for calculating the subscript have to be formulated, all the statements of the compiled program (except the loops) have been converted into three-address instructions. The instructions containing the subscripted variables in the address part will be referred to as *variable* instructions. The subscript to the subscripted variables have already been converted to a canonical form.

In the process of converting the subscript to a canonical form σ statements of formation are laid down for all non-constant steps according to the parameter and the variable component (III.2.4). The σ statement is put directly after the last multi-instruction which calculates the given step h- according to the parameter, or the variable component v or, if the corresponding

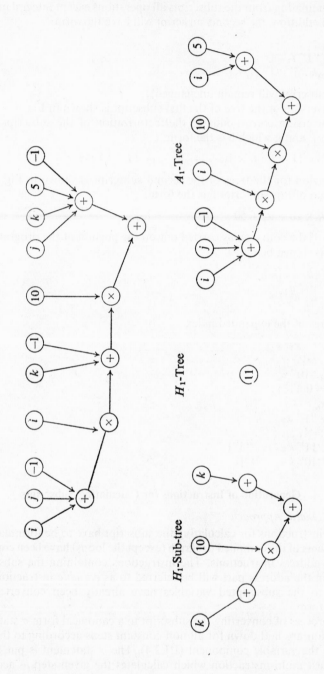

A_1-Tree

H_1-Tree

(11)

H_1-Sub-tree

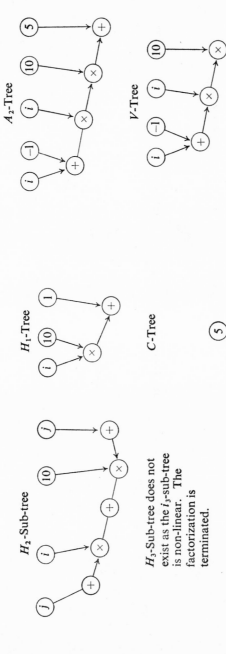

Fig. 4. Conversion of the first subscript

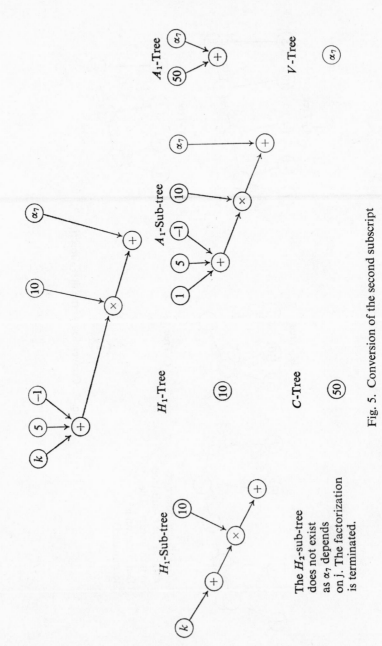

Fig. 5. Conversion of the second subscript

expression H or V in the factorization of the subscript is a simple variable having the weight r, the σ statement is put in front of the loop which has the number r. The σ statement is an indication that in a given place in the program, instructions should appear below which introduce into the subscript the result of calculating h or v (instructions for forming or instructions for calculating the readdress variable). The only exception occurs when the subscript is not dependent on the loops but the variable component depends on a first level loop for the given variable instruction. In this case the σ statement is not applied:

The following procedure is adopted to calculate the subscript:

(1) When the canonical form does not depend on the parameters (i.e. when the initial subscript expression does not depend on the parameters of the considered loops, or when expansion in a linear form according to the latter does not exist), the appropriate address of the variable instruction is formed either by loading the index register with the value of the subscript or—if there is a σ statement for the variable component—by adding the value of the subscript, that addition being made at the point in the program at which the σ statement is located, to the variable instruction itself.

(2) When the canonical form includes the steps according to the parameters, there is always a σ statement for the variable component. The variable component is calculated with the help of the addition instructions as in para. 1) whilst for the steps according to the parameters either the readdress method is applied or the required value is fed into the index register, depending on the type and level of the corresponding loop.

We shall examine the generation of instructions connected with calculating the steps according to the parameters in more detail.

4.2   Generation of Instructions for Loading the Index Register

We shall refer to the set of instructions, in relation to which the loop C is a first level loop, as the *proper body* of the loop C. In other words, the proper body C is the body C from which the bodies and headings inserted into C have been removed.

The index register is used for the steps according to the parameter k of the given loop C only for instructions which enter the proper body C.

To implement the dependence on the parameters with the help of the index register, the latter one must be loaded with the current value of $h \times k$. There may be several steps according to one parameter so that, when the dependence on the parameter is implemented directly with the help of the index register, the number of loads will depend on how the instructions alternate with the various steps according to the parameter k in the proper loop body.

The following method is employed to decrease the number of loads, produced by the alteration of the steps:

A certain step according to a parameter is chosen to make up the so called "main register".

The number of loads of the index register is decreased by modifying some of the variable instructions dependent on the regular loop parameters, with the help of the readdress method.

We shall examine the proper body of a particular loop C and pick out the linear sections in it. A linear section usually signifies a series of instructions not containing labels or branch instructions, such that a label or branch instruction comes before and after it. To form the instructions for loading the index register, each linear section of the proper body C which has the parameter k is divided into segments which are in a certain way of the same type as regards the utilization of the index register.

We shall define a few terms.

A variable instruction dependent on k with the step h is referred to as a *single field of type h*. Generally speaking, the variable instruction in question may belong to several single fields not of the same type. A series of single fields of the type h which belongs to one linear section and does not contain any single fields of another type is referred to as a *field* of type h.

In the linear section it is possible to distinguish the bigger segments of the program and these will be referred to as *quasi-fields*. The algorithm for distinguishing the quasi-fields in the linear section consists of the following. We shall examine the variable instructions in the order in which they are arranged, beginning with the first one. Having singled out a certain field T of the type h, we shall examine all the preceding variable instructions, beginning with the nearest ones. If there is a single field T_1 of the same type amongst them, the whole of the series of variable instructions, from T_1 to T_2 will also constitute a quasi-field of the type h. If there is a quasi-field of the type h, beginning with the single field T_1 and finishing at T, amongst the preceding variable instructions, such that there is no quasi-field of a different type between T_2 and T_1, the whole series of instructions from T_1 to T is considered to be a quasi-field of the type h and the old quasi-field $(T_1 T_2)$ of the type h is not included in the examination. As can be seen from the above, the field of the type h is also a quasi-field of this type.

The main register is only chosen for loops which do not contain calls to procedures and ones where none of the loops, with regard to which the loop in question is a first level one, is a loop with an exit.

For regular loops the main register is chosen in the following way. Assume that all the linear sections of the proper body of the given loop C are divided into quasi-fields and single fields which do not enter any one quasi-field. On the strength of the algorithm for separating the quasi-fields, such a division will be unique. If we assume m_i to be the number of quasi-fields of the type h_i, then n_i will be the number of single fields of the type h_i which do not enter any one quasi-field. The number of all the quasi-fields is

$$M = \sum_i m_i$$

and the number of the single fields

$$N = \sum_i n_i.$$

In the regular loops for the instruction K, which contains the address with the step according to the parameter h_i, the index register is used if K is in the quasi-field of the type h_i and the readdress system is applied if K is in a quasi-field of another type h_j. The index register is used for the instruction K which is in the single field if the latter contains the address with the step according to the parameter h_i whilst h_i is chosen for the content of the main register. In the contrary case, readdressing is applied to K.

With this approach to programming instructions for altering the subscript, the following points must be taken into consideration when choosing the content of the main register. Assume that h_i is chosen as the content of the main register. Then for each quasi-field R of the type h_j different from h_i, load the index register with h_j is put† in front of the entry into R, keeping h_i in the working location. Loading the index register with h_i which has been kept, is put after the last instruction. In view of the preceding paragraph only one readdress instruction is required for single fields of the type h_j as distinct from h_1. Then the total number of instructions for altering the subscripts which depend on k (not counting the readdress instructions for the single fields of the type which are contained in the quasi-fields of another type and the instructions for calculating the values of $h_j \times k$, as the number of these instructions bears no relation to the choice of the main register) will be

$$L = 2(M - m_i) + N - n_i.$$

Let the steps according to k in the subscripts dependent upon k be $h_i \ldots h_t$. Then, in order to reduce L to the minimum h_i is chosen from $h_i \ldots h_t$ for the contents of the main register, so that

$$2m_i + n_i \geqslant 2m_j + n_j (j = 1, \ldots, t).$$

For the irregular loops, the linear sections are divided into fields and single fields only. In this case it is assumed that each variable instruction can be a single field of only one type. If this is not so, then the instruction in question is divided into several instructions, each of which will satisfy this requirement. In fact, the three address instruction of the kind

X	$a[k]$	$b[2 \times k]$	$c[k]$

can be replaced by instructions of the form:

$\Longrightarrow$	$b[2 \times k]$		t_1

X	$a[k]$	t_1	$c[k]$

We shall assume that m_i is the number of fields and single fields of the type h_i and that the total number of all the fields is

$$M = \sum_i m_i.$$

† It should be borne in mind that the statement "load the index register with h_j," signifies that the expression $h \times k$—the values of which are calculated once each time k is altered by the loop heading—is sent to the register.

For fields and single fields of the type h_j $(h_j \neq h_i)$ where h_i is the content of the main register, the same method for loading the index register with h_j at the beginning of the field and for loading the index register with h_i at the end of the field, is used as for the quasi-field in the previous case. Then the number of operations for loading the index register is $2(M - m_i)$. Therefore, h_i is chosen as the content of the main register so that $m_j \geqslant m$ ($j = 1, \ldots t$).

If the main register for the loop C is not selected, the index register is used for the fields and single fields in the event of C being an irregular loop and only for quasi-fields if C is a regular loop. The index register is loaded with h_i at the beginning of the field (or quasi-field) of the type h_i and does not subsequently appear again at the end of the field.

If the main register is chosen for loop C, an instruction for storing the main register in the working location is put in front of every loop in relation to which C is a first level loop, and after such a loop the retained value if restored. Similar instructions for retaining and restoring the main register are laid down for a variable instruction, the variable component of any address of which is introduced with the help of the index register. In some cases the great number of instructions for preserving and restoring indicates that when deciding whether or not to choose the main register, several other circumstances must be considered as compared with those which are taken into account in the ALPHA-translator.

We shall refer to the expressions $I_1 = h_1 \times k, \ldots, I_t = h_t \times k$ as *logical index registers*. The values of the logical index registers for irregular loops are recalculated every time the loop body is completed afresh. For regular loops, not all logical index registers are implemented via the physical index register but only the main one and of the rest only the ones for which at least one quasi-field has been singled out. For all such logical index registers the initial value is zero (cf. note in para. 3.2), but they are altered by the readdress method by the value $h \times D$ where h is the corresponding step according to the parameter and D is the step for altering the parameter.

4.3   Generation of Instructions for Modifying Variable Instructions

Generation of instructions for readdress, restoration and formation follows the generation of instructions for loading the index register and, at the same time, dependences on the parameter are eliminated from the canonical form of the subscript, which are implemented with the help of the index register, then, if the variable component is also formed with the help of the index register, it is substituted by zero. In view of what was said at the beginning of Section 4.1 for all the variable steps according to the parameter and for the variable component not equal to zero, there are always σ-statements at the proper levels of execution.

Below we shall examine only those variable instructions which depend on the loop parameters or which have a variable component not equal to zero. For each variable instruction K, we shall examine the series of loops which envelop it, supplemented by a fictitious loop being the highest loop, which envelops the whole program. Each loop of this series may be linked with the instruction K in three different ways.

If there is a σ-statement for the variable component of at least one subscript in the actual loop body, the loop in question is said to be linked with K by formation.

If the parameter of the loop in question enters at least one subscript belonging to K, the loop is said to be connected to K by readdressing.

If the loop in question is a 1th level loop $(1 > 1)$ with regard to K, whilst the $(1 - 1)^{th}$ level loop is connected to K by readdress, the loop in question is said to be connected to K by restoration.

From the sequence of enveloping loops which has been examined, a series -S- of *connected loops* is chosen, that is to say loops which are connected to the instruction in question in an arbitrary manner: by formation, readdress or restoration. We shall introduce the concept of loop level for a series of linked loops which is similar to the loop level in the case of the enveloping loops (Section 1.1). Below, the term "loop level" should be taken as signifying the level in a series of linked loops.

At the time of completing the analysis of the variable instruction K in question and formulating the instructions for modifying it, the series S of loops linked with K has been determined and the value of the step for modifying the loop parameter is known for each loop in S and also whether or not the loop is repeated a fixed number of times. The loop is called a loop of *constant multiplicity* if the step for modifying the parameter and its upper and lower limits are all constants, and the loop is not one with an exit (see para. 2).

The tag technique for modifying the instruction K during execution of the working program consists of the following. For each loop in S, the instruction K is put in a position in memory which is fixed for the loop in question, but, generally speaking, varies from loop to loop—the *base* of the instruction K. For the first level loop the base coincides with the position in memory which will be occupied by the instruction K in the working program. For the maximum level loop the base coincides with the position which is set aside in the working program for storing the initial form of the instruction K. For the rest of the loops, in the series S, several other memory cells may be bases of instruction K.

For each loop C in the series S, the *formation variable* is calculated if C is linked to the instruction K by formation, and in some cases, if C is linked to K by readdress, the *readdress variable* is calculated. The latter is done only if there are variables amongst the steps according to loop C parameter in the subscripts which enter K, or if the step for modifying the parameter C is a variable. If not, a readdress constant is found by the translator.

The formation variable for the loop in question is made up of the values of the variable components for the subscripts which enter the instruction K. Only those components whose σ-statements are in the actual body of loop C are involved in this. The instructions for calculating the formation variable consist of (1) an instruction for shifting the value of the variable component to the position in the machine word corresponding to the position to be occupied by the corresponding address in instruction K. (These commands are placed in the position of the corresponding σ-statements.) (2) An instruction for adding together the variable components which have been shifted if there are several of them in instruction K (these instructions are also placed consecutively in the positions of the corresponding σ-statements, from the second one to the last).

The instructions for calculating the readdress variable (if it is not a constant) are compiled in the same way as the instructions for the formation variable except that instructions for multiplying the step according to the parameter h by step D for modifying the parameter must first be put in the position of the σ-statement, where, if D is the variable and the σ-statement for D follows the σ-statement for h in the program then these instructions are put into the position of the σ-statement for D.

Among the instructions for calculating the formation and readdress variable, economy of the instructions to be placed in the position of one particular σ-statement and which coincide within the group, is performed.

The instruction K in the first level loop is obtained by adding the contents of the base L_1 of instruction K for the loop in question to the formation variable and by sending the result to the base L_2 of instruction K, set aside for the $(1 - 1)^{th}$ level loop. We observe that if the first level loop is linked to the formation of K, the bases for the first and $(1 - 1)^{th}$ level loops must be different. The formation instruction is placed immediately after the command for calculating the final value of the formation variable of the loop in question. If the first level loop is linked to K by formation (i.e. formation must be carried out in the loop body) then, as distinct from the general rule, the base L of the instruction K is not the position of K in the program but a separate cell which preserves the "pattern" of instruction K, to be added to the formation variable of the formation instruction. Readdressing of instruction K according to the first level loop parameter is always carried out by adding the contents of the base L of instruction K for the loop in question to the readdress variable and by placing the result in L. The readdress instructions are placed before the closing bracket of the loop in question.

When the $(1 + 1)^{th}$ level loop is connected with the formation instruction K, there is no need to restore the 1st level loop according to the loop parameter since, owing to the formation, the instruction K is automatically restored in the original form for this loop, before entering into the 1st level loop. Otherwise restoration instructions are compiled.

An instruction is restored according to the parameter of the loop in question in two ways:

(1) by transferring the original form of the instruction for the loop in question (see para. 4.4);

(2) by subtracting the restoration constant from the instruction to be readdressed. This type of restoration is only used when:

(a) the first level loop is a loop with constant multiplicity;
(b) the readdress variable is a constant;
(c) the $(1 + 1)^{th}$ level loop is not a highest level loop.

This type of restoration is carried out by subtracting the restoration constant created by the translator from the contents of the base L of the instruction K for the first level loop and by placing the result in L. When restoration of this type takes place, the bases of the instruction K for the first and $(1 + 1)^{th}$ level loop coincide. If the $(1 + 1)^{\text{th}}$ level loop is linked with the instruction K by readdress, the possibility of combining readdress and restoration is examined. In addition, the possibility of eliminating the restoration and readdress instructions is considered. The restoration instruction (if it is not possible to combine the two) is placed immediately after the closing bracket of the first level loop.

In the general case, the first type of restoration is used. This restoration is carried out by transferring the contents of the base L_1 of the instruction for the $(1 + 1)^{\text{th}}$ level loops into base L_2 for the loop in question. In the case of restoration of this type L_1 and L_2 must, of course, be different.

4.4 Choosing the Initial Form of the Variable Instruction

We shall assume that the subscript of a certain variable a has the canonical form

$$a[h_1 i_1 \ldots h_s i_s vc]$$

where $i_1, \ldots, i$. are the regular loop parameters and i_1 may be an irregular loop parameter. In accordance with the Note at the end of para 3.2, $i_2, \ldots, i_s$ are converted to their original zero value when reducing the parameters to a canonical form.

This means that the expressions $h_2 \times i_2^{\text{start}}, \ldots, h_s \times i_s^{\text{start}}$. which would normally enter into the expression of the initial form of the subscript, have already been taken into account in the variable or constant components. If i_1 is an irregular loop parameter, dependence on it is implemented via the index-register. In this case, the expression $h_1 \times i_1^{\text{start}}$. is inserted at once into the index register. The variable component is inserted into the subscript at the appropriate moment by the formation instruction.

The above remarks signify that the initial value of the subscript can be given in the form of a subscript without dependence on parameters and with a zero variable component $a\ [0C]$.

4.5 Further Details Regarding the Organization of Checking the Regular Loops for Completion

As stated in Section 2, checking for completion in regular loops is carried out either by the counter or with the help of the index-register.

If step D for modifying the regular loop parameter is a variable, the position "element exhausted" is verified each time the loop body is completed according to the value of the parameter.

If D is a constant whilst the upper or lower limits for altering the parameter are variables, then an additional check is carried out for skipping the execution of the loop in the case of an empty set of parameter values.

If the main register I has been chosen in loop C and the step for modifying it is a positive constant, the loop is checked for completion by checking the value of I, where changing the register I to the step for its modification coincides with this verification. In all other cases instructions for checking the counter are compiled for the constant D, which coincide with the modification of I (if the main register I is chosen in C).

Whenever it is stated that checking for completion is carried out by the counter N, it is implied that $abs\,(B-A)$ is taken as the initial value of N and that $abs\,(D)$ is taken as the modification step on the condition that the FOR clause has the form

for $k := A$ **step** D **until** B

Exit from the loop is carried out when the sign of N is changed.

All the combinations of operations which have been mentioned are achieved by using special machine instructions.

4.6 Evaluation of Results

Thus, when compiling instructions for calculating subscripts, the methods used are those also employed in manual programming. Of course, we were further limited by having to use only certain standard methods, and to arrive at a more flexible use of these methods, we had to carry out an analysis which would be simple to implement. Some of these methods had already been used in previous translators (4.6.8). In the case of the constant readdress variable, the translators described in these papers compile exactly the same instructions as the ALPHA-translator. In the case of the alternating readdress variable in the translator[4, 7] a special variable is compiled which has identical steps in all three addresses instead of shifting the readdress step into the requisite address, and when the moment for readdressing arrives the appropriate addresses are singled out to receive the requisite readdress variable. This increases the number of instructions required for readdress as compared with manual programming or with the methods used in the ALPHA-translator.

The methods of restoring are described in (III.8). The translators described in these papers only use transfer of the initial form of the instruction, when restoring. The same methods of restoring are described in paper (VII) as in the present chapter, although restoration by substruction the constant was applied most generally and this entailed a large number of instructions.

The readdress and restoration mechanism, using bases for variable instructions was suggested by A. P. Yershov in 1957, when modernizing the programming for BESM. The basic difference in formulating the instructions for modifying the variable instructions, as described in the above mentioned papers, compared with the way suggested in this chapter consists of the following. In the ALPHA-translator, instructions for modifying the variable instructions are formulated in such a way that all instructions which change a given instruction are formulated simultaneously, depending on the various loops, whereas in the papers indicated all instructions which change a group of instructions are formulated according to one parameter. We are of the opinion that simultaneous compiling of all instructions which change a given instruction means that better programming is achieved thanks to the interaction of these instructions.

5 Implementation of the Described Algorithms

The algorithms for translating which have been described were implemented in Blocks 11–13 and 15–18 of the ALPHA-translator.

As a rule, each of the major algorithms for converting the program to be translated consists of three parts:

(1) analysing the program to extract information about the structures to be processed;

(2) actually processing the program using a given conversion algorithm;

(3) introducing into the program to be translated any necessary inserts and changes to be determined by the algorithm.

Thus, the three stages which have been mentioned in the process of applying the algorithm for cleaning up the loops and the algorithm for reducing the subscript expression to a canonical form are carried out by Blocks 11, 12 and 13. In addition, a series of functions connected with the described algorithms is implemented by the preceding blocks.

5.1   The Work of the Preceding Blocks

This work consists of either preparing certain information to be used for analysing the loops and subscripts or of preliminarily standardizing the FOR-clauses and subscripts.

When the identifiers are replaced (IV.1), Block 3 marks the loops that have an exit; when the expressions are programmed (IV.2) Block 5 converts the subscripts to reduce all the lower limits to zero and also carries out the subsequent standardization of the FOR clauses.

(1) If an element of the FOR-clause is an arithmetical expression, it is programmed in such a way that at the end of its program it is assigned to the loop parameter and not to the working variable;

(2) The calculation of expression E, in the context: $:= E$ step, is taken out of the FOR clause and placed before it. Block 6 (V.4.2.2) compiles the list of variables to which there is an assignment when the procedure statements are carried out. These lists, which first have to be tabulated, are inserted into the program—by the auxiliary Block 8—at the end of a group of internal language statements which implement the source procedure statement.

Block 8 extracts all the operations from the subscript positions, except for integral addition and multiplication multi-instructions. In addition, if there are both addition and multiplication multi-instructions *and* other operations in the subscript position, all the operations are extracted from this position. Block 8 also inserts into the loop statement sign the information that the loop has a real parameter and not an integral one

5.2   The Block for Compiling the Loop and Assignment Tables

Two main information arrays are filled in in Block 11; the table of loops and the lists of assignments. The number of lines in the table of the loops equals the number of loops in the program. It is determined to which of several possible loop types each loop belongs, depending on the type of FOR clause and also on such factors as the presence of an exit from the loop via the branch statement, the presence in the loop body of calls to a procedure and the use in the loop body of a loop parameter as an argument or result of an expression which is not a subscript. A reference to the list of assignments for the loop in question is also inserted into a row in the table of loops. The list of assignments is compiled as a list of all non-working variables so that in the loop in question there is at least one assignment statement for the value of this variable, otherwise this variable is contained in the list of assignments produced by the procedure statement.

5.3 The Block for Cleaning Up the Loops and Processing the Subscripts

In accordance with the algorithm for cleaning up the loops and using the information gathered in the list of assignments, Block 12 performs the cleaning up the loops, i.e. moves the multi-instructions to the maximum possible level in the order of the enveloping loops. In addition, the operations carried out on the constant arguments are executed, whereas the operations carried out with non-constant arguments are transferred to the common list. The common list (III.3.2) has a list structure and consists of alternate items in a sequence of multi-instructions, on the basis of which each sequence is positioned according to the loop before which it will be carried out.

In Block 12, there is a specially allotted field into which the expanded subscript of any considered subscripted variable is written, in accordance with the algorithm for the conversion of a subscript expression to the canonical form.

Beginning with the innermost loop and following the sequence of the enveloping loops the expressions for the steps according to the parameters for the loops in question are picked out, as far as this is possible. Besides this, the constant part and the remaining variable component of the subscript expression are picked out. The algorithm for cleaning up the loops is applied to each of the expressions obtained.

5.4 The Block for Inserting the Operations Previously Taken Out

Block 13 completes the work of the above mentioned algorithm. For each loop, information taken from a row of the loop table is added to the statement sign for the loop, saying to which type the loop belongs. The series of operations taken out when cleaning up the loops are taken from the common list into the program and are placed in front of the appropriate loop for the series in question.

5.5 Compiling the Instructions for Calculating the Subscripts and Organizing the Loops

Blocks 15 and 17 compile the instructions for modifying the loop parameter, and Blocks 16 and 17—the instructions for modifying the index-register. Block 17 compiles the instructions for modifying the variable instructions.

Block 15 compiles the instructions for modifying the loop parameter for special and irregular loops. Simultaneously the block analyses the loop bodies and selects the main register for all standard loops. On the basis of the table of main registers which was obtained in Block 15, Block 16 separates the corresponding fields and quasi-fields within the loop body, implements the programming methods described in para. 4.2 and for each standard loop it stores the list $h_1, \ldots, h_t$ of steps according to the parameter k, to be loaded to the index register.

Block 17 compiles the instructions for formation, readdressing and restoration and also the instructions for calculating $h_i \times k$ for all steps $h_1, \ldots, h_t$. Besides this, it compiles instructions for checking the completion of regular loops. The instructions compiled in Block 17 are put into the common list. In addition, there appears a table of loops and σ-statements, in which references to the common list are placed. This means that the instructions connected with the loop or σ-statement in question can be selected from the common list. On the basis of the common list, the loop table and the σ-statement table, Block 18 inserts the instructions compiled by Block 17 into the appropriate places in the program.

6   Conclusion

After operating the ALPHA-translator for a period of one year, we are in a position to conclude that the quality of programming the loops and subscript expressions is, in the majority of cases, quite high and closely approaches that achieved by the skilled programmer when writing a program. By cleaning up the loops quite high quality operating programs can be obtained even when the ALPHA-program is compiled by an unskilled person. Removal of the instructions of formation from the loops is most effective. However, it should be noted that in some cases, particularly when using dynamic arrays, the number of formation instructions becomes considerable and the total length of the program may substantially exceed (by 2–1·5 times as much) that of the manual program, although the time figures have the same order.

In this chapter, parts 1 and 3 were written by M. N. Bezhanova, parts 2 and 4 by I. V. Pottosin and part 5 was a joint effort. S. K. Kozhukhina, G. I. Kozhukhin, I. A. Vitkina and R. N. Klyushkova were also involved in implementing these algorithms in the ALPHA-translator.

The authors would like to express their thanks to all these people and also to the programming department as a whole for taking part in discussions about the algorithms which have been mentioned. The authors are also grateful to G. I. Kozhukhin for his help in writing the article.

REFERENCES

1. YERSHOV, A. P. and KUROCHKIN, V. M. (1961). Some of the problems involved in automatic programming. Proceedings of the All-Union Conference on computing, mathematics and the application of computing machinery. Publ. Academy of Sciences of the Azerbaijan Soviet Socialist Republic, Baku.
2. HAWKINS, E. N. and HUXTABLE, D. H. R. (1963). A multi-pass translation scheme for ALGOL 60. In "Annual Review in Automatic Programming", Vol. 3. Pergamon Press, Oxford.
3. VE LIKANCVA, T. M., YERSHOV, A. P., KIM, K. V., KUROCHKIN, V. M., OLEINIK-OVOD, YU. N. and PODDERYUGIN, V. D. (1961). A compiler program for the computer (PPS)—The Third All Union Conference on Computing, Mathematics and the Application of Methods of Computing Techniques. Publ. Academy of Sciences of the Azerbaijan Soviet Socialist Republic, Baku.
4. KITOV, A. I. and KRINITSKII, N. A. (1959). Electronic ciphering machines and computing. Fizmatgiz, Moscow.

5. BERGE, C. (1962). The theory of graphs and its applications. Moscow IL.
6. KAMYNIN, S. S., LYUBIMSKI, E. Z. and SHURA-BURA, M. R. (1968). On the automation of programming—Problems of cybernetics. No. 1
7. YERSHOV, A. P. (1958). A programming program for a high speed electronic computing machine. Moscow, Publ. Academy of Sciences of the USSR.
8. TRIFONOV, N. P. and SHURA-BURA, M. R. (eds) (1961). An automating programming system. Fizmatgiz, Moscow.

VIII ECONOMY OF EXPRESSIONS IN THE ALPHA-TRANSLATOR

I. V. Pottosin

The economy of expressions, i.e. the finding of identical expressions in the program and its re-writing in such a manner that the identical expressions are computed only once as far as possible, is one of the most widespread optimization procedures in automatic programming. In this way, the program to be translated is divided into non-overlapping sections, and expressions are economized in each section separately, without taking into account the expressions contained in other sections. We shall call these sections of the program *economy sections*. Economy of expressions results in a reduction both of the number of instructions and of the operating time and depends on the nature of the algorithm and on the size of the economy section. The algorithm of the economy of expressions implemented in the ALPHA-translator takes fully into account the commutativeness of addition and multiplication. It is, however, not optimal, since it does not investigate all possible breakdowns of the original formulae into sub-expressions. The economy section for this algorithm is a sequence of assignment statements for the ALPHA-program appearing immediately after one another which (sequence) is not interrupted by labels, by symbols **begin** and **end** and by other delimiters, or by other types of statements. In the ALPHA-translator economy of expressions is implemented at the level of internal language.

1 Description of the Algorithm

1.1 Initial Assumptions

Before carrying out the economy of expressions, the initial expressions are converted to a sequence of multi-instructions (III.2). A multi-instruction† consists of the operation, the operands and the result. The operands enter the multi-instruction both with the direct and with the inverse operation (subtraction with respect to addition, division with respect to multiplication). The operands, entering the multi-instruction with the inverse operation, are provided with a special mark in the record of the multi-instruction. We shall denote this mark by the symbol *. Thus, on translation, the statement of the Input language

$$f := (a + b - c)/b \times c/d$$

is converted into two multi-instructions in the internal language:

$$+ \quad a \quad b \quad c^* \quad t1$$
$$\times \quad t1 \quad \quad b^* \quad cd^* \quad f,$$

where $t1$ is the intermediate result.

---

† To simplify the terminology, the term "multi-instruction" signifies here any internal language assignment statement.

6

Conditional expressions, additionally to multi-instructions, produce statements for checking conditions, labels and branch statements.

Among multi-instructions we shall distinguish two kinds: *commutative*, i.e. with commutative operation (addition, multiplication, etc.), and *non-commutative*, i.e. with non-commutative operation (sin (x), $x \uparrow y$, etc.). For clarity we shall provisionally introduce the following limitations:

(1) if some non-operating variable x appears as the result of a multi-instruction, then x does not enter into any multi-instruction as an operand;
(2) non-commutative multi-instructions are unary;
(3) all operands of a commutative multi-instruction differ from each other;
(4) the economy section consists of a sequence of multi-instructions, such that if the first multi-instruction is executed any other multi-instruction is also executed.

1.2   Definitions

We shall number the multi-instructions in the order of their entry in the sequence of multi-instructions, appearing as the economy section. We shall designate the *complex* of the ith multi-instruction for the commutative multi-instruction by a set of three symbols (θ, a, b), and for the non-commutative ones by the pair of symbols (θ, a), where θ is the operation of the ith multi-instruction, and a and b are some of its operands. A complex is called effective, if it appears as the complex of more than one multi-instruction in the sequence under examination. If a sequence of multi-instruction does not contain an effective complex, it is called irreducible.

The problem of the elimination of identical expressions is considered as the problem of the formation of effective complexes in the sequence of multi-commands.

Let us select a given effective complex K. We shall relate to this complex some new variable, which will be referred to as the *result of the complex*. In all multi-instructions, including K itself, we shall substitute operands, entering in the complex K, by the result of the complex. Moreover, if, after substitution, the result of the complex appears in a multi-instruction as the only operand, such a multi-instruction is called a *disappearing multi-instruction* and in subsequent transformations such multi-instructions will not be taken into account. We shall call this transformation *reduction of the complex*.

The successive application of the reduction of the complex finally results in an irreducible sequence of multi-instructions, which, together with the non-ordered set of effective complexes, employed when carrying out reductions, appears as the result of transformations. It is clear that, for a given sequence of multi-instructions, one may obtain different results, depending on the order in which effective complexes are selected.

1.3   Algorithms

In the selection of effective complexes we consider the following obvious equivalences:

$$ab^* = (a^* \, b)^*;$$
$$a^* \, b^* = (ab)^*.$$

Let us select a certain economy section. For each variable, appearing as the operand of at least one multi-instruction of the given economy section, we shall construct two Boolean vectors—the *entries vector* and the *sign vector*. For operations an entries vector is constructed only. For a given variable a (or operation θ) the ith component $L_a[i]$ of the entries vector L_a takes the value *true* if the variable appears as the operand of the ith multi-instruction and otherwise the value *false*; the ith component $S_a[i]$ of the sign vector S_a takes the value *true* if the variable a appears as the operand of the ith multi-instruction and enters into it with the inverse operation, and the value *false* if the variable a occurs as an operand of the ith multi-instruction and does not enter into it with the inverse operation. If the variable a does not occur as an operand of the ith multi-instruction, the value of $S_a[i]$ is undefined.

We start the selection of the complexes from the first multi-instruction of the economy section. For commutative multi-instructions the operands are chosen systematically, beginning with the first. Let the ith multi-instruction be given by $\theta A_1, \ldots, AnP$, where θ is the operation, A_j are the operands and P is the result of the multi-instruction. We consider the complex $\theta A_1 A_2$. For this complex we construct the entries vector $L_{\theta A_1 A_2}$. Taking the operations of conjunction, disjunction, negation and of negation of the equivalence (we shall denote the last one by the symbol $\oplus$) of vectors to constitute componental operations, giving as their result also a vector, we have for $L_{\theta A_1 A_2}$ the relationship:

$$L_{\theta A_1 A_2} = L_{A_1} \, \& \, L_{A_2} \, \& \, L_\theta (\overline{S_{A_1}{}' \oplus S_{A_2}{}'}),$$

where

$$S_A{}' = \begin{cases} S_A, & \text{if } S_A[i] = false \\ \bar{S}_A, & \text{if } S_A[i] = true \end{cases}$$

We determine from the entries vector for the complex whether it is an effective one or not. In fact, if there is a value $k \neq i$, such that $L_{\theta A_1 A_2}[k]$ is *true*, the complex is effective. Having performed in this case the transformation of the reduction of the complex, we shall consider the result of the complex as the operand of the corresponding multi-instructions. In this way, we shall obtain its entries vector. Vector $S_{A_1}{}'$ is the sign vector for the result of the complex $\theta A_1 A_2$. Continuing successively to select the operands of the multi-instruction A_j, we shall investigate all complexes $\theta A_s A_j$ $(s < j)$, where A_s represents either the operands, not entering into any effective complex, or the results of effective complexes (the result of the effective complex $\theta A_k A_m$ $(k < m)$ is thus considered as the kth operand of the multi-instruction). The investigation is conducted with increasing numbers of the operand and is terminated either with the exhausting of all the corresponding operands, or with the discovery of an effective complex. Having obtained the effective complex, we have to modify also the entries vector for the operands of the complex, since these operands disappear from the corresponding multi-instructions after the selection of the complex. Therefore, if A_j is the operand of the effective complex $\theta A_j A$ (or $\theta A_s A_j$) the new value of the vector L_{A_j} will be

$$L_{A_j}' = L_{A_j} \oplus L_{\theta A_j A_s}$$

The survey of the multi-instruction is terminated when all its operands are exhausted. For non-commutative multi-instructions θAP a single complex θA may be considered. The entries vector for this is defined by the relation

$$L_{\theta A} = L_\theta \,\&\, L_A.$$

The sign vector for the result of this complex is undefined. The remaining operations carried out on multi-instructions of this kind are analogous to those for commutative multi-instructions.

It is obvious that, having performed the algorithm described over all the multi-instructions of the economy section, we shall obtain an irreducible sequence. However, the number of reductions performed in the initial sequence may prove to be not a maximum. For example, in the sequence

$$
\begin{array}{cccccc}
\theta & a & b & c & d & t1 \\
\theta & a & b & t2 \\
\theta & a & c & d & t3 \\
\theta & a & c & t4
\end{array}
$$

we shall obtain according to the algorithm stated the effective complexes θab and θcd entering into two-multi-instructions each, in spite of the fact that all possible variants have been examined, we should then select a variant resulting in the effective complex θac, entering into three multi-instructions, and in the effective complex θBd, entering into two multi-instructions, where B is the result of the complex θac.

1.4 Transition to a Real Situation

For the description of the algorithm we considered an ideal situation. We applied some limitations and did not consider the form of the operands. In a real program the following variables may occur as operands of the multi-instructions up to the moment of the economy of expressions (III.2)

(a) scalars;
(b) intermediate operating variables, arising during the construction of the multi-instructions and cleaning up the loops and also scalars, having appeared in place of the operating variables during the cleaning up of the loops (VII.1.2);
(c) constants;
(d) subscripted variables, denoting either components of arrays or formal parameters of procedures called by name, their subscripted expressions having been reduced to the canonical form (III.2).

Results of the multi-instructions may be scalars, operating variables and subscripted variables.

Limitation 1 (see 1.1) may not be fulfilled in the case of variables, appearing as the operands of multi-instructions. While removing this limitation we have to consider: (A) that multi-instructions obtained from effective complexes must not be placed in an arbitrary position of the economy section since the operands of an effective complex must be calculated before the moment of executing the corresponding multi-instruction; (B) that some variable x may enter as the operand into the multi-instruction, both the precedent of some multi-instruction M, of which x is the result, and also into the multi-instruction following after M (obviously, in the economy, it will be necessary to distinguish these entries). We shall say that a multi-instruction produces a given effective complex, if it is the first containing this complex. As regards (A), it is sufficient to place the multi-instruction for the effective complex immediately before the multi-instruction producing this complex. Next we note that (B) applies actually only to scalars and to subscripted variables. In order to take into account this necessary distinction, renaming of the variables is carried out during the operation of the algorithm. If the variable appears as the result of some multi-instruction, it will receive another name in the survey of the following multi-instructions which differs from that which it had before the survey of the given multi-instruction. Scalars and subscripted variables undergo such a renaming, whereupon, if the subscripted variable is an array the name of the array changes; if it is a formal parameter then it changes both its name and the names of all variables—actual parameters, substituted for the given formal parameter.

Limitation 2 is overcome by using as the operand of the n-ary non-commutative operation $(n > 1)$ $\theta A_1, \ldots, AnP$, the sequence of symbols $A_1, \ldots, A_n$.

As regards limitation 3, it should be noted that if a conditional expression emerges in the assignment statement, multi-instructions which cannot always be executed may appear in the economy section. Therefore, if the multi-instruction M, producing a given complex, is contained in some conditional expression, it will not always be correct to place the multi-instruction, computing the effective complex, before M, for example, if this complex enters at least one of the multi-instructions outside the conditional expression. We shall place the multi-instruction, computing the effective complex, immediately before the major conditional expression (i.e. that which is not contained in any other conditional expression) containing the multi-instruction, producing the given complex. In this case the multi-instruction, computing the effective complex, will always be executed, which may in some cases be superfluous, but will always be a true operation. The operands of this instruction will always be computed before executing the conditional expression. In fact, only operating variables may be results of multi-instructions in the conditional expression. If an operating variable appears as the operand of an effective complex, then it has to correspond with a disappearing multi-instruction with this operating variable as its result. This multi-instruction either precedes the conditional expression, or, if it enters into the conditional expression, it precedes the conditional expression owing to this same mechanism of implementation.

Limitation 4 is removed on account of the fact that if a multi-instruction contains several entries of one and the same variable, only the first entry is considered during the selection of the complexes.

2 Implementation

The algorithm described is implemented in the ALPHA-translator by Block 14. It selects the effective complexes and forms an ordered list of their multi-instructions for the whole program being translated. Block 15 places these multi-instructions into the program in the requisite positions as its secondary operation.

2.1 Organization of the Operation

The block carries out a single-stage scan of the program and a repeat scan of each economy section. During the first scan, selection of an economy section, its transfer into memory and the construction of the entries and sign vectors for all variables (besides the operating ones), appearing as the operands of any multi-instruction of the economy section under examination are carried out. For the operating variables the number of the multi-instruction in which the given operating variable is employed must be memorized. During the repeat scan of the economy section, the complexes are reduced. Let us consider a given multi-instruction. The set of its operands may differ from the initial one, owing to the reduction carried out. We shall decide, on the basis of the entries vector for the operand, whether the operand is retained in the multi-instruction or not, and also we include in the set of the operands the results of the effective complexes, entering into the given multi-instruction and reduced during the scan of the preceding multi-instructions. Having selected the effective complex in the multi-instruction thus obtained and having reduced it, we write out the multi-instruction, computing the given complex in the list of the inserted multi-instructions. The multi-instruction under examination (or the main conditional expression for it) is, however, preceded by a note about the subsequent insertion of the written out multi-instruction. In doing so, we endeavour to retain the multi-instruction of maximum length: if K_1 and K_2 are effective complexes ($K_1 = \theta A_i A_j$, and $K_2 = \theta A_{k_1} A_s$ where A_{k_1} is the result of the complex K_1) and $L_{k_1} = L_{k_2}$, then one multi-instruction $\theta A_i A_j A_s$ with the result A_{k_2} is carried out. The following methods of transformation are available for the disappearing multi-instruction:

(1) if the operating variable t, employed within the economy section, appears as the result, the multi-instruction is eliminated, but in the multi-instruction utilizing t, this operating variable is substituted by the result of the complex—with the corresponding modification of the entries vector for the result of the complex;

(2) if the multi-instruction produces a given complex, and its result is a scalar, not appearing as the result of any of the multi-instructions, following the given multi-instruction under examination in the economy section, this scalar is taken as the result of the complex and we then proceed as in case 1;

(3) in all remaining cases, the multi-instruction is substituted by the operation of transfer from the result of the complex to the result of the multi-instruction. If the variable appears as the result of a given multi-instruction, its symbol is provided with a special mark. Therefore, in

the subsequent scanning, the entries of that same variable will not coincide by symbol with the entries preceding it as the result. The renaming is carried out in this manner.

2.2 Organization of the Information

The main informational arrays, used in the operation of the algorithm of the economy of expressions are:

the arrangement field;
the common list;
the array of multi-instructions taken out;
the array of data about the multi-instructions;
the field for the economy section.

All the symbols, analysed in the economy section, and also some information about them are placed into the arrangement field. These symbols are the signs of operation and the variables contained in the economy section. We shall distinguish between simple symbols (signs of operation, identifiers of scalars, of arrays, of constants and of operating variables) and compound ones (subscripted variables and operands of non-unary non-commutative operations). Each symbol is in correspondence with a storage cell of the arrangement field, the number of which is determined by hash addressing the symbol (III.4.1). By virtue of the use of hash addressing, the operating time in the process of the identifying of the symbols is in direct proportion to the number of symbols. All the necessary information about the symbol is placed in the arrangement field and in the common list. Furthermore, the information about the symbol occupies one storage cell in the arrangement field and all the remaining (not "incoming") information is carried into the common list. References to the common list—i.e. the numbers of storage cells in the corresponding storage cell of the arrangement field, starting from which some information about the symbol is placed in the common list are shown.

The symbol itself is placed in the arrangement field (if it is not a compound one) or—in the case of a compound symbol—the reference to the common list, where the compound symbol is written out. For the operating variables, the entries vector and the sign vector may contain no more than one value *true*, since the operating variables have only two entries, being the result of some multi-instruction and as the operand or part of the operand. Therefore, it is not necessary for the operating variables to occupy an additional place for the entries vector and the sign vector, it is sufficient to have the number of the multi-instruction, the operand or part of the operand of which (if the operand is a compound symbol) is the given operating variable, and also the information as to with what sign of the operation it enters. All this information enters into the storage cell of the arrangement field. For scalars, constants, operations signs and compound symbols, entries vectors and sign vectors may be constructed. If these vectors emerge, references are placed in the common list in the storage cell of the arrangement field, and the vectors themselves are placed in the common list.

If during the scan we detect the assignment of some variable, its symbol, located in the storage cell of the arrangement field, is provided with a mark, with the result that when detecting a subsequent entry of this variable we assign to it a storage cell of the arrangement field, different from the old one, because we do not find a variable coinciding with it in the arrangement field. In order to take into account the effect of the assignments to the compound symbols in their identification, we substitute the compound symbol while writing it out in the common list in such a representation, in which all the entries of identifiers of scalars and of subscripted variables into the compound symbol are substituted by the numbers of the storage cells of the arrangement field of these identifiers.

The groups of the multi-instructions for the effective complexes, produced by the given multi-instruction of the program or by the multi-instructions of the given conditional expression enter successively into the array of multi-instructions taken out. Each group is separated from the next by a special delimiter, a mark. This delimiter is placed in the program before the corresponding multi-instruction or before the conditional expression. On insertion of the multi-instructions taken out, the array of the program and the array of the multi-instructions taken out are scanned in turn. The scan starts with the array of the program, and the fact that a special delimiter is met in one of these arrays indicates that it is necessary to switch the scan to another array.

Into the array of information about the multi-instructions are placed the number of the operand of the multi-instruction (taking into account the reduction of the complex), the identifier of the result of the multi-instruction, the identifiers of the results of effective complexes contained in the multi-instruction, and an indication as to whether the given multi-instruction has disappeared.

The program being translated is placed, portionwise, into the field for the economy section.

2.3 Some Remarks and Hidden Snags

2.3.1 Speed of operation of the algorithm. In developing and implementing the algorithm, it is necessary to eliminate a quadratic scan. As previously mentioned, the program must be scanned twice during the operation of the algorithm. However, by employing hash addressing, the identification of identical symbols requires time, depending directly on the number of symbols. A quadratic scan appears only during a search of effective complexes in the multi-instruction. Moreover the time of the search depends on the square of the number of operands of the multi-instruction. Since the number of operands in the multi-instruction may in principle not be very large (in the ALPHA-translator it cannot be more than eight; the multi-instruction with a large number of operands is split up such that the number of operands of each part does not exceed that indicated), even a quadratic survey will not require much time under such conditions.

2.3.2 Quantitative limitations for the economy section. In virtue of the fact that the algorithm operates for a period of time, directly dependent on the length of the economy section, time limitations for the economy section do not arise. However on the strength of the fact that the operation of the algorithm is linked with the storage of a significant volume of information, there emerge informational limitations on the length of the economy section. To lay down the length of entries vector and of sign vector and the length of the array of informations about the multi-instructions, a rigid limitation is introduced—the length of the economy section must not exceed 144 multi-instructions. Moreover, the necessity of allocating the arrangement field, the common list and the field for the economy section altogether in memory is again taken into account. In view of the fact that the selection of the economy section occurs during the first scan, when the exact number of the effective complexes is still unknown, it is necessary to allow for the emergence of the maximum possible number of effective complexes within the given structure of the multi-instructions. This means maximum reserved space in the arrangement field and in the common list which will practically always be larger than is necessary.

As soon as the number of multi-instructions of the economy section reaches 144 or the volume of any informational array (taking into account the maximum reserved space) reaches the permissible maximum, the economy section confines itself to the previously selected multi-instructions. Analysis of some programs, constructed by the ALPHA-translator, has shown that, in practice, the economy section is limited to 70–120 multi-instructions as a result of limitations on the volume of the informational arrays.

2.3.3 Several entries of a variable as operand of a multi-instruction. As stated, the presence of several entries of one and the same variable as the operand of a multi-instruction with commutative operation engenders difficulties in the construction of the entries vector and of the sign vector, since the information about the fact that the variable enters more than once into the multi-instruction is in no way taken into account and cannot influence the selection of the effective complexes. It would be possible to carry out some renaming of the variables to avoid this. However, this would make the algorithm too complicated. Therefore, as has already been said, during the selection of the effective complexes only the first entry of a given variable is considered as the operand of the multi-instruction. The presence of entries of a variable with different operational signs ($a - a$ or a/a) causes especially great difficulties. This special representation of zero or of unity, although meaningless, is nevertheless quite permissible in syntax. Here, it would be possible to apply the mechanism of simplification of identical variables or expressions, where in the presence of identical expressions (but not of variables) it is necessary to conduct a study of each simplification of the complex. There is no such mechanism in the ALPHA-translator. Therefore, in the case of identical variables with different operational signs, only the first entry is taken into account, but in the case of the simplifiable expressions, the resulting program may correspond to the initial algorithm.

2.3.4 Changing the order of actions. By virtue of the representation of numbers in the machine by means of a fixed and limited number of bits, a change in

6*

the order of actions can lead to a loss of accuracy or to the production of numbers not represented in the given machine. For example, if the number 10^{19} is the maximum number in the machine, the expression $a \times b \times c$, where $a \sim 10^{18}$, $b \sim 10^{-18}$, $c \sim 10^{8}$, can be calculated only by proceeding from left to right. Meanwhile, in the selection of effective complexes, we consider that any rearrangements in the expressions, in keeping with the commutatve nature of the operation, are possible. In the overwhelming majority of cases the order of calculating the expression is actually not of importance. In those cases where it is necessary to take this into account, it can be achieved by means of an appropriate arrangement of brackets. Thus, in the above case it is necessary to write $(a \times b) \times c$. Then the expression will produce not one, but two multi-instructions, and no rearrangements are made between the multi-instructions.

3   Conclusion

Economy of expressions is an integral part of the algorithms of the sequence of compiler programs.[2-5] The economy of expressions in those compiler programs occurred simultaneously with the generation of machine instructions. Each newly generated machine instruction was compared with the previously generated instructions[3, 4] or with the expressions not yet programmed.[2, 5] Here, the commutative nature of addition and multiplicaton of two operands was taken into account. The arithmetic was the economy section. The arithmetic statement in refs. 2–4 cannot include checking of conditions. Therefore, in principle, the economy section, separable in the ALPHA-translator cannot be smaller than the arithmetic statement in this sense. The arithmetic statement[5] may include (speaking in terms of ALGOL) both conditional expressions and conditional statements. In virtue of this, the economy section[5] may be both larger, and smaller, than the economy section in the ALPHA-translator.

We shall consider an example: Let a section of the program have the form

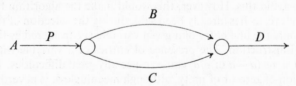

where P is the check of some condition and A, B, C and D are statements or expressions.

In the paper by Yershova et al.,[5] an economy is always effected in sections $A \cup B$, $A \cup C$. The expressions between the parallel sides of branches B and C do not economize. In the ALPHA-translator, the economy will be effected on the section $A \cup B \cup C \cup D$, if P belongs to a conditional expression, but if P belongs to a conditional statement, the scheme will split into four separate economy sections—A, B, C and D.

The difficulties which appeared in these previously described algorithms of the economy, were as follows:

A significant increase in the time of operation of the algorithm with large economy sections on account of the quadratic scan of the information. The complication of the algorithm when wishing to take into consideration the commutative nature of the operation for a large number of operands.

In the paper by Yershov[1] an algorithm of the economy of expressions was put forward, which allows the economy of expressions to be carried out in a time, linearly increasing with an increase in the number of the instructions in the economy section. This removed the first difficulty.

From what has been mentioned above, the algorithm of the economy of expressions in the ALPHA-translator is characterized, in the main, by the following:

(1) the time of operation of the algorithm depends directly on the length of the economy section on account of the utilization of the idea previously proposed[1] during the identification of the variables;

(2) the commutative nature of the operation is taken into account for all operands of identical level within the limits of an arithmetic expression;

(3) the economy of expressions precedes the construction of machine instructions;

(4) the economy of expressions is effected for parallel sides of a branch, if this branch is produced by a conditional expression;

(5) the application of the algorithm described essentially takes into account the multi-instruction structure of the internal language.

The algorithm described was discussed in the seminars of the division of theory of algorithms and programming of the Computing Centre, Siberian Branch of the Academy of Sciences of U.S.S.R., where useful comments were made. The author wishes to express his gratitude for this to the Collective of the Department. A. P. Yershov and G. I. Kozhukhin studied the implementation of this algorithm and gave good advice, for which the author wishes to record his thanks.

REFERENCES

1. YERSHOV, A. P. (1958). Programming of arithmetic statements. *Dokl. AN SSSR* **118**, No. 3.
2. KAMYNIN, S. S., LYUBIMSKII, E. Z. and SHURA-BURA, M. R. (1958). Automation of programming by means of a programming program, "Problems of Cybernetics", Issue 1. Fizmatgiz (Physico-Mathematical State Publishing House), Moscow.
3. YERSHOV, A. P. (1958). "A programming program for a high-speed electronic computing machine". Publishing House of the Academy of Sciences of U.S.S.R., Moscow.
4. KITOV, A. I. and KRINITSKII, N. A. (1959). "Electronic digital machines and programming". Fizmatgiz (Physico-Mathematical State Publishing House), Moscow.
5. YERSHOVA, N. M., MOSTINSKAYA, S. V. and RUDNEVA, T. L. (1961). Arithmetic block. *In* "A System of automation of programming" (eds. N. P. Trifonov and M. R. Shura-Bura) Fizmatgiz (Physico-Mathematical State Publishing House), Moscow.

IX ECONOMY AND ALLOCATION OF MEMORY IN THE ALPHA-TRANSLATOR

A. P. Yershov, L. L. Zmiyevskaya, R. D. Mishkovitch and
L. K. Trokhan

1 Basic Assumptions

1.1 Stating the Problem

Broadly speaking, the expression "economy of memory" signifies that all the operations of the programmer (or the translator) are jointly aimed at obtaining a object program which, in operation, uses the least possible computer memory. In order to separate economy of memory procedure from other programming procedures we shall assume that at a particular stage in the programming we have obtained a program nearly in its final form (say, in symbolic addresses) but compiled without considering the number of memory locations to be used. The task of the economy of memory consists of implementing transformations which make it possible to obtain from this program the solution for the same computer problem, but one requiring the minimum number of memory locations possible.

We shall immediately narrow down the approach to the solution of this task.

In the first place there are several levels of memory in the computer (core memory, drums and magnetic tapes). Sometimes, economy of memory of one particular level is achieved at the expense of a "less valuable" memory of a different level (segmentation). This kind of transformation for programs does not occur in the ALPHA-translator, and economy of memory is only effected within the confines of one memory level.

Secondly, we limit the various program transformations aimed at economy of memory to the different variants of memory allocation. The program can be considered as a combination of three kinds of items: instructions, constants and variables. Memory allocation involves comparing each item in the program with one or (for variable-arrays) a group of memory locations in which the instruction, constant or variable in question will be stored when the program is running. Memory allocation in which a different memory location (or group of locations) corresponds to different items, is a trivial memory allocation. Economy of memory will only be attained when an attempt is made to correspond one memory location to several items in the program (or one or various kinds).

In some cases it is more convenient to treat economy of memory as a two-stage process. Let us suppose that it is possible to correspond location z with several items in the program $x_1, \ldots, x_k$. This will be carried out in two stages. First, we shall—as it were—identify the items in the program $x_1, \ldots, x_k$ by replacing all their entries with a certain symbol X (this may be one from among $x_1, \ldots, x_k$). By means of trivial allocation of memory, the memory location *z* will then correspond with the symbol *X*. It is precisely this method which is used in the ALPHA-translator in the majority of cases since it makes it possible to separate the totality of the individual methods of combining the various items in the program from the homogeneous process of the trivial distribution of memory.

1.2   The Form of the Program before Economy of Memory

Economy and allocation of memory make up the final stage in the operation of the ALPHA-translator. We shall briefly describe the form of the program before carrying out the economy and allocation of memory stage. Using generally accepted terminology it may be said that the program to be translated is in the form of a computer program written in symbolic code or, as it will be referred to—a symbolic program. The symbolic program is a series of instructions. Labels may precede the instructions. The instruction consists of an operation code and the first, second and third address. Certain sections of the program may be enclosed in special brackets. At the end of the program stands the *terminal symbol*. Apart from the actual machine instructions, the program may include groups of *pseudo instructions*, which are calls to the interpreting system for the recall of standard subroutines. At the end of each group of pseudo instructions there is also a special terminal symbol.

Each of the mentioned elements of the program (labels, operation codes, addresses and so on) is in the form of a fifteen-bit binary code; the fifteen bits of any code are divided into a *tag* and an *identifying* part. On the basis of their tags, codes are first of all divided into *absolute* and *symbolic* codes. Operation codes and certain addresses in specific instructions (for example the shift value) are absolute codes. Symbolic codes occupy the position of addresses and (only occasionally in pseudo instructions) of operational codes. The identifying part of an absolute code does not require processing and is inserted directly into the object program. The identifying part of a symbolic code contains the ordinal number of a given item in the program.

Symbolic codes are divided into labels, variables and delimiters. The function of the *label* is to refer to instructions in the program. Labels are divided into transfer labels and instruction labels. *Transfer labels* are referred to in instructions for transfer of control whilst the *instruction labels* are used in all other cases (for example, in instructions for readdress, formation and so on). Variables are divided into single and group variables. A variable which, during the allocation of memory, has to correspond to a single memory location is referred to as a *single variable*. Single variables are divided into constants, operative variables and scalars. A scalar variable whose initial constant value is contained in a special *table of constants* is referred to as a *constant*. The number of the constant is the same as the ordinal number of its value in the table of constants.

Working variables appear when programming expressions and are designed to store intermediate results. Working variables are distinguished by the fact that each of them enters the program only twice—once as a result and once as an argument. The rest of the single variables referred to in the program fall into the category of *scalars*.

Group variables are characterized by the fact that they are represented by two fifteen-bit codes which stand side by side. According to the tags of the first code, the group variables are divided into arrays and "blanks". The first *array* code contains the ordinal number of the array and the second indicates an ordinal number of a given array component, in relation to its first component. The length of each array (the number of scalar components) is shown in a special table of arrays. It enters the table of arrays according to its number. All arrays are divided into normal ones, constant ones and drum ones. An array which is instructed to be stored on a drum is called a *drum* array. The fact that an array is of the "drum" type is indicated by a special sign in the table of constants. The position of the drum array on the drum is not fixed beforehand. A *constant* array is one whose components are all given certain, initial values which are stored one after the other in the table of constants. For constant arrays the ordinal number of the constant which is the initial value of the first component of the array in question is indicated in the table of arrays. All other arrays are all *normal* ones.

The blanks symbolize the addresses which are formed in a special way when running the object program. In the first code the ordinal number of the blank is indicated whilst in the second—the address value which must occupy a blank position before executing the object program. The blanks are divided into those for dynamic arrays and those for formal parameters. The blanks of *dynamic arrays* represent the components of arrays which in the ALPHA-program had variable bound pairs. Memory for these dynamic arrays is allocated by a special administrative system in the course of running the object program. Blanks of *formal parameters* symbolize addresses into which must be put the addresses of the items in the object program which correspond to the actual parameters called by name in the position of the formal parameter during executing procedures. For each blank of a formal parameter, there is—in a special *table of blanks* (entry according to the number of the blank)—a list of *fillers*), i.e. of variables or labels whose addresses must be compiled by adding to the initial address which stands in the position of the blank in question.

Delimiters are divided into the terminal symbol for the program—already mentioned—the terminal symbol for the pseudocode, the statement brackets and the symbol for the return statement. Brackets which include certain portions of the program are divided into *operational* brackets and *switch* brackets. If a certain group of instructions in the object program is enclosed in operational brackets, then this means that the given group is the program of a certain *external block* in the ALPHA-program, i.e. of a block which is destined to be stored permanently in one of the computer's external memories (drum, magnetic tape or punched card) during running the object program and which is read into the core memory only when control is transferred to this external block. The form of memory is shown in 15-bit code which comes directly after the opening operational bracket, the number of the tape or the number of the record on the tape where the given block must be stored also being indicated for external tape blocks, in the same code.

The list of unconditional branch instructions is enclosed in *switch brackets*. The ordinal number of an instruction in a list of this kind equals the ordinal number of the corresponding element in the initial switch list of the ALPHA-program. The opening switch bracket is followed immediately by the scalar or absolute code, according to the value of which the element of the switch list is chosen.

If a certain program location is designed to hold the return instruction, which comes at the end of a certain procedure body, its contents will consist of a fifteen-bit *return statement* code. The ordinal number of the return statement, which serves as an entry into the special *table of returns* is placed in the identifying part of the code. In this table there is a list of labels for each return, on which the transfer of control can take place according to the exit from the procedure via the return statement in question.

2   Fundamental Algorithms of the Economy of Memory

As has already been said, the main items in the program which need to be stored in memory are the instructions and variables, from which it is convenient to separate the constants into a special class. The following six possibilities for combining items in the program can be examined from a purely logical point of view:

constants with constants; instructions with instructions;
constants with variables; instructions with constants;
variables with variables; instructions with variables.

Apart from the last two cases, all other possibilities are implemented in the ALPHA-translator. The algorithms used for this are examined in this chapter whilst in the next one details concerning the actual implementation of the described algorithms in the ALPHA-translator are introduced.

2.1   Combining Constants with Constants

Since all constants are introduced into memory at the same time as the program is introduced, it is obvious that different memory locations must correspond to different constants. Thus, the problem of combining the constants boils down to the problem of detecting and identifying identical constants or to what is termed, in programming, the economy of constants.

Usually economy of constants in the translators is obtained when the table of constants is compiled: when it is necessary to fill a table the next constant is compared with all the constants in the table and is either placed at the end of the table or not included at all if the same constant has already appeared in it. Using this method, the total operating time of the translator, in connection with the economy of the constants, is proportional to the square of the number of constants. In the ALPHA-translator, the constants are placed in the table of constants without economy. Economy itself is achieved after the formation of the table by examining the latter in two stages and applying hash addressing (III.4.1).

Two arrays are used for the economy of the constants: the table of constants and the arrangement field. A scale with the number of n digits equal to the length of the initial table of constants is also used. At first, all the digits in the scale equal zero. Assume that on first examination, the constant C_i $(i = 1, ..., n)$ is chosen from the ith row of the table. The machine word representing the constant C_i is the argument for hash addressing. We shall refer to C_i as a representative if this constant was first encountered when scanning the table of constants. Obviously, if C_i is a representative, hash addressing will compare this constant with the free location of the arrangement field into which the number i of the constant C_i is placed. If C_i is not a representative, hash addressing compares this constant with the location of the arrangement field in which the number j of the constant-representative C_j equal to C_i $(j < i)$ is stored. This number j is inserted into the ith line of the table of constants, whilst a unit is inserted into the ith digit of the scale. Thus, as a result of the first scan all the constant-representatives will be marked by zeros while all the constants which enter the table repeatedly will be replaced by references to the number of the appropriate constant representative. During the second scan, a new table of constants is compiled for which the arrangement field which is no longer required, can be used. Assume that the ith row $(i = 1, ..., n)$ is chosen from the table of constants. If the ith digit of the scale equals zero, the constant-representative C_i will be in the ith row. This constant is directed into the kth row of the new table of constants whilst the number k is put into the ith row of the old table. If the ith digit is equal to unity then according to the number j standing in the ith row, the number m is chosen from the jth row of the old table into which it was inserted when transferring the constant-representative C_i from the jth row of the old table into the mth row of the new table of constants and is directed into the ith row of the old table. Thus, as a result of the second scan, the old table is turned into a table for correlating old and new constant names. This table is later used for translating the names of constants in the symbolic program.

2.2 Combining Constants and Variables

The rules for combining constants and variables are the same as for variables and variables (see below). For this, the constant is treated as an ordinary variable, for which there is a hypothetical assignment statement which gives to the variable a value equal to the constant in question.

2.3 Combining Variables and Variables

Variables are combined with variables in the ALPHA-translator on the basis of the global economy of memory theory.[1, 2] By global, we mean an approach to economy of memory in which the question of the compatibility of any pair of variables taking part in the operating of the program is examined. According to this theory the program is considered as an *statement scheme* consisting of n statements $S_1, ..., S_n$, over m variables $x_1, ..., x_m$. Giving the statement scheme means indicating for each of the statements S_i $(i = 1, ..., n)$ which statements from the number $S_i, ..., S_n$ can be carried out after S_i, i.e. which can be *successors* of the statement S_i, and also indicating which of the variables $x_1, ..., x_m$ are *results* and which are *arguments* of the statement S_i. The *weight* of r_j is compared with each variable x_j $(j = 1, ..., m)$, which signifies that the variable x_j occupies the r_j consecutive locations $(r_j \geqslant 1)$ in memory.

If a certain variable x having a weight r, greater than unity, is the result of the statement S, then, for the given entry of x into the statement scheme there is some indication whether all the r constituent variables in the statement S are recalculated (*fully* calculating x), or only some of them.

According to the theory of the global economy of memory, any permissible variant for combining variables can be used to solve the well known combinatorial problem colouring the vertices of a particular *incompatibility graph*† which is compiled according to the statement scheme. The incompatibility graph has R vertices where

$$R = \sum_{j=1}^{m} r_j.$$

A full sub-graph r_j of the incompatibility graph is compared with each variable x_j in the statement scheme $-r_j$ consisting of pairs of vertices which all connect with one another. Let the sub-graphs $G(x)$ and $G(y)$ be compared with the two variables x and y. If x and y cannot be joined together, all the vertices from $G(x)$ and $G(y)$ are connected in pairs by lines. But if y and x can be joined, not a single line is drawn between the vertices in the sub-graphs $G_{(x)}$ and $G_{(y)}$. Correlation between colouring the incompatibility graph and the variant for combining variables is obtained simply: all components of variables whose vertices are coloured the same colour are combined with one another. Thus, global economy of memory requires three problems to be solved:

(a) that a statement scheme is compiled according to the program;
(b) that an incompatibility graph is compiled according to the statement scheme;
(c) that the incompatibility graph is coloured.

These three problems are examined below.

2.3.1 Compiling a statement scheme

2.3.1.1 Selecting the statement. The following is a provisional‡ solution of this problem: a separate program instruction is a separate statement in the statement scheme, and all variables used in the program are taken as variables liable for global economy. It should be borne in mind, however, that when compiling the incompatibility graph, it is necessary to operate with some Boolean matrices of the order $n \times m$. If it is intended that these matrices be stored simultaneously in memory to increase the operational speed of the translator, special measures need to be taken both to reduce the number of statements and the number of variables. In this connection, it was decided to compile an extended statement scheme in which not just one instruction acts as a separate statement but a particular section in the program, referred to as a *quasilinear section*.

Roughly speaking, a quasilinear part is the section of instructions in the operating program corresponding to the series of statements in the ALPHA-program which meets the following requirements:

† In Yershov's paper[2] the graph of linkages.
‡ The Russian says literally "trivial".

1. One of the following delimiters precedes the first statement:

α) ";", standing after the declaration, the procedure statement, the stop statement, the *go to* statement, the conditional statement or the delimiter **end**

β) **begin**

γ) **then**

δ) **else**

ε) **do**

i) :

2. The last statement of the series is either the *go to* statement, or the procedure statement, or the stop statement, or if none of these, the last statement is followed by **else** or **begin** or **end** or the FOR statement, or the conditional statement, or any labelled statement.

3. The internal statements in the series (i.e. excluding the first and the last ones) are essentially unlabelled assignment statements.

If we assume that implementation of the procedure statement is restricted to the substitution of actual parameters and to the transfer of control to the procedure body, it may be considered that implementation of the quasilinear part reduces to carrying out consecutively (left to right without any skips or repetitions) all statements involved in its formation. It is precisely this "linearity" which accounts for the convenience of considering the quasilinear part as the only statement in the statement scheme. However, if implementation of the quasilinear part is to be considered in terms of machine instructions, it acquires a certain internal structure: it will contain statements for the conditional transfer of control, caused by the presence in Input language of conditional expressions and of loops (so called internal loops) which appear when programming operations on multidimensional arrays and also return transfers of control which occur when programming functions.

Laying aside for the present the question of return transfers of control, we shall analyse the problems which occur in connection with the presence of loops and branches. It should be possible to avoid these problems by taking the sections of the program which have a purely linear structure as separate statements. However, during the development of the translator it was decided to explore the possibility of enlarging the statements as much as possible, at the same time preserving high quality economy of memory. To distinguish internal loops and branches, produced by the translator when programming conditional expressions, from loop statements and conditional statements contained in an explicit form in the ALPHA-program two types of transfer labels are put in: *external ones* and *internal ones*. Internal labels are fed in by the translator only when programming conditional expressions and when expanding internal loops needed to implement componentwise operations on arrays. Each internal label enters the program twice: once simply as a label and once as a designational expression in a conditional or unconditional branch statement. When expanding an internal loop, one internal label occurs whereas when programming conditional expressions there are two. The reciprocal arrangement of the labels when they enter the program is shown for both cases in Fig. 1. Here the squares denote the program instructions and conditional transfers of control stand in the ovals. Henceforth, a set of instructions situated between the entries of an internal label M will be referred to as a range of label M.

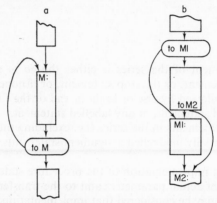

Fig. 1. Layout of internal labels. a = loop, b = conditional expression

If we assume that the quasilinear sections are separated during a systematic scanning of the program, beginning with the first instruction, precise rules for separating statements in the statement scheme may be described simply by listing the instances of a break in the quasilinear section. This break occurs when detecting:

(1) a symbol for the end of the program;
(2) the return transfer of control (excluding calls to standard sub-routines via the interpreting system);
(3) a return statement;
(4) the opening bracket of an external block;
(5) the closing bracket of an external block;
(6) the opening bracket of a switch;
(7) the conditional transfer of control to an external label;
(8) the unconditional transfer of control to an external label;
(9) an external label;
(10) a stop statement.

We may recall here an important definition from the theory of global economy of memory. A portion of an admissible sequence of executing statements (instructions) of the ALPHA-program (object program) in which the first statement (instruction) in the sequence produces the value of x as a whole, the last statement (instruction) takes the value of x as an argument, whilst none of the internal statements (instructions) in the sequence produces the value of x as a whole, is referred to as the *route* of the variable x.

The rules of Input language and the rules for separating the quasilinear sections make it possible to formulate the following two properties of the quasilinear sections.

1st property. The range of any internal label belongs entirely to a particular quasilinear section.

2nd property. The route of any working variable belongs entirely to a particular quasilinear section.

We shall now investigate the influence of the return transfers of control, brought about by the call to the sub-routines for calculating declared functions or—in short—the calls to the functions. Of course, the call to a declared function (i.e. not to the standard sub-routine) must intercept the quasilinear section. However, as distinct from calls to the procedures, the call to the function may be located both in the range of a particular internal label and also be an internal statement for the route of a particular working variable, so that the first and second properties of the quasilinear sections are not satisfied. In order to retain these properties the quasilinear sections are split into two stages.

First, a "provisional" separation of the sections is carried out, during which only the breaks caused by the return transfers of control, interest us. In addition, two stack arrays may be recalled: the first one is for internal labels and the second for working variables. The processing of these stacks takes place when the next entry of the internal label M or the working variable t appears in the program.

The processing of the first stack is determined by the reciprocal lay-out of the internal labels (see Fig. 1) and is set out in a flow chart which is shown in Fig. 2 (S_{1-}, S_{-2} and S_{-3} are the contents of the last three stack cells, counting from the end). When processing the stack of working variables, its content is examined. If the stack contains an entry of the working variable t, this is deleted from it, otherwise t is entered at the end of the stack.

The above described rules make it possible to confirm that when a given return transfer of control is discovered during the provisional scan of the contents of the stack arrays (which may be blank) the given transfer is located in the range of certain labels or within the limits of the route of certain working variables.

If these ranges or routes appear, they are eliminated by changing the resulting internal labels and working variables into external labels and scalars respectively. For this purpose, all the labels in the first stack are marked with an external label tag, whilst the next unoccupied scalar numbers are compared with all the working variables in the second stack. Analogous corrections are also put into the program. This can be done very simply if, when entering the labels and working variables into the stacks, the addresses of the entries of these symbols into the program are also written there. The chart in Fig. 2 and the processing of the working variables are supplemented by the following operation. If on comparing the label M or the variable t with the contents of the stacks, it is found that the latter already contain identical entries for these symbols, these are deleted from the stacks, and in addition a check is made to ascertain whether the label M needs to be changed into an external label or t to a scalar. If these changes are needed they are carried out.

All these operations which are carried out during the provisional scan,

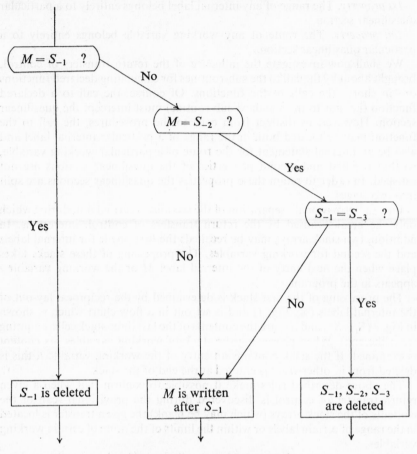

Fig. 2. Processing the first stack

ensure satisfaction of the first and second properties during the actual separation of the quasilinear sections.

To complete the selection of the statements, we shall give some more rules for determining the successors of the selected statement arising from conditions 1–9 for the break of the quasilinear sections.

When the final symbol in the program or the stop statement appears, the successor to the statement is not determined. In the case of the return or unconditional transfer of control, the successor is a single statement labelled with a label indicated in the transfer of control instruction. If the statement terminates in an opening or closing bracket of an external block or an external label, the successor is a statement starting after the appearance of the symbol. When a conditional transfer of control or the opening bracket of a switch appear, all statements to which control can be transferred and also any statement appearing after the conditional transfer of control or after the closing bracket of a switch list are considered to be successors. In the case of a return statement, all statements to which control can be transferred upon removal from the statement according to the given return statement, are looked upon as successors; the necessary information for determining successors is derived from the table of returns.

2.3.1.2   Defining arguments and results. After the program has been divided into statements, the arguments and results must be given for each statement. It will be seen immediately that not all the variables mentioned in the program enter the statement scheme. In the first instance, the blanks of dynamic arrays will not be taken into account since the length of these arrays is not known beforehand and the theory of global economy of memory cannot be applied to them. Economy of memory, allocated for dynamic arrays, is produced by the administrative system during the execution of the working program (X). Secondly, it was decided not to include working variables in the statement scheme, because the routes of the working variables never cut across the statement limits, besides which, experience has shown that the number of cells required to store the working variables is small: as a rule not more than 10. Both these circumstances mean that one can confine oneself to combining the working variables with one another within the limits of one statement using well known and effective algorithms for the economy of working locations in the linear sections. The quasilinearity of the statements poses no problems thanks to the specific entry of the working variables into the program (the first entry as a result and the second as an argument). After economy of the working variables in each statement, one memory array is set aside for all of them; its length is equal to the maximum number of locations required to store the working variables within the limits of one statement. Thus, only constants, scalars and normal, drum and constant arrays and blanks of formal parameters are considered as variables of the statement scheme.

Before describing the selection of the results and the arguments, we should point out one important modification of the notion of an abstract statement scheme. In theory, a statement is an indivisible and basic unit of action in which the arguments are used as it were simultaneously at the moment of entry into the statement, and the results appear also simultaneously on leaving the statement. The actual user of the arguments and the producer of the results (in our case) is not the statement as a whole but individual instructions located "within" the quasilinear section which makes up the statement. In connection with this, the routes of the variables entering the statement are not terminated at the start of it but by some means pass "along" the statement until they reach the instructions which actually use or issue these variables. Consequently, the scheme can contain variables which cannot be considered as either an argument or a result of any statement whatsoever. These are the variables whose routes all belong completely to one specific quasilinear section. We shall refer to these variables as *internal* ones for the statement "inside" which their routes lie.

We are now in a position to define the arguments and results of a given statement. The *result* of the statement S may be any variable y which is not an internal one and to which a value by some instruction from S is assigned.

An *argument* of the statement S may be any non-internal variable x, whose value is used by a certain instruction from S, where if x is the result of S, the statement S can be executed in such a way that some utilization of the value x precedes any assignment to the value x.

The above mentioned definitions which use terms such as "route" and "execution of the statement" and others are non-effective and must therefore be replaced by the equivalent formal conditions. Disregarding the existence of branches in the quasilinear sections, the following conditions for the classification of the variables may be put forward.

The scalar variable x is an internal variable of the statement S if the number of times x enters the statement scheme is equal to the number of times x enters the statement S where x appears as a result for the first time (from the beginning of S) in S.†

A variable x is a result of the statement S if the number of times x enters the statement scheme differs from the number of times x enters the statement S, and x appears in S as the result of any instruction.

A variable x is an argument of the statement S if x appears for the first time in S not as a result.

The presence of branches creates a unique situation in which these criteria do not correspond to the definitions of arguments, results and internal variables as stated. Indeed, when programming a statement, for example

$$y := \textbf{if } a \leqslant b \textbf{ then } y + h \textbf{ otherwise } c$$

the following sequence of instructions is obtained.

	>	b	a	M 1
	⇒	c		y
	TO			M 2
M1:	+	y	h	y
M2:	...	...	...	...

Obviously, in accordance with the criteria, the statement y will be considered only as a result (or an internal variable) here, whereas y should really be considered both as a result and as an argument of the statement. As can be seen, the situation is complicated by the fact that an assignment to the result of the statement occurred at the first branch which "hid" the use of y as an argument in the instruction $M1$. In order to allow for this, it must be remembered when encountering the first assignment to a certain variable at

† This condition is not sufficient for arrays, for if the first assignment to the array is not fully carried out, its route may go beyond the limits of the statement. Therefore, arrays are treated only as arguments or (and) results of an statement, definable only according to use or assignment being contained in the statement instructions.

the first branch of branching that this assignment is produced precisely at the first branch.

Bearing in mind these observations the classification of variables in the quasilinear section can be carried out by the following process. We compare each variable x with two counters n_1 and n_2 and four tags r_0, r_1, r_2 and r_3; n_1 is equal to the number of times x enters the whole scheme and is calculated beforehand. The counter n_2 and the symbols r_0, r_1, r_2 and r_3 are utilized when scanning the statement instructions in the process of collecting information about the variable x. At the start $n_2 = r_0 = r_1 = r_2 = r_3 = 0$. The statement is scanned from the beginning. Every time x appears in the statement, unity is added to n_2. To determine whether we are operating within the first branch of the branching, a special sign C is introduced. At the start $C = 0$. When the conditional transfer of control to an internal label is encountered, this label is sent to C only if prior to this C was equal to zero. When encountering the same label in the program for a second time we assume that the first branch of the branching has been completed and C becomes equal to zero.†

If x appears in the statement as an argument (i.e. in the first or second addresses of the instruction or in the positions of an argument in a pseudo-instruction for call to a standard sub-routine), 1 is put for r_1, and if $C \neq 0$ and $r_0 \neq 0$, 1 is put for r_3.

If x appears as a result (i.e. in the 3rd address of an instruction or in the positions of a result in a pseudo-instruction for call to a standard sub-routine), 1 is always put for r_2. In addition, if $C \neq 0$ and $r_1 = 0$, then 1 is put for r_0; and if $C = 0$ and $r_1 = 0$, 1 is put for r_3.

Thus, as a result of the scanning, n_2 is found to be equal to the number of times x enters the statement, unity at r_1 denotes the appearance of x as an argument, and unity at r_2 denotes the appearance of x as a result whilst unity at r_3 denotes that x first appeared as a result, where, in the case of assignments in a branch, the "buffer" tag r_0 causes r_3 to be filled only on analysis of the assignment at the second branch. Figure 3 determines to which class the scalar variable x belongs. If x is an array, it is declared by an argument when $r_1 = 1$ and by a result when $r_2 = 1$. Further to what has been said, when scanning the statement, one more symbol—r_4—is filled; 1 is put for this if a certain entry of a variable-array as a result was labelled with the symbol "producing fully". This tag denotes that the given instruction, coming into the internal loop, as a result of implementing the loop, recalculates all the components of the given array.

In addition to this, the special features involved in processing blanks of formal parameters should be pointed out. Each blank acts as a representative of all those actual variables which were enumerated in the table of blanks as fillers for the given blank. Thus, if a certain blank entry is analysed when scanning the statement, the addition to the counter n_2 and if necessary the symbols r_0, ..., r_4 are noted simultaneously for all the fillers of a given blank.

† It should be noted that the sign C will, generally speaking, separate not only the first branch of the branching but also the recurrent part of certain internal loops. However, since in such loops assignments can only be produced by arrays (disregarding working variables) which are classified in a special way, this does not lead to errors.

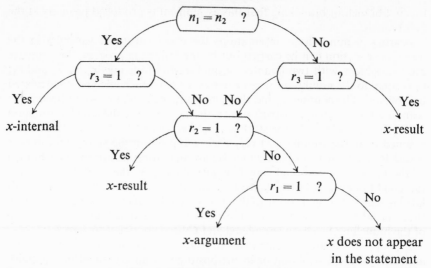

Fig. 3. Classification of variables

2.3.1.3   Representation of the statement scheme. Since the abstract statement scheme is an oriented graph with labelled vertices, the question rests on the presentation of the graphs. From among the graph presentations which are the most prevalent, mention should be made of the matrices of adjacency and the explicit lists of pairs of adjacent vertices on the graph. Taking into account the fact that the order of each vertex in real statements is not great as a rule, so that the volume of information about the graph is proportional to the number of vertices rather than to the square of the number of vertices, it was decided to concentrate on the second method of presenting the statement scheme. It is supposed that this presentation of the scheme will occupy less space (than matrix presentation) and will ensure satisfactorily high speed operation of the subsequent algorithms for compiling an incompatability graph. Approaching it in this way, the statement scheme is in the form of a single list, the number of sections of which is equal to the number of statements. The natural numbering of the sections determines the numbering of the statements. In a section which corresponds to a given statement *S*, five lists are generally shown: successors, predecessors,† arguments, results and internal variables of the statement *S*. The lists are separated from one another by delimiters and any one of the lists can be vacant. The presentation of the statement scheme is described in more detail below.

2.3.2   Constructing an incompatability graph

2.3.2.1   Theory. According to the theory, the entry of the variable *x* and the entry of the variable *y* are not compatible, if the operational fields $D(x)$

---

† The statement *B* is a predecessor of the statement *A* if *A* is a successor of *B*. Information about predecessors, which is fundamentally superfluous, is included in the presentation of the statement scheme only to increase the speed of algorithms for compiling the incompatibility graph.

and $D(y)$, to which the variable entries under consideration belong, are linked. The connected components of the *carrier*—the set of routes of the variable x in the statement scheme—are referred to as the *operational* field of the variable x. We notice at once that the algorithms for subdividing the carrier into connected components were not implemented in the ALPHA-translator, because of the cumbersome nature of these algorithms and also because the need for them is weakened to a considerable extent by the principle of localization operating in ALGOL and in Input language. It is natural to suppose that, in many cases, subdividing the carrier of the variable x into connected components will merely confirm the obvious indication that the ALPHA-program contains two parallel blocks in each of which the variable x is described. However, in this case the identifier of x will be translated by various names in accordance with the principles for translating identifiers which were adopted in the ALPHA-translator (IV.1). On the strength of what has been said, the concepts of the carrier and the operational field are identified, the number of operational fields being equal to the number of variables in the statement scheme.

Let us recall that two operational fields $D(x)$ and $D(y)$ are linked if, and only if, the set

$$H(x) \cap (H(y) \cup B(y)) \cup H(y) \cap ((H(x) \cup B(x))$$

where $H(x)$ is the set of statements which forms the start of at least one route of the variable x, and $B(x)$ is the sequence of statements which are internal statements of at least one path of the variable x, is not empty.

The set $H(x)$ is defined as a set of all statements which produce the variable x, i.e. the ones where x is shown as a result. The set $B(x)$ is constructed as an intersection of two sets $E(x)$ and $L(x)$ where $E(x)$ is a set of all statements which can be reached by moving along the arrows, in the statement scheme starting from any statement which produces x whilst $L(x)$ is a sequence of all statements which can be reached by moving in the opposite direction to the arrows, in the scheme, starting from any statement which receives x (in the case of $L(x)$ it is also suggested that movement is terminated when the statement which produces x is reached).

We must add to these principles the condition when the variable x, which is internal for a particular statement S in the scheme, is incompatible with the arguments and results of other statements (internal variables of different statements are always compatible). Obviously, x will be incompatible with the variable y, if and only if $S \in B(y)$. The question of the incompatibility of arguments, results and internal variables in one statement, arising out of the fact that the statement has an internal structure, will be discussed below.

2.3.2.2 Constructing the sets E and L. All the sets in question, and also the incompatibility graph, are represented in Boolean binary matrix form. The sets H, L, E and B are represented as matrices (denoted by the same symbols) of the order $n \times m$, where m is the number of variables and n is the number of statements.

Unity in the ith row and in the jth column denotes that the ith statement belongs to the corresponding set of the jth variable. The incompatibility graph is represented as a matrix N of the order $m \times m$. Thus, as distinct from abstract theory, one vertex of the graph N corresponds to each variable, but on the other hand this vertex is taken with a weight equal to the weight of the variable, that is equal to the number of memory locations required to store it.

It should be noted that the number of variables m in the statement scheme does not include variables which have a zero number of entries into the program. Such variables occur in quite a large number because, in the first place, in the programming process the translator sometimes has a particular variable "in reserve", not actually using it, and in the second place, because some intermediate statements (e.g. formation statement) are introduced by the translator using the names of subsidiary variables, and then disappear from the program with the variables.

To preserve the correspondence between the ordinal number of a variable of this kind and the number of the row in the matrix of incompatibility, when the statement scheme is compiled all the variables are renumbered, on the basis of the calculation of the number of times they enter the program.

The matrix E is compiled according to the following algorithm. At first e_{ij} is taken to be equal to 1, if the ith statement succeeds the statement which produced the jth variable. Next, a loop for scanning all the statements in the scheme is executed. The ith row of the matrix E is scanned for the ith statement $(i = 1, \ldots, n)$. When unity appears in the jth component of the row $(1 \leqslant j \leqslant m)$ units are added to the jth column of the matrix E namely to those components whose numbers are equal to the numbers of the statement-successors in the ith statement. After completing the loop according to i, all the elements in the matrix E are added up and if the sum of the elements is equal to the sum calculated when the loop according to i was previously executed, then the structure of the matrix E is taken as final.

The matrix L is compiled in a similar way. At first, 1_{ij} is taken as to be equal to 1, if the ith statement precedes the statement which receives the jth variable. Next, a loop for scanning all the statements is executed. The ith line of the matrix L is scanned for the ith statement $(i = 1, \ldots, n)$. When unity appears in the jth row $(1 \leqslant j \leqslant m)$, units are added to the jth column of the matrix L and also to those components whose numbers are equal to the numbers of the statement-predecessors in the ith statement which do not produce the jth variable completely. The criteria for completing the formation of the matrix L is the same as for E. The matrix for the graph of incompatibility is compiled exactly according to the criterion for linking the operational fields. At first, only the upper triangle of the matrix is constructed after which it is "transposed" to the lower one. The diagonal elements of the matrix are taken as equal to unity.

    2.3.2.3 Consideration of the structure of the statements. Obviously, a graph of incompatibilities thus compiled takes into account only incompatibilities caused by linking the routes of the variables which pass from one statement to another. We ought to add links between routes of variables which pass within the statements, to the links which have been considered. For any i^{th} statement in the scheme, these links are made up from links of the following routes:

(1) internal variables amongst themselves;
(2) internal variables with transient routes passing through the statement;
(3) internal variables with arguments of the statement;
(4) internal variables with results of the statement;
(5) arguments of the statements amongst themselves;
(6) arguments with results of the statement;
(7) results of the statement amongst themselves.

We shall first examine the second case. Obviously, any internal variable of the ith statement S_i ($1 \leqslant i \leqslant n$) will be incompatible with a particular variable y, only if $S_i \in B(y)$. Thus, if the jth variable ($1 \leqslant j \leqslant m$) is an internal one for the ith statement, the jth row and the jth column of the matrix of graph N will for the latter be equal to the ith row of the matrix B.

To consider the other cases, so-called *lists of links* are compiled for each statement in the scheme, in which the pairs of incompatible variables are explicitly shown. These lists are compiled at the same time as the statement scheme and only after this are the links which they produce added to the matrix in the graph of incompatibilities.

In cases 1, 5 and 7 all the corresponding variables are assumed to be incompatible with one another. In case 7, in fact, all the results of a given statement must be compatible due to the fact that their routes are linked, though in cases 1 and 5, the apparent incompatibility may prove to be false, although in the given case it was decided not to complicate the algorithms. In order to discover the links in cases 3, 4 and 6 a simplified analysis of their routes along the statement is carried out. This analysis takes the form of a reverse scanning of the quasilinear section, i.e. starting with the last instruction and working upward. Simplifying the analysis involves, for certain types of variables, not examining in detail their routes, according to the formal definition, but only certain sequences of instructions in the quasilinear section which can be developed more simply and which are known to include precise routes. Thus, the route of any external variable in the quasilinear section consists of the whole sequence of instructions in the section from its first instruction as far as the instruction in which the given variable enters as an argument for the first time before the end of the section. The route of any internal variable consists of the sequence of instructions starting from the instruction which produces the first (from the beginning of the section) assignment of the value to the given variable (it is also the first time generally that the given variable enters the section) as far as the instruction in which the given variable enters as an argument for the last time before the end of the section.

In the light of these definitions, the lists of links are compiled in the following way. For each variable in the statement scheme the binary tag r is introduced; for all the variables these tags are scanned when analysing the next instruction K (when the quasilinear section is scanned working upwards, as has just been mentioned) which produces the assignment to the variable x. The purpose of the tags is as follows: at the moment of analysing the instruction K the tag r is equal to unity for all variables whose routes cross the instruction K.

Obviously, all these (and only these) variables are linked with the variable x and it is just these variables which are included in the list of links for the given entry of the variable x. The tags r themselves, which are all equal to zero at first, are given values at the same time as the reverse scanning of the section according to the following rule; the value 1 is assigned to the tag r for the variable y once, when the entry of y as an argument appears. In addition, for internal variables all their entries are calculated (to be more precise, unity is subtracted from the number of entries found earlier when previously scanning the quasilinear section); when the last entry of an internal variable appears the tag r is taken as equal to zero. These general rules for calculating the links are enforced in cases 4 and 6, when one of the linked variables is a result-array. Result-arrays are considered linked with all internal variables and all arguments, without being analysed.

We note, finally, that during the reverse scanning of this quasilinear section economy of the working locations in the section may also be created; this economy was produced in the ALPHA-translator by a modification of the standard algorithm for the economy of the working locations [3].

2.3.3   Colouring the graph of incompatabilities

2.3.3.1   *Initial premises.* We note that the combining of variables in the statement scheme is equivalent to the classic problem of colouring the vertices on the graph of incompatibilities, only when all the variables in the scheme are scalars, that is they have a weight equal to zero. If all these variables have equal weight which is more than unity, the task of colouring can also be reduced to the classic one if it is limited to colourings in which any two compatible arrays coincide with each other in all their locations, since in these the number of colours is reduced to a minimum. In general we must limit ourselves to the so-called regular colours [2] that is colours in which any chosen variant for combining arrays does not conflict with the need to place the combined arrays in computer memory in such a way that all the locations relating to one array are put into memory in succession.

The authors consider it to be impractical to find algorithms for colourings which would give the least amount of colouring for an admissible number of elementary operations even in the case of the classic formulation of the problem of colouring.

Therefore it is necessary to work out some kind of an approach to an approximate solution, one perhaps which cannot be strictly proved but within the boundaries of common sense and in accordance with the experiment. The approach adopted in this article is based on the so-called "principle of non-uniformity" which, in the authors' opinion can be applied to a considerable proportion of problems to do with computing. The principle consists basically of the following observation: it can be said of most of the problems of the kind mentioned above that they have many scalars (up to several hundreds) and considerably less (tens) arrays. Arrays are split up into small groups so that the weights of all the arrays in one group have the same, or very nearly the same, value whilst groups differ sharply from one another as regards weight. If we apply this principle, the choice of the following simplified strategy when solving the problem of colouring, seems to be a reasonable one: variables of the same weight must as far as possible be combined but as for variables of differing weights, here the basic economy of memory must be obtained by simply "packing" arrays which weigh less into an array which weighs more. The operations whereby a particular array is combined partly with one array and partly with another may be of a limited nature since they do not contribute any substantial improvement to the allocation of memory.

    2.3.3.2 Combining variables of a given weight. The combination of variables of the same weight, that is, the ordinary colouring of vertices on the graph which is carried out in the ALPHA-translator is based on the following theorem from the theory of graphs. Two vertices of a graph are said to be unicoloured if there exists a minimum colouring of the vertices of the graph by which these vertices can be coloured in one colour. The least number of links which must be passed in order to get from one vertex to another is referred to as the distance between the two vertices on the graph. The theorem attributed to G. I. Kozhukhin[4] applies: for every vertex of the graph which is not adjacent to all the other vertices, there is a similarly coloured vertex the distance between them being equal to two. In order to find the minimal colouring, according to this theorem, it is necessary to have at one's disposal a criterion allowing at least one of the unicoloured vertices amongst those situated at the distance two from the given vertex, to be found. However, we have no such criterion at our disposal and we therefore choose the vertex which is to be coloured the same colour as the given vertex, using other reasons for our choice, which do not necessarily, however, mean choosing a unicoloured vertex.

    Before discussing the rules for choosing a vertex which can claim to be of the same colour, we shall indicate the overall arrangement for colouring the vertices on the graph, based on the search of unicoloured vertices. The vertices are in some way numbered. Vertex A is the one with the lowest ordinal number. If it is adjacent to the rest of the vertices, it is omitted and the vertex which follows next in numerical order is taken. If A is not adjacent to all the peaks, peak B, the next claimant to being unicoloured is chosen from among the vertices which are situated at the distance two from A. After this, vertices A and B are "merged", i.e. only one vertex remains in the graph, taking the higher number B and this new vertex is linked to all the vertices which were adjacent to both A and B. Information about its merger with B is kept for the vertex A which is disappearing from the graph. This merger may be regarded as the actual implementation of combining corresponding variables.

    As a result of this single sorting out of all the vertices on the graph, every vertex on the graph either disappears or becomes adjacent to all the rest, i.e. the original graph G is changed into a complete graph $G*$. The number of vertices in graph $G*$ gives the number of colours and next to each vertex C in graph $G*$ there will be a list of the vertices which have disappeared from G and merged with C, i.e. coloured in the same colour as C. We note that since, when changing the graph, peaks A and B which are situated at the distance two from each other, are merged, implementation of this merger in the original graph results not only in the disappearance of one vertex but also at least one link (to be more exact, as many links as there are vertices separating A and B, i.e. adjacent to both A and B). This means that another interpretation, arising from the results of Yershov and Kozhukhin's paper[4] can be given to the minimum colouring of graph G: when changing graph G into $G*$ we obtain graph $G*$ with the minimum number of vertices (i.e. the minimum colouring of graph G), if the total number of links which has disappeared when carrying out the conversion was the maximal one when compared with any other means of merging pairs of vertices.

Such an interpretation provides some kind of a lead in our attempt to arrive at rules for choosing pairs of vertices A and B to be merged. The authors examined three variations on such rules.

1. With vertex A in a fixed position, the vertex having the lowest ordinal number, i.e. being first in the sequence amongst the vertices at the distance two from A is chosen as vertex B.
2. With vertex A in a fixed position, the vertex on the graph giving the highest number of vertices separating A from B is chosen as the vertex.
3. Amongst all the pairs of vertices in the graph, a pair of vertices A and B is chosen which has the highest number of vertices separating them.

For a comparative evaluation of these rules, experiments in colouring random graphs at the 45th order using all three methods were carried out on a computer.[5] The results showed that the first method gave between 11 and 12 colours, the second between 9 and 10 and the third between 8 and 9. Tests were carried out manually on graphs of lower orders (between 10 and 15 peaks) and on planar graphs, in which, on the whole, there was no appreciable difference in the given rules (for example, several tens of colourings of planar graphs which had 50 vertices, using the first rule, did not give more than five colours). Since this rule is by far the simplest, it was decided to adopt it.

2.3.3.3 Combining variables of equal weight. We shall now examine the general procedure for colouring the graph of incompatibilities. To explain the algorithm it will be convenient to consider the graph as a multi-storey building situated in space. On each floor there are vertices which have one weight and links connecting the vertices of equal weight ("corridors"). Passing from one floor to the next there are "staircases"—links connecting vertices of different weights. On the first floor there are the heaviest vertices; the higher up the building, the lower the weight of the vertex. At first vertices of equal weight are merged on each floor, according to the rule described above. In addition, it must be borne in mind that although only vertices on the same floor are merged, the space between them is measured not only by the "corridors" but also by the "staircases". As a result of the mergers, all the remaining vertices on each floor will be connected by a complete system of "corridors".

When considering vertices with differing weights the merger operation cannot be interpreted as literally as in the case of vertices of equal weight. Therefore we shall first consider briefly the combination of corresponding variables. Variables of differing weight are combined in two stages. At the first stage, the variables are scanned consecutively, starting with the heaviest. For every variable x_1, with a weight p_1, on the top floors starting with the next one, there is a first variable x_2, with a weight of p_2 ($p_2 < p_1$) so that the corresponding vertices A_1 and A_2 on the graph are not joined by a "staircase". If such a variable exists, it is combined with a variable x_1, i.e. the variable x_2 is fed with information stating that it is now a sub-array of the variable x_1 occupying its first p_2 locations. Vertex A_2 on the graph is joined by "staircases" to all vertices to which peak A_1 is adjacent, and neither A_1 nor A_2 disappear from the graph, being joined together by a "staircase". After this first "insertion" of the variable x_2 into the variable x_1 we shall carry on with our investigation of variables compatible with x_1 but now on floors whose weight does not exceed $p_1 - p_2$. If a variable x_3 with a weight p_3 appears then, like x_2, it is "inserted" into x_1, but now into the next p_3 cells following the first p_2 cells of the array x_1. This filling up process of the variable x_1 with lighter variables continues until peak A_1 is no longer adjacent to all the variables on the graph, or until the remainder of the cells in the variable x_1 are too small to hold any one of the remaining variables. When this moment is reached the work with the variable x_1 is completed, and we pass to the variable y which is next in weight, regardless of whether this variable was previously inserted into one of the heavier variables from the lower floors or not.

Thus, as a result of the first stage of the combining process, the reciprocal arrangement of the arrays is reminiscent of a set of "matryoshki".† There are some first class variables which are never inserted, filled entirely or partly by second class variables into which, in turn, third class variables can be inserted. We note that the second class variables may include variables which were not inserted into any of the heavier arrays because the range of unfilled locations in each of these arrays was too small to accommodate the given variable. Nevertheless, in order to try and insert these variables into heavier arrays, the following operations are carried out at the second stage of the combining process. The first two first-class arrays are taken, which have the unfilled remainders, and they are joined together. Let p_1 and s_1 be the weight and the volume of the blank part of the first array x_1 and p_2 and s_2 be the corresponding values for the second array x_2. The joining operation then signifies that the weight $p_1 + p_2$ is attached to the array x_1, peak A_2 on the graph of incompatibilities corresponding to x_2, is merged with A_1, whilst the variable x_2 is provided with the information that it has become a sub-array of the variable x_1, occupying its last p_2 locations. If any lighter cells were found to have been inserted into the variable x_2 they are also declared to be sub-arrays of the variable x_1, and are placed into x_1 starting from the $(p_1 + s_2)^{th}$ location of the array x_1. In other words, variables inserted into x_2 are moved to the end of the array so that blank locations in x_2 are at the beginning. Thus, when x_2 and x_1 are merged, the resulting array will contain a "window" of the size $s_1 + s_2$ locations, situated $p_1 - s_1$ locations away from the beginning of the array. After this window has been obtained, an attempt is made to insert into it the rest of the second-class arrays, compatible with x_1. When this is done, x_1 will be considered to be completely filled, regardless of whether or not anything is found to have been inserted into the window which has been

---

† Translator's note: Wooden dolls which fit inside each other.

7

constructed. If after this two more blank arrays are found amongst the remaining first-class arrays, these are treated in the same way until all the possibilities for joining arrays have been exhausted.

2.3.3.4 General organization of the algorithm. We shall add a few remarks about the actual organization of the described algorithms for combining. The graph of incompatibilities is represented as a Boolean adjacency matrix. In addition, a so-called colouring table is compiled for all variables. Entry into this table, as into the adjacency matrix, is according to the ordinal number of the variable. At first, only the weight of each variable and information about its type is stored in the table (a distinction is made between constants, constant-arrays, and drum arrays, and also between scalars and normal arrays). When combining variables of equal weight, the first vertex which at the distance two from the given i^{th} vertex is examined by examining the first zero located in a particular j^{th} position in the ith row of the graph adjacency and satisfying the following conditions:

(a) $j > i$;
(b) the Boolean componentwise product of the ith and j^{th} rows of the matrix do not equal the zero row and
(c) the weights of the ith and j^{th} variables coincide.

Joining up the ith vertex on the graph to the jth results in the ith row and column of the adjacency matrix being logically added to the jth row and column respectively. To show that the ith variable is combined with the jth, the name of the jth variable is put into the ith row of the colouring table. If, when combining variables of different weight the ith variable is inserted into a jth array, the name of the jth array and the displacement, are placed in the ith row of the colouring table, i.e. the indication as to which location in the jth array to begin from when arranging the ith variable. If, when making such an insertion it is found that the jth variable was actually inserted into a certain K^{th} array, the name of the Kth array and the displacement of the ith variable, converted with respect to the beginning of the Kth array, are labelled in the ith row.

Thus, after completing the colouring of the graph of incompatibilities the colouring table becomes a table for replacing the names of variables, with regard to the combinations carried out. The total volume of memory which needs to be allotted for storing the variables, equals the sum of the weights of those variables for which the corresponding row in the colouring table contains no references to other variables.

Finally, we shall point a few peculiarities in the combination of variables. As previously mentioned, economy of the working variables is carried out amongst these themselves in the quasilinear sections. A separate section of memory, with a dimension of the maximum number of working variables needed according to all the statements in the program, is set aside for storing the working variables. This section does not coincide with any other variables. When combining variables of equal weight with constants or with constant arrays, a variable with the name of a constant or a constant array always remains a non-interchangeable variable. Consequently, when combining equal weights, all the constant arrays are found to be first-class arrays, i.e. are not inserted into any heavier arrays. Drum arrays only coincide with one another.

2.4 Combining Instructions

The presence of several memory levels in the hardware representations of Input language means—as has been pointed out earlier—that certain blocks in the ALPHA-program can be declared to be external. The instructions in the object program which implement a certain external block B, always occur in the external memory of that kind which was assigned to block B by a special declaration. The external block B is read into core memory when transferring control to block B from the block which directly surrounds block B. Since the outermost block, which makes up the ALPHA-program, cannot be an external one, this means that the instructions for reading the external block and for the transfer of control to it, at the time they are executed are located in core memory. Thus, the possibility arises for economy of memory by reading various parallel (i.e. not nested) external blocks into the same section of memory. Generally speaking, the mechanism for allocation of external blocks in memory is similar to the dynamic allocation of memory: when there is entry into the block, the administrative system must reserve an array of locations in the dynamically allotted section of memory, equal in length to the number of instructions in the program of the external block, read the external block into this array and make an adjustment in it according to the position selected. However, rejection of recursive procedures meant that in the ALPHA-translator the position in memory which the external block may occupy could be predetermined (i.e. still during the translation) by analysing the layout of the external blocks in the ALPHA-program, and the object program could be issued with external block instructions already adjusted to the position assigned to them in memory.

Apart from economic allocation of memory for external blocks in the ALPHA-translator, another process for reducing the volume of the program was implemented, known as "cleaning up the program", which, although it had nothing to do with economic allocation of memory, was found convenient to carry out at this particular stage in the translation. The question concerns the combining of instructions which (combining) could be carried out because of certain peculiarities in the machine instruction code, and also the discarding of "superfluous" instructions from the program, which appeared during the programming.

2.4.1 Allocation of memory for external blocks.
External blocks in the program are introduced into the section of machine memory to be dynamically allocated, which we shall henceforth refer to as "section D". The top part of section D is used for dynamic allocation of memory for arrays which have variable bound pairs, which is implemented by the administrative system. The external blocks are read into the bottom part of section D. Since various sets of external blocks are stored in section D at different moments during operation of the object program, both the upper limit of the bottom part and the lower limit of the top part can "float". The administrative system observed the

fluctuations in the limits and if they occur one after the other, a control stop comes into operation which interrupts the operation of the object program.

By the time the allocation of memory for the external blocks takes place (after the global economy of the variables and the "cleaning up" of the program) the external blocks have become arranged with regard to each other and with regard to the remaining part of the symbolic program, exactly as they were arranged in the ALPHA-program.† Since the delimiters of all blocks, other than the external ones, do not appear in the symbolic program, the programs of the external blocks seem to be submerged in the remaining part of the program, separated from it by statement brackets. We shall refer to the remaining part of the program as the *main block*.

For the external blocks, memory is distributed according to the following algorithm. The symbolic program is scanned from left to right and all the external blocks are numbered in succession, starting with 1, in the order in which the opening statement brackets appear. The main block is given the number zero. On scanning, two tables are compiled—the *blocks table* and the *nesting table*. The length of these tables equals the number of external blocks (k) and entry is according to the block number. When scanning Δ_i—the length of the ith external block is entered into the ith row of the blocks table ($i = 1, \ldots, k$); the pair of numbers (n_i, i) where n_i is the number of the innermost, or main block surrounding the ith block, is entered into the ith row of the nesting table.

Now let α be the start and ω the finish of section D. A series of scans is carried out on the nesting table. During the first scan, the external blocks for which $n_i = 0$, i.e. inserted directly into the main block, are found. Let the numbers and lengths of these blocks equal $i_1, i_2, \ldots, i_r$ and $\Delta_i, \Delta_{i_2}, \ldots, \Delta_{i_r}$ respectively. Then the block with the number i_j ($j = 1, \ldots, r$) is given as its start the address $\omega - \Delta_{i_j}$ which is entered into the blocks table. During the next scan of the nesting table the external blocks for which $n_i = 1$ are found. The starting points for the latter are established as in the previous case, except that the address of the start of the n_i^{th} block, decreased by 1, is taken as the initial point instead of ω. During the ith scan of the nesting table the external blocks nested into the $(i - 1)^{th}$ block are found and so on until the starting points are attached to all external blocks. If the starting point of at least one block is found to be less than α, a control stop, indicating exhaustion of section D, is brought into operation.

2.4.2 Cleaning up the program. In the M-20 computer it is possible to combine unconditional transfer of control (operation code 56) to the second address with transfer of the contents of the first address to the third address. In the

---

† If the blocks were shown as external ones in the ALPHA-program, contained in the procedure declaration bodies, this statement is not wholly accurate. When programming expressions in the ALPHA-translator (IV.2) procedure bodies are rearranged and collected at the end of the program. However, on the strength of the clause which states that if an external block is part of the procedure body F, calls to F cannot take place from any other external block, this rearrangement of the external blocks does not affect the accuracy of operation of the algorithm to be described.

programming phase, the ALPHA-translator does not take this possibility into account and consequently all instructions having operation code 56 come out with first and third address empty. During the cleaning up of the program, when instruction K having operation code 56 appears, the instructions preceding it are scanned. If within the sequence of instructions which is always executed in succession and which closes with instruction K, an instruction of transfer Z (operation code 00) appears, with the result x, and no instruction between Z and K receives x, the instruction Z is discarded from the program and its first and third addresses are added to instruction K.

The other operations involved when cleaning up the program arise out of the fact that in the programming phase, the machine instructions which implement the internal language statements are compiled for each statement separately, regardless of context. This leads to the possibility of incoherent and obviously unnecessary instructions appearing in the final program, which can be discarded without altering its meaning. In the first place, unlabelled instructions, standing immediately after the instruction for the unconditional transfer of control, are discarded. Such instructions may appear when programming conditional statements. Secondly, a group of instructions of the following sort may appear when programming complicated conditions: the calculation of an expression of which the final instruction is one for addition, subtraction or subtraction of modules, then an instruction for checking the sign of the expression just calculated, and finally conditional transfer of control. Since the binary tag ω produced by the above mentioned arithmetical instructions, is defined precisely as the sign of the result, there is no need to check this symbol specially and the corresponding instruction can be discarded. Thirdly, when programming transfers of control the following configuration of instructions might arise:

	KOP	A_1	A_2	A_3
	36 (or 76)		M_1	
	56		M_2	
M_1:				

Each configuration of this sort is replaced by the following type of instruction:

	76 (or 36)		M_2	
M_1:				

Finally, transfer instructions which have the same first and third address are discarded when cleaning up the program. Such instructions are likely to appear as a result of combining variables in the economy of memory.

3 Implementation of the Described Algorithms in the ALPHA-Translator

The algorithms for economy and allocation of memory, the composition and issuing of the final object program are carried out by six blocks in the ALPHA-translator. The names of the blocks correspond to the separate stages into which the algorithms as a whole are divided: Block 19 economizes on the constants and compiles the table of entries; Block 20 compiles the statement scheme; Block 21 compiles the graph of incompatibilities; Block 22 colours the graph of incompatibilities; Block 23 cleans up the program and Block 24 compiles and issues the object program. All these blocks operate within the framework of the general organization of the ALPHA-translator (III). At the start of its operation, each block carries out its own allocation of memory, using the facts about the length and position of transferable information arrays, as well as several previously used numbers for variables and labels, and any other information stored in the communication cells which permanently occupy the last 64 locations in memory.

Before the economy and allocation of memory stage, all information is arranged in the computer in the following way: symbolic program on the first and second drums, table of constants and communication cells in memory, table of blanks, table of arrays and *scale of constants* on the third drum. The scale of constants is a table of binary digits, entry according to the ordinal number of a constant. The units in this scale correspond to the constants, in the table of constants, which are values of the constant arrays.

3.1 Block for Economizing the Constants and Compiling the Entry Table

Block 19 consists of two parts, which operate consecutively. The first part economizes the constants. There is one more feature to be added to the above described algorithm: if a constant is a component of a constant array (this is defined according to the table of constants), then it is always treated as a constant-representative and is not identified with any other constant equal to it. In addition, all these constants are transferred to the beginning of the table. As a result of the operation of the first part, a new table of constants enters the third drum whilst the old table which is now a table for correlating old and new constant numbers, remains in memory.

The second part of the block scans the symbolic program. In the course of this scanning, the constants are renamed in accordance with the economy produced. The constants both in the table of arrays (in ordinal numbers of the first components of constant arrays) and in the table of blanks (if the filler of the blank was a constant) are renamed. When working with the table of arrays, to fill the requirements of the following blocks, the ordinal numbers of constant arrays are extracted from it and made into a separate *table of constant arrays*.

The work of the second part of Block 19 consists chiefly of compiling a *table of variable entries* into the symbolic program. The length of this table is equal to the sum of the used ordinal numbers of arrays, constants and scalars. In the table of entries one location is designated attached to each variable.

For each variable, Block 19 fills in the 15 right digits of the location, by inserting in them the total number of times a given variable enters the symbolic program (this is the same as the "counter of entries into the statement scheme" n_1 in para. 2.3.1.2).

As a result of the operation of Block 19 the table of constant arrays and the table of entries are left in memory; the remaining tables are put on to the third drum.

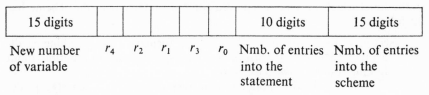

Fig. 4. Format of the table of entries

3.2   Block for Compiling the Statement Scheme

When compiling the statement scheme Block 20 renames the variables. In the new numbering of variables (which is done separately for constants and scalars) variables whose entry into the symbolic program totals zero are not taken into consideration. Numbering of arrays is preserved for technical reasons. The new number of each variable with non-zero number of entries is placed in the left fifteen digits of the corresponding location in the table of entries.

The statement scheme is compiled in accordance with the algorithm described in para. 2.3.1. We shall just show in a little more detail how information obtained during the operation of the block is stored and represented. The counter n_1 (already obtained), the counter n_2 and the tags $r_0, \ldots, r_4$ are shown for each variable in the table of entries. Complete contents of one line of the table are shown in Fig. 4.

During the third scanning of the quasilinear section, the digit r_1 is used for the tag r. After qualifying the variables in the statement, r_1 becomes equal to unity for arguments of the statement, r_2 for results and r_3 for internal variables of the statement. After completely separating the next statement in the scheme, the positions $r_0, \ldots, r_4$ and n_2 in the table of entries are cleaned up. The variables in the symbolic program are renamed during the third (backward) scanning of the instructions in the quasilinear section.

As has already been pointed out, the statement scheme is compiled by Block 20 in the form of a single list. Each section in the list, corresponding to one statement, has the following structure which can be described in ALGOL 60 metalinguistical language:

⟨section⟩ ::= ⟨statement heading⟩ ⟨separator 1⟩ ⟨list of successors⟩ ⟨separator 2⟩ ⟨list of results⟩ ⟨separator 3⟩ ⟨list of internals⟩ ⟨separator 4⟩ ⟨list of variables⟩

The statement heading is a complete list of labels marking the first statement instruction, or (if the statement is not labelled) the statement number coded in a special way. A separator is a particular fifteen-digit symbol, which differs from the other symbols used in the record in question. The list of successors is a list of all the statement-successor labels, or (if they are not labelled) their numbers. The remaining lists are lists of variables. Any of the lists can be empty. A statement in which all the constants and constant-arrays are shown as results is placed as the first section in the statement scheme.

Block 20 also compiles the list of links. The lists of links are filled in succession and are divided into sections. A single section which corresponds to the links which may be recognized for one statement in the scheme has the following structure:

⟨section of the list of links⟩ ::= ⟨start of information about linking result-arrays⟩ ⟨delimiter 1⟩ ⟨list of arguments⟩ ⟨close of information about linking result-arrays⟩ ⟨list of pairs⟩

⟨start of information about linking result-arrays⟩ ::= ⟨empty⟩ | ⟨delimiter 2⟩ ⟨list of internals⟩

⟨close of information about linking result-arrays⟩ ::= ⟨empty⟩ | ⟨delimiter 3⟩ ⟨list of results-arrays⟩

⟨list of pairs⟩ ::= ⟨blank⟩ | ⟨list of pairs⟩ ⟨element of the list of pairs⟩

⟨element of the list of pairs⟩ ::= ⟨delimiter 4⟩ ⟨linked scalar⟩ ⟨list of scalars⟩

⟨list of scalars⟩ ::= ⟨blank⟩ | ⟨list of scalars⟩ ⟨internal scalar⟩ | ⟨list of scalars⟩ ⟨non-internal scalars⟩

The following explanation should be made with regard to these formulae. The list of arguments is always referred to and denotes linking arguments amongst themselves. The start and close of information about linking result-arrays, together with the list of arguments denote linking result-arrays with all the internals and with all the arguments of the statement. In the element of the list of pairs, a linked scalar is considered as being linked with all the scalars shown in its list of scalars and with all the internal scalars shown in previous lists of scalars, which refer to the given section. The last rule means that the volume of the list of links can be reduced without repeating the same internal scalars in the elements of the list of pairs. Internal scalars are differentiated in the lists from external ones by a special tag.

As a result of the operation of Block 20, the statement scheme is left in memory, and the lists of the table of constants and the table of arrays—on the third drum. The rest of the tables disappear since they are of no further use.

3.3 Block for Compiling the Graph of Incompatibilities

The operation of Block 21 starts with the statement scheme being transformed to a form convenient for compiling the graph of incompatibilities. First of all, the statement headings are converted. Instead of a group of labels marking the statement in question, or a conditional number (for unlabelled statements) each statement is given a number which is put into the heading and which is equal to the ordinal number of the statement in the statement scheme. The lists of successors are altered accordingly.

Secondly, lists of internal variables which form an individual list with sections which have the following structure, are taken out of the statement scheme:

⟨section of the list of internal variables⟩ ::= ⟨statement number⟩ ⟨list of internals⟩

In addition, a binary scale of internal variables is compiled equal in length to the number of all the scalars and which contains unity in digits which correspond to the internal variables.

Thirdly, a list of predecessors is fed into the operator scheme for each statement. To achieve greater speed of operation of the algorithms for compiling the graph of incompatibilities, the best method proved to be labelling the predecessor with the address of the start of the section of the statement scheme which referred to the statement-predecessor instead of with the statement number. Since the introduction of the list of predecessors entails an extension of the statement scheme, the list structure was used for the list of predecessors. In the case in question this means that for the list of predecessors each section in the statement scheme is only extended by one memory location. If the number of predecessors is greater than three, the third symbol in the inserted location is converted into an address for continuation the list of predecessors which are accumulated in a separate continuation list. Each location in the continuation list is filled up in the same way as the inserted location in the statement scheme.

In order to establish a correspondence between ordinal numbers of statements and their previous labels and conditional numbers, the correspondence table, the length of which is equal to the number of labels plus the number of conditional numbers, and entry into which is according to the number of the label or the conditional number, is used. The ordinal number of a statement which contains the corresponding label or conditional number in its heading, is put into the table position.

Thus, the sections of the statement scheme finally have the following structure:

⟨section⟩ ::= ⟨ordinal number⟩ ⟨separator 1⟩ ⟨list of successors⟩ ⟨separator 2⟩ ⟨list of results⟩ ⟨separator 4⟩ ⟨list of arguments⟩ ⟨separator 5⟩ ⟨list of predecessors⟩

After converting the statement scheme, the graph of incompatibilities is compiled according to the algorithm described in para. 2.3.2. It should be mentioned that the lists of links are not used by Block 21 but are put into the graph of incompatibilities by the next block.

As a result of the operation of Block 21 the matrix for the graph of incompatibilities is left in memory. The lists of links are still on the third drum. The symbolic program is not used during the operation of Block 21.

3.4 Block for Colouring the Graph of Incompatibilities

At the start of its operation, Block 22 reads in the list of links from the 3rd drum and inserts information about the links into the matrix of the graph

7*

of incompatibilities. After this, colouring of the graph of incompatibilities is carried out according to the algorithm described in para. 2.3.3. As a result of the operation of Block 22, the table of substitution for names of variables in accordance with the combinations which have taken place, remains in memory. Furthermore, the table of arrays is modified and rows which correspond to the arrays which have disappeared are discarded from it and it is then written onto the third drum. The symbolic program is not used during the operation of Block 22.

Finally, it should be mentioned that Blocks 21 and 22 do not operate always in the translator. Since the algorithms for global economy of memory take up quite a lot of time, it was decided to carry out global economy of memory only where this is really necessary, i.e. either when the symbolic program together with all the variables in the form assumed after completion of operation of Block 20 is not placed into memory,† or when the problem requires dynamic arrays. If, going by these rules, there is no need to carry out economy of memory and if there is no switch "on" on the operating panel which requires obligatory economy of memory, Block 20 immediately calls Block 23 into operation.

3.5 Block for Cleaning Up the Program

Block 23 scans the symbolic program and cleans it up, in accordance with the rules described in para. 2.4.2. If global economy of memory has been carried out the variables are renamed in accordance with the table of substitution of names.

Block 23 also carries out other additional operations. First of all, the pseudo-instruction for raising in an integer power is replaced by a corresponding sequence of machine instructions. It proved to be convenient to delay the completion of programming integral powers until Block 23, to avoid difficulties arising out of the fact that working variables may only have two entries each in the program. Secondly, the following are removed from the symbolic program: return statement symbols, terminal symbols in pseudo-instructions for calls to standard sub-routines, and also switch brackets-machine instructions carrying out a control transfer according to the switch being introduced instead of an opening bracket. Finally, to satisfy the following block in the translator, the total number of external blocks in the symbolic program is calculated.

3.6 Block for Compiling and Issuing the Working Program

Block 24 is composed of three parts which operate consecutively. The first part, by scanning the symbolic program, calculates the true number of instructions (the length) of the main block and the external blocks, at the same time filling the table of blocks and the table of "nesting" for them (see para. 2.4.1). An extra "zero" is added to the table of blocks, showing the length of the main block. Furthermore, when scanning the symbolic program, the first part compiles the following tables which will be used when calculating the absolute

† Since the symbolic program consists of symbols which have a fifteen-digit format, it was estimated that the object program would take up ¾ of the length of the symbolic program.

addresses and when compiling the object program: *table of transfer labels, table of instruction labels, table of memory types, table for the order of issue (issuing)*. The table of labels is entered according to the number of the label. The ith row of the table shows the ordinal number of the instruction labelled with a label having the number i, and also the number of the external or main block in which the given instruction is situated. The table of memory types is entered according to the number of the external block; the jth row of the table shows the memory type in which the jth block ought to be situated. The numbers of the external blocks are listed in the table for the order of issuing, in the order in which their opening brackets occur in the symbolic program. In the absence of external blocks, the tables of "nesting", of memory types and for the order of issuing are also omitted.

The main purpose of the second part is to allocate core memory and memory on the drum (see diagram below). The memory allocation diagram requires some

Allocation of memory for the object program

Allocation of core memory	*Allocation of memory on drums*

0 000		00 000
0 017	Service locations	Drum arrays (may be absent)
	AS (may be absent)	
	Master block	Drum external blocks (may be absent)
	Constants (together with constant arrays which may be absent)	The place for storing own dynamic arrays (may be absent)
		17 777
	Formed constants (may be absent)	
	Working locations (may be absent)	
	Scalars (may be absent)	
	Normal arrays (may be absent)	
	Section D (may be absent)	
	Operational field IS (may be absent)	
7 500		
7 777	IS (may be absent)	

explanation. The "service" locations are reserved throughout and used during the operation of the administrative and interpreting systems (AS and IS). The AS is included in the working program when dynamic arrays or external blocks are present. The memory is allocated according to the increasing ordinal numbers of variables. All the constants in the program which assume the form of instructions and which can be referred to with the aid of instruction labels, relate to the *array of formed constants*. The IS is included in the object program when there are calls to standard sub-routines in it (i.e. practically always, since most operations for input and output of information are carried out with the aid of standard sub-routines). The size of the *operational field* for IS is established by the ALPHA-translator in the following way. If the AS is absent, a place is not allotted for section D and $\omega = \alpha$. If the program contains external blocks but no dynamic arrays, an attempt is made to take the sum of the lengths of all the standard sub-routines used in the problem, as the length of the operational field. If this attempt results in a control stop during the allocation of memory for external blocks, the length of the largest standard sub-routine will be taken as the final size of the operational field. During the allocation of memory on drums only the first two physical drums are taken into consideration and are treated as one logical drum with addresses from 0 000 to 17 777. Memory is allocated for drum external blocks in the order in which they occur in the table for the order of issuing. The third physical drum is allotted to storing standard sub-routines which are to be used.

The results of the allocation of memory are stated in a special table in which the number of items is equal to $5 + n$ where n is the number of arrays. The start and the length of the main block are placed in the first row, and in the 2nd, 3rd, 4th and 5th rows—the "pre-starts" of constants, formed constants, working locations and scalars respectively. The start of the ith array (including any drum array) is placed in the row which has the number $5 + i$. The table obtained is printed. If allocation of memory conflicts with the size of memory or of the drums, appropriate control stops are put into operation.

Apart from general allocation of memory the second part allocates memory for external blocks according to the algorithm described in para. 2.4.1, prints the table of blocks obtained after doing this, and transforms the ordinal numbers of the corresponding instructions in the tables of transfer labels and instruction labels, into their absolute addresses.

The third part of the block scans the symbolic program to replace the symbolic addresses with absolute ones, reducing the program to computer format, and "extracting" external blocks from the main block. The main block is put onto the third drum, forming a continuous array with the constants and formed constants, and the external blocks are put on the first and second drums. When an external block is removed, the corresponding instructions for calling a block from external memory and for control transfer to it, are left in its place. In addition, when scanning the program, the numbers of all standard sub-routines to be used in the program are extracted and an array of formed constants, also to be entered on the third drum, is actually filled.

When the operations of scanning and assigning absolute addresses are completed, the object program is issued, that issue being in one of two modes:

punching the object program on to punched cards or preparing the program in a working position in memory followed by an immediate transfer of control to the start of the program. The mode is prescribed by the operator by making the appropriate switching on the computer console.

Punching on to punched cards is done in the following sequence.

(1) Card of the call to *IS* and the adjustment of it to the given operational field (if necessary).

(2) Input card and chart for recording the next tape or drum block on to the appropriate type of memory followed by output of punched cards with the program of the block in question (if necessary). The input cards and the cards for the external block programs are delivered in the order in which they occur in the table for the order of issuing.

(3) Card for input AS, the main block, the constants and the constants formed (in one package) as well as for transferring control to the main block; then the punch cards that form the mentioned package are punched.

(4) The programs of the punch card blocks.

In this sequence of the issue a few details have been omitted for the sake of simplicity, but it is important to notice that in order to start the work it is sufficient to put the entire punched package onto the reading device and press the "input button". Furthermore, there are ways of checking the accuracy of punching the object package.

For the immediate execution mode, it is assumed that all the necessary magnetic tapes which have marked record spaces (including the tape with IS and library sub-routines) have already been placed on tape units. When the program is brought into the position for operation all the tape blocks are recorded on tape and then the punched card blocks are punched. The drum blocks which are left on the first and second drums are put together so as to form one continuous array. Since the external blocks were taken out of the main block and put onto the third drum in the same order as they appeared in the table for the order of issuing, the corresponding arrangement of the drum blocks will be exactly as required according to the allocation of memory. Thus, after bringing together the drum blocks all that remains is to transfer them to the start as directed by allocation of memory. After allocating the external blocks, the AS, the main block, the constants and the formed constants are extracted from the third drum and are written into the memory. Finally, the IS and the necessary standard sub-routines are read from the tape and placed on the third drum. The IS with the necessary adjustment is read into its position in memory, after which control is transferred to the start point of the object program.

3.7   A Simplified Algorithm for Economy of Memory

All the above described algorithms have been implemented to the fullest extent in the ALPHA-translator. The first few months of the experimental operation using the ALPHA-translator showed, however, that the time spent on global economy of memory was too great (more than half the time spent on translation), whereas the volume of available memory was too small, with the result that in large problems when economy of memory was particularly important, global economy could not be used.

From the point of view of operating time, compiling the matrix L proved to be time consuming whilst from the point of view of memory capacity it was the allocation of the lists for linking internal variables and (for large problems) the matrices H, B, L and E. Difficulties which cropped up could be partially explained by programming deficiencies in the implementation of algorithms.

However, the main way to increase the operational speed of the algorithms fundamentally and to remove the quantitative limitations would be to simplify to some extent the algorithms used.

3.7.1 First, the way of compiling the matrix L was simplified: the check up on the break in operation, on appearance of the statement which produces the variable for which the set L is compiled, was removed. Generally speaking this simplification gives rise to unnecessary links but, on the other hand, it meant that operations on single bits of memory locations could be excluded from the algorithm for compiling L, thus increasing more than tenfold the speed of operation of the corresponding algorithm.

3.7.2 The most radical simplification, by the way, and one which did not cause any noticeable worsening of the economy was found to be the exclusion of internal variables from global economy of memory; after being separated in the quasilinear section, the latter were readdressed as working variables and economized with one another and with original working variables within the limits of the quasilinear section, using ordinary algorithms for the economy of working locations. This simplification greatly reduced the volume of the lists of links and substantially reduced the size of the graph of incompatibilities.

This simplification proved to be even more useful because, if too large number of statements or variables in the statement scheme does not allow a global economy of memory to be applied, the partial economy of memory could still operate thanks to the combination of internal variables from various quasilinear sections in the program.

3.7.3 In the original version of the algorithms for global economy of memory, information regarding scopes for declared variables, which said that variables could be combined if they were declared in parallel blocks in the ALPHA-program, was disregarded. There was no need for this so long as the matrix L was compiled exactly in accordance with the definition of the set L. However as the following example shows,

```
begin
   ...
   for : 1, ..., n do
      begin
      Block 1 : begin
               array A[1 : 2000]
               ...
            end;
```

Block 2 : begin
      array $B[1 : 2000]$
      . . .
      end;
    end
  end

the presence of the *FOR*-statement containing both Block 1 and Block 2, results in arrays A and B being linked, although they are declared in different blocks. Unfortunately, the situation demonstrated in the example is fairly typical, particularly for large problems of the iterative type. Therefore it was decided to develop a technique for the ALPHA-translator which would take into account information about the localization of non-own arrays in the ALPHA-program, for direct use by the block for colouring the graph of incompatibilities.

The proposed technique consists of the following. During substituting the identifiers and processing the declarations, (IV.1), Block 3 also compiles for the arrays a table *LOC* of information about localization. Each line of table *LOC*, which corresponds to a certain array A, contains two numbers—n_1 and n_2, where n_1 is the number of Block B containing the declaration of array A, and n_2 is the number of the outermost block, situated furthest to the left in the ALPHA-program, not contained in B. Since the blocks are numbered in the order in which the opening brackets occur, whilst the rows in table *LOC* are filled up in the order in which array declarations in the ALPHA-program are distributed, table *LOC* obviously has the following characteristics:

(a) the numbers n_1 increase monotonically as they move along the table from its start to finish:

(b) if the information (n_1, n_2) corresponds to the non-own array A, then any non-own array A', with the information (n_1', n_2') for which $(n_2 \leqslant n_1')$, can be combined with A during allocation of memory.

Table *LOC* is used by Block 22. If Block 21 had worked and compiled the graph of incompatibilities, the information obtained is used in such a way that, for any pair of arrays A and A' which are compatible according to table *LOC* in question, zero is inserted into the appropriate elements of the matrix of the graph. If Block 21 had not worked, table L is changed into a reduced graph of incompatibilities, and the technique for combining arrays is applied to it.

3.7.4   The final simplification in economy of memory, based on an analysis of the experimental operation, was to exclude drum arrays from global economy of memory. This is because drum arrays are often used by programmers when solving large problems which can be programmed from separate blocks with the help of a complexator (II.2.6). In this case it turned out to be more convenient to allow the programmers full control of the allocation of memory on the drum.

Finally, the authors would like to express their thanks to M. R. Shura-Bura for drawing attention to the importance of taking into account the localization of arrays in economy and allocation of memory.

REFERENCES

1. LAVROV, S. S. (1961). Economy of memory in closed statement schemes. *J. Comput. Math. Math. Phys.* **1**, No. 4.
2. YERSHOV, A. P. (1962). Reducing the problem of memory allocation when compiling programs to one of colouring the vertices of graphs. *Dokl. Akad. Nauk. S.S.S.R.* **142**, No. 4.
3. KITOV, A. I. and KRINITSKII, N. A. (1960). "Electronic computers and programming". Chap. X, Sect. 49, para. 5. Fizmatgiz, Moscow.
4. YERSHOV, A. P. and KOZHUKHIN, G. I. (1962). The estimation of the chromatic number for connected graphs. *Dokl. Akad. Nauk S.S.S.R.*, **142**, No. 2.
5. TROKHAN, L. K. (1962). Colouring graphs of the 45th order. A report from the Computing Center of the Siberian Division of the Academy of Sciences of the U.S.S.R.

X ADMINISTRATIVE SYSTEM IN THE ALPHA-TRANSLATOR

G. I. KOZHUKHIN

The administrative system (AS) in the ALPHA-translator is intended for the dynamic allocation of memory for arrays with calculated bound pairs (*dynamic arrays*) and for *external blocks* (II.2.3).

Blocks, in which dynamic arrays are declared or which directly envelop the external blocks, will be called *dynamic*.

Since the AS is not concerned with adjustment of the program to calculated base addresses of dynamic arrays (IV.1.3.2.1) and with the relocation of the external blocks (IX.2.4.1) its functions include only the allocation of memory in the dynamics of operating the program and, in appropriate situations, assigning the base address of a section of memory, allocated for an array.

Since the operational schemes of AS in allocating memory, both for the external blocks and for the dynamic arrays, practically coincide, the algorithm for the operation of AS will be described for the case of dynamic arrays.

According to the semantics of the Input language, a given variable arises at the moment of entering the block in which it is declared, and disappears on leaving this block. This makes it possible to organize the operating field ["section D" in (IX.2.4.1)] of AS as a stack. With such an organization of memory, it is necessary to dispose of information about the moment of formation of the array and about the moment of its deletion. Obtaining information of the first type does not involve difficulties, since entry into the block is easily shown by static analysis of the translated program. Obtaining information about the moment of deletion of some array in exact conformity with the semantics either leads to significant difficulties in implementation (during static analysis of the program), or requires analysis of all *go to* statements in the dynamics of operation, which, evidently, may aggravate the time characteristics of the object program.

It appears, however, that if the deletion of the array is not linked to the exact instant of exit from the block, it may be comparatively easy to organize the operation of AS, without in this way impairing the object program. In this manner the relationship between implementation and the semantics of the Input language is somewhat disturbed, since the deletion of the array occurs not at the moment of exit from the block, but after this, at the moment of entry into some other block.

1 Algorithms of Operation of AS

The operation of AS is organized in the following manner. Let us examine some moment of execution of the object program. Let N_1, N_2, ..., N_k be a list of numbers of blocks, arranged in order of their nesting (i.e. N_k enters directly into N_{k-1}, N_{k-1} enters directly into N_{k-2} and so on), and let us assume that at a given moment entry must take place into Block N_{i+1} from block N_k. The numbers N_1, N_2, ..., N_k will then certainly include the number N_i (this follows from the fact that on leaving a block it is possible to pass only into an enveloping block). It is readily seen that if $i < k$, we will already have passed through all blocks with numbers standing to the right of N_i in the list, when entering into N_{i+1}, consequently, memory reserved for dynamic arrays declared in these blocks, may be released.

In its operation AS always holds the current list N_1, N_2, ..., N_k.

In order to provide AS with numbers of blocks at the time of operating the program, the statements AS0 and AS1 of calls to AS are inserted by initial blocks of the ALPHA-translator in the corresponding places. The statement AS0 transmits to AS the number of the Block N_i statically enveloping that block in which the statement AS0 is placed. The statement AS1 transmits the number of Block N_{i+1} in which this statement is situated.

In these cases, when there are no procedures in the ALPHA-program, the static picture of nesting blocks coincides with the dynamic one, and therefore it is sufficient to place the statements AS0 and AS1 in succession at the start of each dynamic block. If the program contains procedures, certain sections of the program will be inserted, as it were, into others during the operation, according to the semantics of the Input language. In order that the list of the block numbers of AS corresponds to the dynamic nesting, the statements ASO and AS1 are in such cases placed into different positions of the program. That section, in which the insertion occurs (for example, call statement to the procedure), is considered as it were a dynamic block by including it in specific "brackets of the dynamic block", and the statement AS0 is placed into it. The section of the program to be inserted elsewhere is also included in the brackets of the dynamic block but the statement AS1 is placed into it.

It is readily seen that, as before, the static numeration of blocks of the ALPHA-program (taking into account those which have just appeared) allows, by means of the statements AS0 and AS1, for the transmission of the lay out of the dynamic nesting of the blocks by AS.

For example, if the program is in the form:

$$\{procedure\ F; \{...\}; ... F; ... F; ...\}$$

it will, after arrangement of the statements AS0 and AS1 assume the form:

$$\{AS0\ (0); AS1\ (1); procedure\ F; \{AS1\ (2); ...\};$$
$$... \{AS0\ (1); F\}; ... \{AS0\ (1); F\} ...\},$$

where the number in the brackets after the call statement to AS, shows the number of the block which it (call) transmits to AS.

It should be noted that this scheme of operation of AS may also be applied in the presence of recursive procedures. However, in connection with the fact that on the return of the recursion we may pass from some block into that same one, there appears the necessity of introducing one more call statement to AS. This statement must be placed at the end of the body of the recursive procedure and must pass on the number of the Block N in which it is situated, so that the administrative system, when executing this statement, will erase the numbers of all blocks to the right of the one on the extreme right, coinciding with N, including N itself. Here, it should further be noted that in the list of numbers N_1, N_2, ..., N_k held in AS, one and the same number may occur in several entries.

Besides the mentioned calls to AS, supplying it with information about the dynamic nesting of blocks, there are three further types of calls. In these calls, the number of the block, in which the corresponding call statement is situated, as well as the length of the required section of memory, is communicated to AS. As a result of the operation of AS according to the algorithm described above, either the initial address of the free section of memory is given out, or the blocking stop is operated. These three calls are "strengthened" as follows:

(1) statement AS2—for dynamic arrays;

(2) statement AS3—for external blocks;

(3) statement AS4—for dynamic own arrays (in this case the bound pairs with respect to all dimensions are passed on as well as the necessary storage space. AS assumes the principle possibility of employment of dynamic own arrays in the ALPHA-program. The main problem in this case lies in storing the components of dynamic own arrays at the exit of the block in which they are declared, and in transcribing the stored values (with possible re-arrangement because of modification of bound pairs) into the section of memory reserved for the own array, at the entry into the block in which it is declared.

The values of dynamic own arrays will be stored at the end of the drum. When transcribing the stored values into memory a "coupling" of own arrays being held on the drum, is provided in order to prevent gaps in the arrangement of information on the drum.

2 Implementation of Algorithms in the ALPHA-Translator

The call statements to AS during working of the translator are arranged, as far as necessary, within Blocks 3–7. The final programming of statements to AS is carried out in Block 15. The nature of the operation of these blocks is as follows.

2.1 Block 3 analyses the declarations of all arrays, entering into the ALPHA-program. On discovering declarations of a dynamic array, the necessary operations for calculating the length of the array are put in place of the declaration, corresponding call statements to AS (AS2 or AS4) and statement x, indicating the necessity for forming the base address of the given array (IV.1.3.2.1).

Simultaneously, for all blocks, a scale is set up, in which the dynamic blocks are marked.

2.2 Blocks 4 and 5, according to the information, obtained from Block 3, mark brackets of dynamic blocks (all remaining block brackets other than external ones are discarded from the program by Block 8.) Simultaneously, statements AS0 and AS1 are placed at the start of each dynamic block. Besides, where it is necessary to introduce intermediate dynamic arrays, these blocks carry out the same operation as Block 3.

2.3   Block 7 in the programming of procedures arranges the statements AS0 and AS1 according to what has been described above.

2.4   Finally, Block 15, in addition to its main function, numbers successively all brackets of dynamic blocks. The storage of numbers of blocks is carried out in a stack, which at first "is loaded" with zero (numeration of blocks is conducted from unity). In this case the last number in the stack is taken as the number in communication with AS at a given call to it (except for AS0), and for AS0—the penultimate number.

2.5   The program of AS is inserted into the object program of Block 24. During its operation, AS is placed in memory starting from storage location 0020. Numbers of blocks $N_1, \ldots, N_{k-1}$ are stored in the operating field, the reference to the storage location storing the number N_{i-1} is placed into the storage location storing the number N_i, and the storage location with number N_k is held in a working location of AS.

The operating field of AS consists of two stacks: the upper one is for dynamic arrays and the lower one for the external blocks. In joining the stacks, the blocking stop occurs. The location r_i with block number N_i is always placed at the start of the section of the upper stack, to be reserved for arrays, declared in N_{i+1}, the start of the section of the lower stack for the external blocks, contained in N_i, is stored in r_i.

At the end of the operating field "beyond the lower stack" a table is placed which indicates the current allocation of own arrays (on drum or in memory).

2.6   AS exists in two variants—with or without own arrays. The first variant contains 35, and the second 270 instructions. It should be noted that not one of the real programs run during a year's period of experimental exploitation of the ALPHA-translator involved the use of dynamic own arrays. At the same time dynamic arrays were employed in more than 80% of programs, though not everywhere was there an actual necessity to use it, since in the majority of programs the variable bound pairs, assigned by the input statements, change from variant to variant, but remain constant within the single run.

XI THE ALPHA-DEBUGGER

M. M. Bezhanova and Yu. I. Mikhalevitch

It has already been explained (I) that in the ALPHA-system of automated programming a special program is used to debug ALPHA-programs, which is called the ALPHA-debugger and which takes the form of a zero Block in the ALPHA-translator.

The following principles were taken as a basis upon which to construct the ALPHA-debugger:

the debugger has its own source language, the units of which are statements of a given class; each statement is a formal record of operations which usually have to be carried out when debugging computer programs;

feeding information to the debugger (in terms of the ALPHA-debugger source language) has the following purpose: to make the necessary alterations to the ALPHA-program which is to be debugged, without rewriting the latter, and in the process of running the program to obtain alphanumeric information about the progress of the solution in terms of the original ALPHA-program, information which describes the order in which statements are executed as well as values of pertinent variables obtained when running the program.

The course of the ALPHA-program to be debugged starts with all the necessary changes being made in the ALPHA-program by the debugger, on the basis of information fed to the latter before the said program is translated. If necessary, a so-called *code array* is compiled. The amended ALPHA-program is translated and a method of solving is then executed using the code array compiled by the ALPHA-debugger as its working array.

1 Input Language of the ALPHA-Debugger

We shall consider the ALPHA-program as a sequence $A = \{a_1 \ldots a_z\}$, made up of basic Input language symbols.

We shall refer to any subsequence of the sequence A in the form

$$M = \{a_i \ldots a_{i+m}\} \ (i \geqslant 1, i + m \leqslant z)$$

as *a context*.

A context $(M, N) = \{a_i \ldots a_{j+n}\}$ will be referred to as an *interval* defined by the contexts $M = \{a_i \ldots a_{i+m}\}$ and $N = \{a_j \ldots a_{j+n}\}$ $(i \leqslant j, m, n \geqslant 0)$; we shall refer to the contexts M and N as *start* and *finish* of the interval, respectively.

We shall refer to a set of intervals in the ALPHA-program which are used in the definition of a certain statement as the *scope* of that statement.

The following two rules for shortening may be applied when defining the intervals:

(1) if for a certain interval (M, N) $i = j$ and $m = n$, the context (M) may be indicated instead of the interval (M, N);

(2) if for a certain statement the interval (M, N) is such that $i = 1$, $n = z$, that is to say, such that the interval coincides with the whole ALPHA-program, the description of this interval may be omitted from the statement.

From now onwards $(A_1, \ldots, A_n)$ will be used to denote a list of the identifiers for certain variables declared in an ALPHA-program under consideration. The following types of statements are permissible in the ALPHA-debugger.

1.1   Print Values of Variables
Syntactical definition:

   Print values $(A_1, \ldots, A_n)$ **in** $(M_1, N_1), \ldots, (M_k, N_k)$.

In its scope this statement causes the printing of names and the values of the variables $A_1, \ldots, A_n$ immediately after the assignment statements have been executed, left parts of which are these variables.

1.2   Print Labels
Syntactical definition:

   Print labels in $(M_1, N_1), \ldots, (M_k, N_k)$.

This type of statement causes printing of labels of the labelled statements which are situated within its scope, directly before the execution of these statements.

1.3   Print Labels and Values of Variables
Syntactical definition:

   Print labels and values $(A_1, \ldots, A_n)$ **in** $(M_1, N_1), \ldots (M_k, N_k)$.

This statement is a combination of types 1.1 and 1.2 statements.

1.4   Print Values of Variables in a Fixed Position
Syntactical definition:

   Print values $(A_1, \ldots, A_n)$ *after* $(N_1), \ldots, (N_p)$.

The statement causes the printing of names and values of variables as indicated after the last statement of each context $(N_1), \ldots, (N_p)$ has been executed.

1.5   Print the Number of Loop Repetitions
Syntactical definition.

   Print the number of loop $(r_1, \ldots, r_k)$ **repetitions.**

Here, r_i is the r_ith entry of a FOR-statement, counting from the start of the ALPHA-program. The statement calculates the number of times the loop body is repeated during execution of each of the specified FOR-statements and prints this number when the loop is completed.

Henceforth, statements of types 1.1–1.5 will be referred to as *debugging statements*.

1.6 Substitution Statement

Syntactical definition:

change ⟨the list of equivalents⟩ **in** $(M_1, N_1), \ldots, (M_k, N_k)$.
⟨list of equivalents⟩ ::= ⟨list elements⟩ | ⟨list of equivalents⟩
⟨list element⟩
⟨list element⟩ ::= ⟨fragment to be replaced⟩ *to* (Q)
(fragment to be replaced⟩ ::= (R) | **identifier** (X).† where R is a context;
X is a identifier; Q is a sequence of the basic symbols.

This type of statement changes specified sections in to the corresponding Q, in the specified scope. The rules for substitution are examined in Section 2.

In the information given for debugging, the ALPHA-debugging statements are put in any order. However, substitution statements take precedence over debugging statements, i.e. the ALPHA-program, altered by substitution statements is the initial ALPHA-program for the operation of debugging statements. This should be borne in mind when indicating the scopes for the debugging statements.

If the information for debugging is absent, the work of the ALPHA-debugger is reduced to executing a single statement which may be implicit by any information for debugging (including empty), namely, a statement for including non-declared procedures. The presence of this statement is governed by the possibility of using in an ALPHA-program calls to a certain procedure, not declared in the program but present in the library of standard procedures (II.2.2). This library is a collection of procedure declarations written in Input language. The library is stored on tape and is available during operation of the ALPHA-debugger. The statement for including non-declared procedures is put into the program of declarations of those procedures, call statements to which are present in the ALPHA-program.

2 Description of the Algorithm for the Work of the ALPHA-Debugger

Taken as a whole, the algorithm for the work of the ALPHA-debugger falls into three stages which are executed consecutively.

2.1 First Stage

During the first stage, information for debugging is decoded and tabulated in special list form which is convenient for subsequent processing and which allows the operation of the ALPHA-debugger to be speeded up during subsequent stages. Thus, during the first stage the following are compiled for each of the subsequent stages:

(1) a scale of context lengths;
(2) a table of references;
(3) a common list;
(4) a scale of starting symbols.

† Inclusion of the identifier as a special case is done, for instance, to simplify substitutions of the type

change (n) **to** (5) **in** $(\sin (n))$

since universal substitituon would give si5(5) instead of sin (5).

A scale of loops to be printed is also compiled for operation at the third stage, giving the ordinal numbers of those loops for which an indication of the number of times they are repeated must be printed.

The scale of context lengths gives the context lengths of interval starts and ends which appear in the information for debugging, and also lengths of sections to be altered and identifiers of variables to be printed.

This is done to shorten the time spent on scanning the ALPHA-program so that in future, attention may be concentrated solely on ALPHA-program contexts, the lengths of which coincide with the lengths marked on this scale.

All contexts given by the debugging information are entered in the common list as well as the connection between them, which is fixed by each of the debugging information statements.

To shorten the time which will be subsequently taken to find these contexts in the ALPHA-program, a table of references is compiled in which the Nth row corresponds to each of the contexts in the common list, N being calculated according to the context with the help of the hash addressing function (III.4.1). If, when filling in the table of references, it turns out that several contexts $K_1, ..., K_s$ all give the same value N of the hash addressing function then, in contrast to the procedure described in (III.4.1), information for contexts $K_1, ..., K_s$ is stored systematically in the locations of an additional continuation table of references, in which information about context K_i contains a reference to information about context K_{i+1} ($i = 1, ..., s - 1$). One row in the table of references will contain information about the type of context (interval start, section to be altered, interval end) and its length, a reference to its start in the common list and also, if need be, a reference to the continuation table of references.

The scale of starting symbols contains marks on those ALPHA-program symbols which start contexts entering into the table of references. The scale can be entered according to a nine-digit alphanumeric code, in which the first four digits denote the number of the location on the scale and the remaining five—the number of the location bit, a unity in which indicates that the symbol which has the specified number is the first one for some context from the debugging information.

Furthermore, to speed up operating time, only information about contexts of interval starts is introduced in the first stage in the table of references; the information about the ends of interval sections to be altered and variables to be printed is introduced into the table of references in the course of scanning the ALPHA-program only at the second and third stages. The same is done to the scale of starting symbols.

The ALPHA-program is adjusted at the second and third stages, in accordance with the debugging information. In view of the fact that new variables are being introduced into the program, it will be necessary to introduce declarations of these variables, as well as a description of the statement for input of the code array into memory and declarations of non-declared standard procedures which are to be used in the ALPHA-program to be considered.

The requisite non-declared standard procedures are found by comparing the identifiers which occur in the program with the list of names of non-declared standard procedures which are located in the library, and by subsequently inserting procedure declarations for which names have been found.

2.2 Second Stage

The main part of the second stage consists of the algorithm which carries out operations assigned by the substitution statements.

We shall now describe the procedure for implementing substitution statements.

When information about contexts can be found at a given moment in the table of references, such contexts will be referred to as *available contexts*. Let us assume that at a particular moment when scanning the ALPHA-program the symbol a is examined. Let a be called the starting point for comparison. From the contents of the scale of starting symbols it can be determined whether, amongst the available contexts, there is any context beginning with a. If there is not, we pass on to the next symbol in the ALPHA-program,† which is taken as the starting point for comparison.

We shall assume that a is the start of one of the available contexts. Then a repetitive process of comparing current contexts, starting with the symbol a, with available contexts, will begin. The loop will pass along the length i of the current context, from $i = 1$ to $i = l_{max}$, l_{max} being the maximum context length. Let us assume that a current context K of length i is isolated in the ALPHA-program. From the scale of context lengths it can be determined whether, the available contexts include a context of the same length. If not, i is increased to unity with subsequent checking on completion of the loop according to i.

Let us assume that the available contexts include one with a length i. The value of the hash addressing function $f(K) = N$, will then be calculated and the context K compared in turn with all the available contexts, next to which is placed the location N from the table of references. If N is empty or the available contexts should turn out not to coincide with K, i is increased to unity.

Assume that K does coincide with certain available contexts. Further operations are determined by the type of available context.

If an interval start is found, information about sections to be changed in this interval, and about the end of the interval is entered into the table of references. The scale of starting symbols will be filled up in an appropriate way. Information about the interval start is eliminated from the table of references.

The following should be noted, in connection with the operation for eliminating information from the table of references. If the information I to be eliminated contains a reference to information I', which is in the continua-

---

† The idea of using a scale of basic symbols to speed up the procedure of checking contexts in the ALPHA-debugger was suggested by I. V. Pottosin. A more general scheme for a similar method is described by V. V. Martynuk.[1]

tion table of references, then information I' will now take the place of information I. If no such reference was made then information I is simply removed.

In what follows it should be borne in mind that implementation of the substitutions is equivalent to reprocessing the ALPHA-program, which takes place according to the scheme "read—process—write" (III.3.4). Where it is necessary to distinguish between texts in the ALPHA-program which have been reprocessed and those which have not, we shall refer to the former as the old ALPHA-program and to the latter as the new one.

If the available context is found to be a replaceable section, then in accordance with the table of references the substituting text Q is taken from the common list and inserted into the new ALPHA-program for the context K.

After carrying out the substitution, reading the old ALPHA-program symbols reverts to a special mode (note that available contexts are always compared with the old ALPHA-program), in which contexts are compared only to discover interval bounds, whereas substitutions—even if they coincide—are blocked. This special mode is removed as soon as all the symbols which constitute the amended section K have been read as starting points in the old ALPHA-program.

If an available context is found to be an interval end then information about that interval end as well as about all sections to be amended relating to the closed interval, is eliminated from the table of references.

At the end of the second stage, if need be, a control print is made of the interval numbers (in the order in which they appear in the debugging information), the starts or ends of which were not found when scanning the ALPHA-program. In this case a control step is brought into operation.

Let us look at an example of implementing substitutions.

Task for debugging†

```
    begin
        change "n" to "15"
        change "; entry (n);" to ";" in "integer" "begin";
        change " : n × (n + 3)/2" to " : 135",
    "until n × (n + 3)/2" to  "until 135" in "a" do";
        end of debugging
The old ALPHA-program;
    begin integer n;
        input (n);
        begin integer i, j; real element, total;
        real arrays x [1 : n], a[1 : n × (n + 3)/2];
        for i := step 1 until n × (n + 3)/2
                    do a[i] := 0
    end
```

---

† In the hardware representation, round brackets for limiting sections and also commas for separating contexts within the section are discarded. Each context is put in inverted commas.

The new ALPHA-program:
> **begin**
>> **begin integer** i, j; **real** element, total;
>> **real array** $\times$ [1 : 15], a[1 : 135];
>> **for** $i := 1$ **step** 1 **until** 135 **do** $a[i] := 0$
>
> **end**

Note. In the task for debugging there was no indication that the declaration "integer n;" had been eliminated from the ALPHA-program. But after substitution, the debugger scans the ALPHA-program and at the same time removes from it "declarations of numbers" which crop up as a result of substitution.

3.3 Third Stage

Operations assigned by the debugging statements are carried out at the third stage. Intervals are found in the same way as at the second stage. As soon as a particular interval start is found, assignment statements are obtained such that the identifier of the variable to which assignment is carried out coincides with the identifier of the variable mentioned by a statement of the type 1.1 or 1.3, the interval of which is open. In addition, if the variable is a scalar, only statements for printing the identifier of the variable and the statement for printing the value of this variable are inserted (after the assignment statement to be examined). Since there is no device in the ALPHA-translator for executing operations with strings, a variable name is inserted not by stating this name as a print statement argument but by arranging it in the code array which is compiled in the course of the third stage and by indicating in the print statement the appropriate component in this array. In this context and subsequently the term "print" signifies printing on triple register teletype.

If the variable in question has subscripts which are not blanks, the following information is provided in addition to the print statement indicated:

(a) statements for assigning to certain variables which are to be introduced anew, the value of each expression in the subscript positions:
(b) statements for printing the values of these variables.

The form of the information to be issued during the work of the statements is described below.

If the variable in question is a multi-dimensional array (by the declaration or because of empty subscript positions), all the scalar components of this variable are printed in the order in which they are arranged in memory.

If the interval opened during scanning at the third stage belongs to the scope of a certain statement of type 1.2 or 1.3, the entries of all the labels for this interval, which precede the statements labelled by these labels are found. The identifier of each label of this type is entered as the next component in the array, whilst the statement for printing the components of this array is put into the ALPHA-program between the label and the statements which it labels.

A 1.4 type statement brings about the insertion of the above mentioned statements for printing identifiers and values of selected variables in a specified position in the ALPHA-program.

A 1.5 type statement demands a recognition of the headings of *FOR*-statements. In the event of the ordinal number of the *FOR*-statement coinciding with one of those to be mentioned by the 1.5 type statement (marked in the scale of loops to be printed) the following are inserted:

(a) the statement for assigning a zero value to one of the variables to be introduced anew in front of the *FOR*-statement;

(b) the statement for increasing the value of n by 1 in front of the closing bracket of this statement (if there are no brackets, opening and closing brackets are put in);

(c) statements for printing the loop number and the value of n after the *FOR*-statement.

Information about undetected intervals of debugging statements can be printed in a similar way as in stage 2.

The code array, compiled as a result of the third stage operation, is put onto tape, if the object program will run immediately after translation or on punched cards if the execution is to be postponed.

When running the object program the code array will be called to memory and when the print statements arranged by the ALPHA-debugger are carried out they will print the current values of the given variables giving the indication of their identifiers (and subscript values) to facilitate the analysis of information which is obtained. Similarly, labels will be printed when the statements which they label are executed. This allows the progress of the object program to be followed.

As an example, let us examine an algorithm for ordering components of an array made up of three positive numbers

$$a[1:3], \text{ where } a[1] := 5{\cdot}7341, \ a[2] := 3{\cdot}14159265 \text{ and } a[3] := 4{\cdot}61987541.$$

Task for debugging:
```
begin
    print the number of loop (1) repetitions;
    print labels and values (M) in "for" "end"
end of debugging
```

Original ALPHA-program:
```
begin (declarations omitted)
    for j := 3 step − 1 until 1 do
    begin i := 1;
    SEND: M[j] := a[j]; K[j] := i;
    SUM: i := i + 1;
go to if i > 3 then KOVO else if a[i] > M[j] then SEND
    else SUM;
    KOVO: a[K[j]] := 0
    end
end
```

ALPHA-program with ALPHA-debugger insertions:

begin integer EVA; $EVA := 0$;
    begin (declarations omitted)
    for $j := 3$ **step** -1 **until** 1 **do**
    begin $i := 1$
$SEND$: print ("$SEND$"); $M[j] := a[i]$;
    print ("M","(", "j", ")", $M[j]$);
SUM: print ("SUM"); $i := i + 1$
go to if $i > 3$ **then** $KOVO$ **else if** $a[i] > M[j]$ **then** $SEND$ **else** SUM;
$KOVO$: print ("$KOVO$"); $a[K[j]] := 0$; $EVA := EVA + 1$
end;
print ("loop", "1", "is repeated", EVA, "times"); $EVA := 0$;
end
end

Print out of information during the trial run of the object program (the subscripted brackets are printed as round ones)

```
SEND
M(3)
+++01 573410000
SUM
SUM
SUM
KOVO
SEND
M(2)
+++00 000000000
SUM
SEND
M(2)
+++01 314159265
SUM
SEND
M(2)
+++01 461987541
SUM
KOVO
SEND
M(1)
+++00 000000000
SUM
SEND
M(1)
+++01 314159265
SUM
SEND
KOVO
LOOP 1 IS REPEATED 3 TIMES
```

3   Conclusion

The system examined in this chapter which aims at debugging ALPHA-programs at Input language level, has features in common with other systems[2, 3] These systems are based on a compiler program which places special marks in the ALPHA-program or compiles a dictionary which determines the correlation between certain sections of the source ALPHA-program and the object program obtained from it. Information about how the solution of the problem is progressing is reached in the process of solving the program obtained as a result of translation and processed prior to this compiler program.

The special features of the ALPHA-debugger depend, on the one hand, on its adaptability to the ALPHA-system (namely, the creation of a code array, inclusion of declarations of standard procedures, and the arrangement of special print statements), and on the other on a desire to make this system as convenient and flexible in its application as possible. This is achieved in our opinion by the system of assigning scopes to ALPHA-debugger statements by context indication without introducing into the considered ALPHA-program advance notification.

It should be noted, however, that the process of comparing contexts demands that the program of the ALPHA-debugger be implemented with very great care since if this, essentially trivial, algorithm is implemented in a straightforward manner it will lead to a slowing down in the operation of the debugger. The observant reader will notice, in the description of the algorithms for carrying out comparisons, a means for increasing the speed of operation. Most of these means were included only in the second version of the ALPHA-debugger which was developed after it was discovered that the first version operated too slowly. The potentialities permitted by the substitution statement, prove to be far wider than is necessary for debugging purposes. So with the help of the substitution statement, alterations can be made in the program depending on: elimination of errors found in the program; the necessity of assigning a trial variant (alteration of constants, array bounds, branch statements, steps for changing parameters and so on); the ease of making alterations taking into account the various versions of the problem, which make small but repetitive alterations in the programs (different variations in the formula, procedure, FOR-statements, switch declarations, giving numerical values for symbolic parameters and so on).

Finally, the authors would like to express their thanks to everyone who took part in the development of the ALPHA-translator and who took an active part in the discussion on the ALPHA-debugger, especially to I. V. Pottosin for checking the manuscript and for making some valuable suggestions.

REFERENCES

1. MARTYNUK, V. V. (1964). Economic organisation in the search and retrieval of information using surplus memory. *Comput. Math. Math. Phys.* **4**, No. 3.
2. VER STEEG, R. L. (1964). TALK—a high level source language debugging technique with real-time data extraction. *Commns Ass. comput. Mach.* **7**, No. 7.
3. FERGUSON, H. E. and BERNER, E. (1963). Debugging systems at the source language level. *Commns Ass. comput. Mach.* **6**, No. 8.

THE PROGRAMMING PROGRAM SYSTEM

A. P. YERSHOV AND G. I. KOZHUKHIN

(Paper presented at a conference on "Constructing Programming Programs based on ALGOL" held from the 22nd to 24th December, 1960, in Moscow)

The suggestions put forward in this paper cannot be regarded as a complete scheme for the PP, based on "Input Language"[1]—a somewhat modified version of ALGOL 60,[2] since it is impossible, in a single paper, to set forth all the questions connected with compiling the PP. We shall hardly touch on questions which are, in our opinion, purely technical nor on problems, which no one as yet has apparently attempted to solve. Our main consideration will be for problems which we hope to solve (or which we shall be forced to solve) when working on the programming program.

The paper consists of four main parts:

1. Choosing an internal language and unifying initial information.
2. A series of problems relating to optimization of the operation of the PP and of the object programs.
3. Questions relating to the operation of the PP.
4. Some details relating to the operation of the PP.

Some of the basic ideas in this paper have already been put forward in a more general form in an earlier paper.[3]

1 Selecting the Internal Language and Unifying the Initial Information

1.1   Any language represents a "double edged weapon" and is intended for the transfer of information between corresponding ends. Therefore, in the assessment of a language, the interests and wishes of both sides must be considered.

1.1.1   Experience gathered in constructing a PP shows that the language in which programming is conducted must on the one hand be as uniform as possible in its structure and on the other hand, the symbols of the language must carry as much information as possible about themselves.

1.1.2   Experience gained in constructing source languages for a PP shows that it is advisable that the source language should have a system of representation which is as flexible as possible, and requiring in particular, a wide variety of possible symbols.

As to the question of the symbols containing information about the objects which they denote, here man is like the machine in that he too welcomes such information but ..., as a rule, he does not want to be compelled always to include such information in the symbol. This is clearly in evidence in the case of scientific literature, where even in mathematics—not to mention physics and engineering—the use of characters and signs is far from always being standardized.

1.1.3   This conflict of interests between man and machine which arose in the early programming programs was solved in the USSR mainly in favour of the machine. All the source languages in these programs had symbols of a fixed length and a fairly restricted choice of statements.

ALGOL represented one of the first steps towards meeting the interests and needs of the human being. In ALGOL, identifiers of any length are allowed, there is an extensive choice of statements, statements alternate with declarations, etc., etc.

It is impractical, in our opinion, to conduct coding directly from an ALGOL-type language. It is wiser to carry out a preliminary translation from the external language into an internal language, i.e. to carry out a sort of "conversion to a form suitable for coding".

1.2   What does Translation into an Internal Language Involve?

1.2.1   We have already stated that uniform type of information is more suitable for a machine. In this connection, there arises the need to establish the length of the basic unit of information in the internal language. The actual length of the unit of information will depend on the solutions of several other problems about which something will be said below; however, it will clearly not exceed 5–9 binary bits. We wish to replace by standard symbols units of information such as identifiers, numbers, variables with sub- and superscripts and so on. This will simplify the subsequent operation of the PP considerably.

However, during such a substitution, we would certainly not want to lose the information about what the given symbol itself represents. In PPs constructed in the USSR, the source language has been based on a symbol of fixed length (usually one address), which, however, did not as a rule contain any information about its significance. This was quite understandable and was due to the fact that the human operator should introduce this information. Furthermore, in view of the poorness of the means of representation, the need for such information hardly ever arose in these languages. In ALGOL 60[2] and in Input language[1] we have a completely different picture. In these, as a rule, there arises a multitude of questions about whether a given syntactical unit of language belongs to one or other syntactical subclass of information. For example, about an identifier we wish to know whether:

it is a variable;
or a label;
or an identifier of a function;
or an identifier of an array.

A variable may be:

simple;
have a subscript;
have a superscript;

may have a **real** type;
or a **Boolean**;
or an **integer** and so on.

As can be seen from the examples given, whether a given syntactical unit belongs to one or another subclass of information is often determined by the whole of the subsequent course of programming and it is therefore very important to dispose of such information.

It may be thought that when translating from the source language into the internal one, it will be easy to obtain part of this information and then to include it directly into the internal language symbol. Thus, the basic internal language symbol will be divided into information and identifying bits. (We notice that this principle is often employed when, for instance, using different figures for different subclasses of information, and different letters to identify the items within the given subclass).

For coding the identifying bits, we shall try, as far as possible, to use the principle of coding a symbol by the address of its value or by the address of additional information about it.

It is clear that in defining the precise structure and length of an internal language symbol, we should seek a solution which compromises the following three requirements:

(1) The symbol must be as short as possible;
(2) it must include as much important information as possible;
(3) the information included in the symbol must be relatively easily accessible.

1.2.2   Standardizing the form of the program schemes. Second in succession—but not in importance, to the problem of choosing an internal language is the construction of a uniform program scheme.

1.2.2.1   ALGOL 60 and particularly Input Language, comprise a large number of operations, a number of which can easily be expressed through the rest thus reducing the number of operations to a minimum. Naturally this makes the task of programming easier. However, with this kind of minimization, care must be taken since, generally speaking, it is not clear to what degree standardization can be used without at the same time impairing the operating program to be issued by the PP.

1.2.2.2   The second aspect of the standardization of schemes is the elimination of declarations from them. The fact is that declarations constitute foreign bodies, and up to the instant of carrying out coding it is in our opinion better to place them in separate tables so as to have only statements in the scheme. It is possible that part of the information in the declarations can be successfully put into internal language symbols (for example, information about the type of variable) and the remaining part used to standardize the scheme (for example, substitution of identities).

The question of which tables to compile and in what form to compile them will be decided in the course of work on the PP and possibly not first but as the programming algorithms are compiled when it is more definitely apparent what form will be most useful for these tables.

8

1.3   Finally, before leaving the problem of the internal language, mention should be made of two important problems which crop up in connection with the two-phase programming operation:

(a) when to start taking into consideration the special features of the computer;

(b) how to distribute the optimizing algorithms between the first and second programming phase.

We have raised these questions because minimization of descriptive means inevitably leads to a partial loss of information about the original structure of the scheme. Disregard for this fact may lead to the PP giving a program of a far worse standard than that of which it is capable.

2   Problems of Optimization

When compiling a PP all questions relating to optimizing the operation fall logically into two fields: optimizing the operation of the programming program itself and creating the best possible object program.

2.1   Optimizing the Operation of the PP

Although it is clearly important to create a PP capable of operating at high speeds, it is nevertheless far from clear *what* factors influence the operation speed of the compiler program and, more especially, *how* they affect it. The quality of operation of the PP is usually characterized on the one hand by its operating time and on the other, by the quality of the object program it produces. Obviously, these two requirements are contradictory, and in practice a compromise must be sought. The level of optimization at which we are aiming will be explained below. However, we think that even with fixed demands on object programs, there are certain basic points in the PP which, if properly settled can greatly accelerate the work of the PP. We think that these basic points consist of the following.

2.1.1   Analysis of the source information on the basis of which the plan of work for the PP is constructed. It is perfectly obvious that if the PP is always started according to a single plan, dealing with many problems will be like breaking a butterfly on the wheel. For example, if a problem is put completely in memory there is no point in summoning the block which organizes exchange between different memory levels. To take another instance, when all the variables in a loop depend on the loop parameter there is no point in "cleaning up" the loop (i.e. in eliminating from the loop all operations which can be implemented before the start of operation) and so on.

The questions which we are going to settle in this connection consist of the following: how exactly to carry out the analysis and how to organize the work of the PP. It is possible that in certain instances we will even go so far as to create duplicates of blocks (i.e. blocks which fulfil one and the same operation but which differ in capacity).

It is worth considering providing programmers with means for indicating additional information, by which the PP will be able to establish its operational procedure.

The actual analysis of programs will most probably be carried out when translation into the internal language takes place.

2.1.2   The careful balance in the distribution of memory between the PP and the information. Here, the problem consists of the following: whether to keep the PP on tape and the information on a drum, or vice versa. Possibly, at different stages in the operation this question will need to be settled differently. Thus, when translating into the internal language when all information has to be processed at once, it will obviously be better to store it on a drum whilst the block (or blocks) of PP can be seen read from tape. But possibly later on it will be more sensible to do it the other way round. We must confess that the merit of one solution or the other is not clear to ourselves, but in any case we shall try to put forward reasonable grounds for our choosing one alternative or the other.

2.1.3   Reducing search and sorting time. Everyone is aware how much time is spent, on investigation and sorting out of information in operation of a programming program.

2.1.3.1   However, a lot of the sorting out has already prompted ways of cutting down on it. The fact is that programming algorithms usually implement the search for a highly specialized type of information. In doing this, a considerable amount of information which could be obtained incidentally and which might prove to be very useful for subsequent blocks, is left aside.

We shall try to apply this idea of obtaining information incidentally as widely as possible in the programming program, and we believe that in many cases a great deal will be gained by it.

2.1.3.2   Finally, to reduce the amount of search and sorting out, the algorithm for identification, based on the so called hash-addressing functions, will be used wherever possible. The essence of this method is put forward in a paper by A. P. Yershov[4] and briefly consists of the following.†

Let us examine a particular set of numbers $A = \{a_1, \ldots, a_k\}$. For the sake of simplicity we shall assume that each element in this set can, by being coded in a certain way, be placed in one memory location. Now assume that some device distributes the elements of this set, one by one, in the form of a provisional sequence (possibly with repetitions). The problem which must be solved is having obtained the next element in the sequence, to determine whether this element is appearing for the first time or whether it has occurred earlier. In the first case, the element is sent into one of the group of locations $L + 1, \ldots, L + n$ $(n \leqslant k)$, intended for storing the elements of the set $A = \{a_1, \ldots, a_k\}$ whilst in the second case the element may for example be disregarded. This problem is encountered in different forms in many programming algorithms (for example in the economy of instructions, in the formation of every kind of table and so on).

The ordinary method used in the case in question is one in which the elements of the set A are placed in the locations $L + 1, \ldots, L + n$ one after the other and each new element is in turn compared with all the rest already being stored

† It should be noticed that a similar idea was discovered independently by I.B.M. and used in the compiler program SOAP 2.[5]

in memory. This method gives the operation time of the algorithm proportional to k^2.

If the work is organized in the following way, quadratic sorting can be omitted in this problem. Let us suppose that a certain integral function F is determined on the elements of set A such that $L + 1 \leqslant F(a_i) \leqslant L + n$ for all a_i. We shall refer to this function as the "hash addressing function". The algorithm will be used in the following way: before starting the work, the array $L + 1, \ldots, L + m$ is cleaned up. Let us take the next element a_i. Let $F(a_i) = L + m$. Let us try to place a_i into the $L + m$ location. If this location is empty then a_i occurs first and is put into $L + m$. If the element a_i fills $L + m$ then the current a_i is disregarded. If $L + m$ is occupied by an element other than a_i then, by examining one by one the locations $L + m + 1$, $L + m + 2$ and so on, we can find either the first empty $L + m$ location or a location occupied by the element a_i. In the first case a_i is placed in $L + M$ and in that second, it is disregarded. It is easy to see that quadratic sorting is obtained when $F(a_i) \equiv L + 1$. It appears that if the hash addressing function is selected so as to give uniformly distributed values in the section $L + 1 \div L + n$, on random sequences of A elements, and if on this condition we assume that $n \simeq 1.5.k$, the mathematical expectation of operation time of the algorithm will be proportional to k. For different actual identification problems which crop up in the PP, it is possible of course to select hash addressing functions which are quite close to the ideal one required.

2.2   Optimization of the Working Program
2.2.1   Questions relating to limited memory

2.2.1.1   It might be assumed that the problem of segmentation, i.e. of allocating the program and information to different memory levels, has by now become a classic programming problem. Nevertheless, a satisfactory solution to this problem has not yet been reached. At the same time it would be unwise to develop such a powerful unit as the PP, based on Input language, only for computing problems which can be wholly accommodated in memory. Taking into account the fact that we cannot entrust the allocation of statements and information in memory entirely to the computer, we are inevitably forced to introduce into the source language some method of showing allocation of information in memory.

At a meeting of the Association held in June a report was put forward relating to the modification of ALGOL by introducing exchange operations. Briefly, this proposal boiled down to the following: to introduce certain exchange operations, the arguments of which may be labels and variables. Furthermore, appearance of a label indicates that the block, labelled by this label, is read from or written to the memory of the indicated kind. If the argument of the exchange operation is a variable, then the value of this variable is read or written.

Another way for introducing into ALGOL means of indicating exchange, with which we are familiar, is the method used in DASK ALGOL. It consists briefly of the following. Each block to be recorded onto a drum has the label "comment drum program" and correspondingly, information recorded onto the drum has the label "comment drum data". Summons to memory is initiated, as far as can be gathered from the report, by call to the appropriate block or information.

It is difficult to say at this stage which of these methods is the best. At all events, irrespective of the form a means of indicating exchange will be provided for in the PP.

In addition to segmentation, to be implemented by the human operator, an "obtuse" version of segmentation will be provided for in the PP. In the event of the block to be programmed not entering memory, the PP will attempt to transfer onto a drum one or several of its sub-blocks. The computer informs the programmer of this fact and thus the human operator bears the entire responsibility for the complete operation of the PP.

2.2.1.2   In the planned PP there is to be economy of variables throughout the whole scheme. Since the special papers, by A. P. Yershov and S. S. Lavrov, are devoted to this topic, only brief mention will be made of this in the present report.

2.2.1.3   The essential difference between ALGOL type languages and previous languages lies in the fact that in the former there has to be dynamic allocation of memory. The problem involved here consists of the following: according to ALGOL and Input language, all subscript bounds must be calculated before entering the block. This means that the value of the subscript bounds and consequently the dimensions of the variable arrays too, will not be known before running the program, though they will be known before operating the block. They are only established when they enter the specified block. Thus, the section of memory for a subscripted variable can only be allotted when the working program is implemented.

Dynamic allocation of memory results in some of the programming processes being shifted onto the object program. The need will arise for a certain administrative program which will allocate memory and at the same time will carry out exchange operations using other memory levels. We are still not clear as to whether the administrative system will take over the function of the IS-2 or whether it will operate in conjunction with it. Most probably we shall pass on to the second version, i.e. we shall simply regard the IS-2 as part of the computer, since now all standard programs are so bound up with the IS-2 that it would be very risky to interfere with anything in it.

2.2.2   Questions related to optimizing the running time of the working program

2.2.2.1   The temporary characteristics of the object program are largely determined by the way the loops are implemented. In the PP the possibility of improving the schemes compiled by a programmer, using the following means, will be examined:

   (a) by cleaning up the loops (i.e. taking out from the loop, operations which can be implemented before the start of the operation of the loop);
   (b) broadening the loops (i.e. amalgamating as many *FOR*-statements as possible into one).

In addition, when programming loops, better known procedures such as the expedient use of the index-register when programming internal loops, combining readdress according to an external loop parameter with restoration according to an internal loop parameter and so on, will be widely used.

2.2.2.2 The quality of programming operations on arrays exerts a pronounced influence on the program running time. Of the most essential problems which have to be solved in order to achieve high quality programming of operations on arrays, we should like to mention the following.

(a) Flexible programming of matrix operations. The basic choice here is whether to program an operation by means of an open or closed subroutine. In some cases using closed sub-routines economizes on memory and simplifies the actual programming algorithms, whereas inserting open sub-routines and subsequently analysing the connection between this sub-routine and neighbouring sub-routines (for the purpose of detecting unnecessary references and the appearance of loops which could be combined) opens up wider possibilities for raising the quality of the working program.

(b) Operations on logical vectors are easily programmed when all the components of a vector are placed in one memory location. However, the task becomes much more complicated when the number of components in the vector exceeds the number of digits in the location. The chief difficulty is to find a universal algorithm for programming these operations which would break up into the least number of individual cases possible.

(c) Formation and composition operations, generally speaking, involve the need to program transfer instructions which actually carry out formation or composition. However, in some cases, these transfer instructions can be put into the programming phase thereby relieving the object program of unnecessary transfers of information. For example, if the vector is made up of several variables, then perhaps, during the allocation of memory these variables could be arranged one behind the other in the requisite order. By the same token, the vector is formed while still at the programming stage. If the fullest possible account is taken of possibilities of this sort, it may save a considerable amount of time and space in memory.

3 Problems of Operating the PP

It may seem strange to speak of operating the PP without having written a single programming program instruction for it. Experience shows, however, that thought should be given to future operation of the PP right from the beginning, and at all stages of the work. The question of ease and reliability of operation should be the starting point for whatever decisions are made. In this section, we shall consider the following points.

3.1 Organization of Coding and Input

This question will not present any difficulties when we have at our disposal the keyboard input device and printing apparatus. However, making an optimistic estimate we shall have to spend at least a year working with manual coding. In manual coding, in contrast to earlier automatic programming systems, we adopt the principle of strictly letter-by-letter coding. This means that each of the 128 symbols (we work on the assumption of a 128 character alphabet) will be given a fixed number which the coder will insert into a blank when reading the given symbol. We believe that letter-by-letter coding is convenient because it is simpler even though it leads to quite a considerable expansion of information.

We also want to test the method suggested several years ago by V. D. Podyeryugin but which so far has not been put into practice anywhere. This method is worthy of note in that it avoids three prominent mistakes which occur at the coding stage—remembering the code, recording it on to a blank and manual perforation. The method is based on the typesetting principle and consists of the following: the coder has in front of her a typesetting case made up of 128 symbols. In each pocket there is a pile of punch cards with a single symbol punched on each of them. Reading the text, the coder compiles a punch card array, selecting the symbols in the order in which they appear in the scheme. As a result, a very long punch card array is obtained which is condensed on some kind of punch-card machine (for example, on a reproducer) and is then fed into the computer. The type of result given by this is as yet not clear, but the actual idea seems very attractive.

3.2   Operation of the PP

The main feature in this paragraph is organizing the behaviour of the PP when processing information which contains syntactical errors. We know that formal rules can be laid down for detecting all syntactical errors (and also for many semantic ones). Naturally, all these formal rules will be included in the PP. The compiler program will contain a great number of control stops the appearance of which warns against the presence of an error. This is the normal procedure familiar to everyone. However, we must first examine a number of aspects.

3.2.1   In the first place, situations which lead to looping of the PP must be avoided completely. To do this, all the loops should, for an indefinite number of repetitions, have blocking comparisons which means that they cannot be repeated more than a limited number of times.

3.2.2   In the second place, the following occurrence should be eliminated. In existing PPs, as a rule, every error which is detected automatically by the PP, regardless of the point during programming at which it is detected, throws the program back to the very beginning. After correcting the error, the problem has to be programmed right from the beginning. This results in the loss of a great deal of time. There are three ways of avoiding this, each of which we shall attempt to implement to the greatest possible extent.

(a)   *Initial control block.* Before the commencement of operation of the main part of the PP a special block reads the information and immediately extracts all the errors which can be detected after one pass. There may be several such errors. We shall save a lot of time if we correct by the one method all the errors which are found.

(b) *The possibility of going further on.* If an error is found somewhere in the "depths" of the PP, this error can in many cases be corrected in the current information instead of in the original information. In that case, the correction of the error does not require a return to the beginning of the program. The syntax of the language must be analysed thoroughly so that errors which can be corrected without going back can be put into a separate class.

(c) *Automatic correction.* A certain amount of redundancy is inherent in ALGOL 60 and in Input language. This means that quite a lot of the errors are automatically corrected without stopping the computer or with a brief stop during which the operator is informed that such and such an error has occurred and that it will be corrected in such and such a way. If the solution worked out by the computer satisfies the operator, operation can continue.

3.3   Debugging

Although the PP will detect most of the errors in information, the working program may still contain errors introduced into the scheme by the programmer himself. These errors are of such a kind that the original information which contained them is syntactically the scheme for a particular algorithm, but not for the one the programmer had in mind. The natural way of detecting such errors is by debugging—by implementing the program on a certain set of initial data and by trying to obtain additional information about how the implementation of the program is progressing. By analysing this additional information, conclusions can be drawn as to the nature and position of the error.

The commonest way of obtaining such additional information is the interpretation method, which is applied in most debugging programs. However, in the case of programs compiled with the help of a PP, this method must be used quite differently. The fact is that the additional information to be issued by the control program must not be expressed in terms of computer language—location addresses, instructions, instruction forms and so on, but must be described in Input language terms, i.e. in the form of statements, blocks, variables and so on. This circumstance alone will greatly complicate the debugging program, since it does not allow the abundant stock of control programs which have been devised, to be applied directly.

There are several ways of tackling the solution to this problem. We shall limit ourselves to two of them—the commonest.

3.3.1   Constructing an interpreting system.
A program can be constructed which will shape the implementation of program schemes, written, for instance, in ALGOL 60, exactly as it is defined in ALGOL 60. In view of the fact that any examination is conducted at original scheme level, it will be easy to issue additional information in terms of ALGOL-language. We wish to work seriously for a while on these lines and the first step in this direction is to draw up precise rules for implementing program schemes at reference language level. We believe that a purely functional description of ALGOL and Input language of this nature will be useful, not only for constructing an interpreting system.

3.3.2   Compiling a dictionary.
The following method should also be examined. The compiled computer program is interpreted, by means of the usual

debugging programs. However, the additional information obtained is translated into source language. This is done by means of a dictionary, compiled in such a way as to link together the elements in the computer program with the corresponding elements in the scheme. This dictionary will be compiled by the PP during programming. It should be mentioned, however, that this idea—straightforward when put in general terms—becomes less clear if considered in greater detail. The main problem here is actually compiling the dictionary which will be difficult to carry out, because of the levelling of original information which will occur during translation into the internal language.

3.4   The task of **operating the PP** will be much easier if the latter can be made to include all standard programs from the library as standard procedures. We shall try, as far as we possibly can, to put this into practice although in the given task—which is at first glance a purely technical one—difficulties do occur.

3.5   Greatest attention will be paid to the **teaching of the language**. It is psychologically important to teach source language to all mathematicians even before the PP is fully completed. Later on it will be necessary to progress to certain, perhaps, administrative measures, although we are sure that source language will speak most effectively for itself.

4   Carrying out the Work and Planning Characteristics

Finally, a few words about carrying out the work to do with compiling the PP and about its general features. Work will proceed in two stages: developing programming algorithms and actually compiling the PP. The product of the first stage, completion of which is planned within six months,† will be accurate flow charts for all the PP algorithms. A special symbolic language will be devised (or used being developed by someone) to describe these flow charts. It is proposed to allot the work at the first stage to eight or nine people. There will be two "managers": the project leader and the "chief engineer". Without becoming involved in technical details, the project leader will concentrate his attention on the most difficult or most important problems and if necessary will help the rest of his colleagues. The chief engineer is the only man who keeps the whole of the PP in front of him and, without becoming involved in the necessity for developing one block or another of the PP, will give particular attention to the current planning of operation and to the linking up of the separate blocks. He will, above all, keep an eye on the smooth transfer of information between the sections of the PP.

Upon completion of the first stage, there will be a "general mobilization" to increase programming speed and to debug the PP. It is proposed that between fourteen and sixteen people will participate at this stage.

Finally, the main features of the PP are:

1. total PP length—up to 15,000 instructions;
2. the length of tasks being programmed—up to 3,000 instructions in a block to be stored wholly in core memory;

† At the time of reporting.

3. the output of the PP—not less than 100 to 150 instructions per minute (excluding the final print out);
4. the work involved in the procedure—15 man-years;
5. date of surrender for operation—first quarter of 1962.

REFERENCES

1. YERSHOV, A. P., KOZHUKHIN, G. I. and VOLOSHIN, YU. M. (1961). Source language for an automatic programming system (Preliminary report). Computer Centre of the Academy of Sciences of the USSR, Moscow.
2. BACKUS, J. W., BAUER, F. L. *et al.* (1961). A report on the algorithmic language ALGOL 60. Computer Centre of the Academy of Sciences of the USSR, Moscow.
3. YERSHOV, A. P. (1959). What must the next programming program be? A report submitted at the All-Union Conference on computing mathematics and computing machinery. MSU, Moscow.
4. YERSHOV, A. P. (1938). Programming arithmetic operators. *Dokl. akad. nauk S.S.S.R.* **118**, No. 3.
5. YERSHOV, A. P. (ed.) (1961). SOAP 2. *In* "Programming Automation". Fizmatgiz, Moscow.

BASIC PROBLEMS ENCOUNTERED IN CONSTRUCTING A PROGRAMMING PROGRAM

A. P. YERSHOV

(Institute of Mathematics, Siberian Branch of the Academy of Sciences of the U.S.S.R., 16th March, 1961)

The construction of a complicated mechanism such as a programming program (PP) for Input language,[1] not only demands a thorough study of all the individual problems confronting those engaged on the project, but also means that every such person must be as familiar as possible with the project as a whole and able to extract from this knowledge all the information which might be useful to him when dealing with the particular problem with which he is concerned.

In connection with this, the main aim of this article is to bring together all the main problems which have to be solved when constructing a PP. In addition, this article will form the basis of a document showing how the work is to be planned and divided amongst the researchers. Finally, a complete enumeration of the main points of one problem or another will mean that the researcher can be more certain that, when dealing with the task in hand, he will not omit anything of importance.

To understand this article some knowledge of earlier papers connected with the project[1-3] is required, and it should therefore be borne in mind that questions which were examined in some detail in these earlier papers are only discussed briefly in this one.

The bibliography given is not a full one. Of the available sources the only references given are those directly related to the corresponding problem and at the same time accessible to us.

Problem 1: The Choice of Internal Language

As was pointed out earlier[2, 3] the process of translating the program scheme into a computer program will be divided into two phases. The language in which the scheme will be written after the first translation phase is called the *internal language*.

All information about the program written in the internal language must be divided into two parts: the statement scheme and tables of additional information, arranged separately from the statement scheme.

The main requirements as regards the syntax of the statement scheme are that it should be simple and that there should be as few different types of statements as possible.

8**

The main requirement for the syntax of the auxiliary tables is that all the necessary information contained in them should be as easily and as quickly available as possible. The connection between the arguments (entries into tables) and functions should, as far as possible, be such that the required functions can be extracted without examining the whole table.

It should not be forgotten that the major optimization of the object program will occur at the second programming phase. In this connection, the syntax and semantics of the source language must satisfy the following additional requirements:

(1) Analysis of the topological structure of the statement scheme must be as simple as possible. In particular, the linear sections,† loop bounds and scopes for values of variables must be easily separable within the scheme. For any pair of linear sections, a quick solution must be sought to the following trilemma:

(a) One linear section always follows another linear section;
(b) One linear section may follow another linear section, but not always;
(c) Linear sections may never occur together;

(2) Levelling and standardization of the form of statements in the statement scheme ought not to result in a loss of information, arising from the diversity of forms of Input language, which might be useful for optimizing the object program. In this connection, the tables which are to be written in the internal language, must contain means for retaining information, which disappears from the statement scheme. The program representation in the internal language is the point which divides the first and second programming phases. Therefore, constructing the internal language, especially the syntax and semantics of the statement scheme, is a task of paramount importance since it is precisely the form of the statement scheme which actually determines what will be done at the first and second phases. At the same time, the syntax of the table part will obviously be defined more precisely during work on the PP, as demands for one or other kind of information are specified. Taking all this into account, the internal language must be constructed independently of the specific features of the computer.

Sources. The internal language is by nature a primitive language for program statement schemes. Therefore, a knowledge of the languages of earlier automatic programming systems will most certainly be useful.[5-13] In particular, one would be well advised to acquaint oneself with the "Supervisors" developed in the Leningrad division of the Mathematical Institute of the Academy of Sciences of the USSR, since it was there that the question of representation of multidimensional variables was examined.[14-15]

At the same time one should not be influenced excessively by earlier automatic programming systems. The internal language has a very important feature in that it is internal and not intended for the formulation of problems by the human operator. Therefore, a constructor of the internal language is fortunate in that he is able to be free of the necessity for clarity and richness

† For a definition of the term "linear section" see for example ref. 4.

of language needed for descriptive purposes, merely making sure that the language wholly satisfies the demands given above.

Problem 2: Constructing a Functional System of Input Language

This problem consists essentially of the following: constructing an algorithm which, assuming the entry of a certain algorithm A in Input language to be syntactically accurate, would reproduce a whole sequence for execution of the basic statements of the algorithm A, corresponding to the particular data set for A. In terms of the theory of algorithms language, it is a question of constructing a universal algorithm for a class of algorithm to be expressed in Input language. In programming terms, the problem consists of developing a flow chart for an interpreting system which would interpret the execution of algorithms written in Input language.

This problem must be solved, chiefly in order to standardize the rules for executing algorithms written in Input language. The fact is that the description of Input language, while giving extensive information about the syntax of Input language, contains far fewer precise indications as to how the basic language statements are to be executed. There is no exact definition, even in the rules for calculating the values of expressions, as the discussion conducted in the pages of the ALGOL Bulletin shows. In the description of Input language, the rules for carrying out steps for executing algorithms—such as finding a label from a given value of a designational expression, substituting actual parameters for formal ones and keeping the value of variables of the **own** type —are not described accurately enough.

Without actually standardizing the rules for executing algorithms in Input language, the programming algorithms, and their equivalence, must be fully and precisely defined, which is necessary if the rules for converting statement schemes are to be applied correctly, when obtaining the best possible program.

A functional Input language scheme should contain the following:

(a) an accurate list of the elementary and independent steps for executing algorithms, written in Input language;

(b) an accurate chart showing possible branches from one elementary step to another and with exact wording of the conditions under which a branch can take place;

(c) a full list of the conditions under any one of which, subsequent execution of an algorithm becomes impossible (e.g. a request for a value not yet calculated);

(d) an accurately worded result of an executed algorithm;

(e) a definition of the equivalence of the algorithms written in Input language, based on the result of executing the algorithm.

When working out points (d) and (e) one should bear in mind the following characteristics of Input language: strictly speaking, block entries in Input language cannot be counted as algorithms in the usual sense, since they do not contain original data which can be modified. In connection with this, when defining equivalence either the idea of original data must be formally introduced, thereby widening to some extent the limits of Input language, or the idea of executing algorithms and comparing the results must be adapted to this feature of Input language; it contains no indication of the precise rules for the approximate execution of arithmetic operations on numbers. In this connection, either a description of operations on numbers will have to be added to the language, or the given definition of equivalence will need to be formulated in such a way that it does not take into account the manner in which operations on numbers are actually carried out.

The development of a functional scheme for Input language is closely linked with the construction of the internal language for which a functional scheme also has to be obtained.

This will in fact be simpler for the internal language than for Input language. Finally, definitions must be given of the equivalence of algorithms expressed in the internal language (to apply the transformations of the statement schemes correctly) and of the equivalence of algorithms expressed in Input language and in the internal language respectively (to apply correctly the rules for translating from Input to the internal language).

Sources. The problem of describing accurately the rules for executing algorithms is not a new one in the theory of algorithms, but with regard to its size and to the fact that it relates to a formal algorithmic system such as Input language, this problem has no precedent. Generally speaking, problems of this magnitude do arise when developing any non-trivial automatic programming system. However, no papers specially devoted to the strictly logical analysis of programming languages have appeared to date.

The reader can acquaint himself with the idea of the universal algorithm by reading paper.[16] Paragraph 3 in the article by Yershov[17] which describes the rules for executing "statement algorithms"—an algorithmic system similar to program statement schemes but somewhat simplified—might be useful. Yershov's paper[18] examines ways of defining the equivalence of algorithms.

Finally it should be noted that this problem is very important since the functional scheme, together with the description of Input language, will be a starting point for the construction of programming algorithms.

Problem 3: Algorithms of Syntactical Analysis of Input Language

The essence of the problem is expressed in its title. All that is necessary is to explain in more detail what is meant by syntactical analysis. In this connection, the problem consists of the following:

(a) checking that a word, being considered as a value of a particular syntactical unit of Input language, is syntactically correct;

(b) separating the syntactical units of the language;

(c) correcting the mistakes in the program scheme, which have arisen as a result of a redundancy in the language.

Clarification of the above points. (a) a particular word P is referred to as a *correct unit* (A) of Input language if, in accordance with its syntax the word P can be the value of a metalinguistical variable A. In connection with this, one can speak for example of a correct expression, a correct *FOR*-statement, a correct block and so on. The purpose of the algorithm in point (a) is to check whether any word in the alphabet of basic symbols can be the value of a particular given language unit. The necessity for such algorithms is due to the fact that the recording of problems in Input language may contain errors which may upset the syntax of the language. All such errors must be detected.

Point (b) contains the analysis proper, i.e. the subdivision of a word, which is the value of a particular unit of the language, into parts (sub-words) which represent the values of the "smaller" units of the language. For example, a block must be divided into declarations and the statement part, the statement part into separate statements, the statements into their components and so on. The need for this kind of analysis is quite obvious. Points (a) and (b) are closely interlinked since, obviously, syntactical errors will be detected precisely at the time of subdividing a larger unit of the language into smaller ones.

Point (c). We know that a text written, say, in Russian and containing very few mistakes can be corrected, because of the fact that information contained in the "intact" sections of a particular wrong word tells us that this is the word and that it should therefore be written correctly. This property is referred to as "redundancy". Source language also possesses this feature, which should be used to the fullest extent. For example, without the writer of the scheme having to supply any further information, we can—as a result of the above feature—correct such errors as distortion in the writing of basic symbols and certain discrepancies between procedure headings in statements and declarations (e.g. when the name of a procedure in an statement is an abbreviation of a procedure name in a declaration and so on). It would be a good idea to pick out all errors of this kind which can be easily rectified and give rules for correcting them. The value of rules of this kind lies in the fact that they can be applied automatically without taking the problem out of the programming.

The particular feature of Problem 3 is that the results of its processing will be scattered throughout the blocks of the PP. In particular, algorithms for syntactical analysis are needed when constructing a functional scheme of Input language (Problem 2), when programming the interpreting system (Problem 10), during the preliminary processing of the program (Problem 4) and for control service (Problem 9). In this connection, the person working on this problem will have to make a special decision as to how to distribute the algorithms of syntactical analysis throughout the blocks of the PP.

Sources. In order to become "familiar" with this problem, the reader should acquaint himself beforehand with the rules for syntactical analysis of certain simpler formal systems (cf. e.g. Burks *et al.*[19]). Specific papers which deal with the syntactical analysis of certain programming languages: ALGOL 58,[20, 21] ALGOL 60,[22] and also arithmetical statements in the PPs[23] should be studied.

Problem 4: Preliminary Processing

The preliminary processing of a program scheme constitutes one of the elements for translating information from Input language into the internal language. The main purpose of preliminary processing is to impart information of a uniform and standard nature and also to compile certain tables to present the program in the internal language. When compiling algorithms for the initial processing, the following steps should be taken.

(a) An algorithm for renaming identifiers and labels should be derived.

(b) Algorithms for transferring constants from expressions into initial value declarations and for presenting them in standard form should be obtained.

(c) A method for introducing arithmetical and logical expressions into assignment statements should be devised.

(d) A method should be found for introducing into the program scheme symbols for additional variables.

(e) It should be made clear how identities are to be dealt with—whether they are to be eliminated or given a standard form.

(f) A way of presenting variable declarations and initial value declarations in tabular form, should be sought.

(g) A method of presenting, filling and converting should be obtained for tables containing information about the nature, structure and position of variables.

(h) It should be established which sections of syntactical analysis will be carried out during the preliminary processing phase, and ways of signalling errors which may come to light should be worked out. In addition, an effort should be made to find as many errors as possible during the initial processing.

(i) An algorithm should be found for establishing a plan for the subsequent operation of the PP depending on the degree of complexity of the program scheme. A list of possible plans, and simple criteria for choosing them, should be compiled. At the same time, it is desirable to exclude, as far as possible, from any specific plan, the operation of blocks which, according to this plan, will run idle.

(j) Before the statement scheme in the internal language finally takes shape, the symbols for variables should be expanded so that any pair of x_1 and x_2 entries of a particular x variable can be denoted by different symbols, if the situation should arise in which the variable x has one value when using x_1 and another when using x_2. For example the sequence of assignment statements

$$x := x + a; x := x + a; x := x + a; y := x^2$$

after being expanded will look like this:

$$x_2 := x_1 + a; x_3 := x_2 + a; x_4 := x_3 + a; y := x_4{}^2$$

This expansion is necessary for allocation of memory and for programming arithmetic expressions. However, provision will have to be made so that the information lost in this expansion can be stored in special tables.

Sources. The main object to be achieved from the compiler blocks for the preliminary processing is their high speed operation. Therefore, the person engaged on this part of the project might find useful papers in which special attention is given to questions of faster processing of information.[5, 9, 24-29]

When developing algorithms for renaming identifiers, it is a good idea to be familiar with the papers on compression of codes.[30] Some reference is made to the algorithm of expanding in paper.[31]

Problem 5: Allocation

This is a central problem in the development of the PP since it contains great possibilities for raising the quality of the object program. The following questions must be answered when dealing with this problem.

(a) How to find a way of introducing into the program schemes the concept of an external medium, internal memory, magnetic drum and magnetic tape and how to describe standard procedures for transferring information amongst the memory forms mentioned above.

(b) How to find algorithms for dynamic allocation of memory, i.e. allocation of memory at the moment of execution of the object program. How to define the functions of and give an algorithm for constructing, an "administrative program" which will actually produce this dynamic allocation of memory. At the same time it is undesirable to construct a rigid scheme for dynamic allocation of memory, i.e. to construct algorithms which at the programming phase would analyse the possible specific situations which arise upon removal from the block, in order to leave in the administrative program only those cases of allocation of memory in which there is really insufficient information to carry out this allocation when programming a problem.

(c) How to find working variants of algorithms for optimum allocation of internal memory for scalar variables. In addition, the question must first of all be decided whether to construct a general economy algorithm, applicable to the scheme as a whole or whether economy will be produced "in fragments", starting with the linear sections and simplest blocks making the maximum use of information about the position of variables.

(d) How to find algorithms, even if only very approximate in form, for economic allocation of memory for arrays. In addition, one should make a special point of examining the possibility of "exchanging" a certain array (when it is no longer required) between scalar variables or smaller arrays.

(e) How to find approximate algorithms for segmenting the problem by transferring certain blocks onto a magnetic drum, in the event of the assignment not containing any information about distribution of blocks on the drum and on tapes. At the same time, the PP must give an indication that segmentation has been carried out so that the programmer can confirm that it has taken place or prevent it from taking place.

(f) How to work out a system of tables to contain information about variables, which would make memory allocation easier. It is suggested that these tables be filled when translating the program scheme into the internal language and when analysing the statement scheme. In connection with this, to work out a request for contents and formulation of the tables.

(g) How to clarify the question of the actual allocation of computer memory, i.e. either to issue programs in symbolic addresses, indicating memory allocation for arrays, or to issue programs in absolute addresses.

Sources. A description of technical problems of memory allocation and also several useful algorithms may be found in the papers.[5, 24, 31-39]

Problem 6: Programming of Expressions

The programming of expressions falls naturally into two types of problem: programming of calculating expressions and programming of designational expressions.

The following problems must be dealt with when programming calculating expressions.

(a) On the basis of the form of the internal language it must be established which of the programming algorithms will occur when translating from Input language into the internal language, and which at the second programming phase.

(b) When programming expressions containing various types of components, rules must be devised to minimize the number of transformations of variables from one type to another when evaluating the value of the statement.

(c) When programming expressions containing formation and composition operations, algorithms must be found which result in the least possible number of transfers of variables from one location to another when actually implementing formation and composition. Where possible, transfers by appropriate preliminary allocation in memory of components of arrays to be formed or composed should be avoided.

(d) When programming matrix operations, some criteria should be derived to show when the corresponding sub-routine ought to be inserted into the program scheme in open form and when—in closed form.

(e) When programming componentwise operations on arrays, one should make sure that the loops are spread as widely as possible over the whole collection of componentwise operations which can be joined into one loop.

(f) When programming operations on Boolean arrays, a universal algorithm should be devised for programming such operations, starting with the requirement that one Boolean value should occupy one digit of a location in memory. Ways of positioning arbitrary Boolean arrays in computer memory should be found.

(g) When programming Boolean expressions, for the purpose of transfer of control, there should be some criterion devised as to when it is advisable to program a Boolean statement in the form of a chain of instructions for transfer of control and when it is preferable to construct it in the form of a program for calculating the value of a Boolean expression—and one transfer instruction depending on the value calculated.

(h) During programming one should ensure economy in computing expressions which coincide. When developing the corresponding algorithms, a request should be devised for information which might facilitate bringing about this economy. A way of obtaining and using this information should be sought.

(i) When programming expressions containing only constants, provision should be made for them to be calculated during programming.

When programming designational expressions, the chief, and only, problem (presenting any difficulty) is the economic programming of switches. Apart from a general algorithm it is necessary to devise special methods for programming simple switches with a small number of components.

Sources. Programming expressions is one of the most studied questions in automatic programming.[5, 11, 24, 40-49]

Problem 7: Programming Loops

The chief object to aim at when programming loops is to increase the operational speed of the loop by cutting down on the number of auxiliary control instructions and by eliminating from the loop body everything which can be executed before starting the operation of the loop. When working out algorithms for programming loops, solutions must be found to the following problems:

(a) To achieve a flexible programming system to calculate sequential values of the loop parameter, and specifying a suitable way of processing the *FOR* clause depending on the form of the latter.

(b) To develop a flexible readdress system making maximum use of the index register, especially in internal loops.

(c) To find criteria for deciding the most advantageous arrangement of control instructions: at the start of the loop body, at the end or, perhaps alternately with instructions forming the loop body.

(d) To consider thoroughly all possible opportunities for simplifying the whole programming scheme by joining together the control instructions for several loops (e.g. joining together into one instruction restoration according to an internal parameter and readdress according to an external parameter).

(e) To find algorithms for "cleaning up" a loop.

Sources. Programming of loops is examined by several authors,[5, 42, 50, 51] particularly in the paper by Velikanova *et al.*[32]

Problem 8: Programming Procedure Statements

A whole complex of questions, connected with the use of sub-routines, enters into this problem which falls into two sections: programming declared procedures and programming non-declared procedures.

The term "**declared procedures**" signifies procedures for which there are—in the program scheme—declarations expressed in terms of Input language statements. For such procedures the following problems must be dealt with.

(a) To establish criteria for deciding whether a given procedure is to be used as an open sub-routine (i.e. literally according to the rules for implementing procedures given in the declaration of Input language), or whether it is to be programmed as a closed sub-routine.

(b) To find rules for programming auxiliary control operations for open type procedures (retaining values for variables of the **own** type, substituting values of actual parameters which enter the **value** list and replacing formal parameters by actual ones for parameters which do not enter the **value** list.

(c) To find similar rules of operation as for point (b) for closed type procedures taking into account the fact that for closed type procedures, replacement of formal parameters by actual ones will occur, not when programming but when executing the program. To devise algorithms for analysing actual parameters in call statements to closed type procedures in order to obtain all the information needed to program the procedure.

The term "**non-declared procedures**" signifies procedures which are considered as standard, an inherent part of the PP and not requiring their declarations to be added to the scheme in terms of Input language statements. The following problems must be solved with regard to such procedures.

(a) A final list (for the first version) of standard procedures to be compiled showing a call to the latter in terms of procedure statements.

(b) The list of standard procedures to be sorted into three classes, the first to include procedures whose programs must be taken from the library of standard programs in finished or half finished form (programs to be compiled), the second to include procedures whose program will be formulated by the PP itself (programs to be generated) and the third to include procedures whose declarations, expressed in Input language, are added to the PP itself.

(c) Criteria to be found for standard procedures similar to those for declared procedures as in point (a) for using standard procedures as open ones or closed ones.

(d) A method to be found of adding supplementary information to the basic text of the program for procedures of the "programs to be compiled" type, in order to ensure that this program is properly linked to the main one. This information ought to help the PP to produce maximum economy of memory to be used for the procedure.

(e) Algorithms for constructing programs to be found for procedures to be generated. To establish the stage of programming at which these programs will be generated.

(f) A method for inserting declarations of standard procedures of the third type into the original scheme to be found, thus reducing them to declared procedures.

Finally, a problem which is common to all procedures is the distribution of algorithms for programming procedures over the first and second stages of programming.

Sources. For general guidance on this question and an understanding of the terminology see ref. 52 and 53; a knowledge of several automatic programming systems[11, 39, 54] will provide some background information. In connection with using libraries of standard programs in large scale PPs. [9, 12, 36, 55]

Problem 9: Organizing the Work

The complexity and interdependence of the blocks in the programming program demands maximum co-ordination between those engaged on the project as well as the capacity to share information and an ability to pass on to one another the results of their research in a clear and concise form. Special steps must be taken to ensure this.

(a) Work on compiling PP must be clearly divided into two stages. As a result of the first stage, a whole range of questions to do with developing programming algorithms will be solved and a detailed and logical PP scheme will be drawn up. Only when the flow-chart has been completed, fully worked out and thoroughly checked will it be possible to proceed to programming, which constitutes the second stage of work.

(b) For an accurate description of the logical PP scheme, a system of standard symbols must be devised, or in other words a special language must be found, for describing programming algorithms. If this language can be made easy and accurate, then it will be possible to try and construct a "super PP" for compiling the PP automatically. In the latter case, it will be possible to shorten considerably the period of time taken to program the PP.

(c) Experience shows that by far the greatest number of errors when programming the PP are those caused by discrepancies between the blocks as regards the transfer and intake of information. To avoid this, a special "communication service" must be established. Its functions will include the following:

to produce a single, universal method of recording which information is fed to the block before the start of operation, and which is issued;
to make sure that no block obstructs information which might be needed later by the operating blocks;
to choose a structure for the PP which reduces as much as possible the informational link between the blocks, provided that this decrease does not conflict with the guarantee of some of the PPs more important features;
to devise some special "transit" test specifically designed to check communications between blocks.

(d) When compiling the PP a close watch must be kept on the sections of the general programming algorithm which are used in several PP blocks, in order to avoid possible duplications or omissions. The system of control stops in the PP is particularly relevant to these sections. It has been mentioned earlier that when analysing source information it is important that rules should be found for actually tracing errors which are to be formally notified.

In connection with this, an original "control service" must be created which must ensure that every block which is capable, by the nature of its work, of revealing an error of a given type, actually stipulates the appropriate control checks and stops. The following points should be taken into account when introducing this "control service".

Since the discovery of a mistake in the source information, as a rule, necessitates the removal of the problem from the programming operation and a repetition of programming after the mistake has been rectified, the time spent by the computer on programming up until the discovery of the mistake is time wasted in the majority of cases. In this connection, it is desirable that every mistake in the information should be found as early as possible, in addition that the PP should not stop when only one mistake is discovered but—as far as possible—should point out all the mistakes in the information in one operation. There is, however, one important obstacle standing in the path of the fulfilment of this natural requirement, which is that algorithms of analysis may be rather complicated and the fact that they must be inserted in the initial blocks of the PP leads to duplication of blocks and an increase in the operation time of the PP. Therefore, a reasonable compromise must be found and it must be made quite clear what kind of mistakes it would be advisable to look for at the very beginning of the operation of the PP during the initial processing of the material, and what types of mistakes are better left to the later blocks of the PP in which an appropriate analysis of the information fed in is an integral part of the algorithms to be implemented by these blocks.

The "control service" must pay special attention to mistakes in the information which could cause looping in the PP. All mistakes of this sort must be shown up before they are able to cause looping. In the logical scheme of the PP, each loop with an indefined number of repetitions must be analysed and it must be ascertained whether the preliminary analysis of the information can be relied upon to provide the correct operation of the given loop or whether a special comparison needs to be put into the loop to prevent it from being repeated more than a given number of times.

(e) Finally, to ensure a well organized and reliable debugging of the PP a special "debugging service" should be introduced. The service should cover the following points:

finding a single form for the presentation and documentation of any tests which can be applied for debugging the PP;
carrying out a special analysis of the PP scheme, in order to foresee by means of tests, as many opportunities as possible for the operation of individual blocks, paying particular attention to such aspects of the operation of programs as ensuring the necessary number of loop repetitions, correct usage of the locations, checking the correct form of the information which is to be left to the other blocks, correct work of control transfer statements for "boundary" values of compared variables;
by means of special tests designed to carry out an isolated debugging of individual blocks, preparing at least fifty actual problems to serve as final control tests on which the ultimate debugging of both the PP scheme and the PP itself as written in the instructions, will be carried out;
considering the possibility of compiling some special debugging programs which might facilitate the process of debugging the PP.

Sources. Unfortunately, with the exception of ref. 56 no papers could be found dealing exclusively with questions related to organizing the work when developing large, complex programs. For working out the structure of the PP and regarding its organization, articles dealing with the general organization of earlier compiler programs are useful.[5, 32, 36, 39, 42, 57, 58] Constructing a language for describing programming algorithms and compiling a "super PP" are connected with the whole question of the automated programming of non-arithmetical problems on which there is a fairly wide amount of literature available.[8, 10, 59-75]

Problem 10: Preparing for Operation

Preparations for operating the PP should be started early and should proceed along the following lines:

Ensuring that the PP itself has the necessary operational properties; providing the PP with the necessary equipment and auxiliary programs, and training the staff to use the PP.

Main operational properties of the PP. Speed of operation and high quality programming must be guaranteed by the project as a whole. In addition, there are some smaller but equally important points which must be provided for in the PP.

(a) As simple a system as possible must be devised for arranging the PP and introducing it into the computer, with special provision for recording and storing the PP.

(b) A system must be worked out for making it possible to alter the operational modes of the PP, for example so that the PP would or would not be able to carry out a given program optimization, depending on the programmer's choice. It could also be required that the PP deliver the program in symbolic address instead of in its final form. In order to do this, possible operational modes for the PP must be fixed and a simple and convenient way of incorporating the required mode in the PP must be given.

(c) A flexible system for issuing diverse information during the operation of the PP must be devised. This information should include the following:

information concerning syntactical mistakes in the problem, discovered during the preliminary processing;
information concerning mistakes automatically rectified by the PP through language redundancy.
at the occasion of every control stop, information must be given to help analyse the situation, which has caused this stop;
any information concerning allocation of memory and internal coding of identifiers;
information concerning segmentation brought about by the PP itself.
Special care should be taken to impart this information in a simple, graphic form.

(d) A "double computation" scheme must be implemented in the PP, which eliminates the effect of possible bugs in the computer on the operation of the PP. However, this scheme must be "detachable" to avoid wasting time in the case of a computer which operates reliably. The PP should be provided with a certain number of **supplementary facilities and special auxiliary programs** to simplify the use of the PP.

(a) An alphanumeric device for input and output, using an alphabet of the basic symbols (128 characters). If there is no line printer with the standard line length of 96-120 symbols, an automatic type-writer can be used although this slows down the output speed considerably.

(b) When there is no alphabetical mechanism, it will be necessary to devise a temporary method of manual coding paying particular attention to the simplicity of the coding and deciphering operation which ensures the maximum guarantee of absence of errors, particularly when coding.

(c) From the auxiliary programs, apart from the above mentioned programs for input and input control by the PP, a system of debugging programs compiled with the aid of the PP, must be worked out. This problem is discussed in considerable detail above. It need only be mentioned here that obviously the interpreting system will be the most convenient means of debugging, and particular attention should therefore be paid to this point.

Special preparation of the staff for using the PP should be along the following lines.

(a) Following a course of lectures on Input language for supervisors of laboratories and institute departmental groups engaged in solving production problems.

(b) After agreeing on a final form for Input language, writing a manual of Input language which should serve as a basic handbook for using the PP.

(c) Organizing courses for programmers to make a systematic study of Input language, beginning in the academic year 1961/62.

(d) Training and instruction for punch card operators and initial data coders and preparation of computer operators for working with the PP.

(e) Training of the maintenance group leader of the PP project—a man who must have a perfect knowledge of Input language and a near perfect knowledge of the whole PP. Having an expert present is especially important during the period of the initial operation of the PP.

Sources. Katz's paper[76] is devoted to questions relating to the debugging of programs to be compiled on computers. Finally, the results of problems 2 and 3 are used fully to compile an interpreting system. In addition, ref. 77 and 78 might prove useful. The popularly accepted accounts of several algorithmic languages[79, 80] might be useful in seeking the best method of expounding Input language.

REFERENCES

1. YERSHOV, A. P., KOZHUKHIN, G. I. and VOLOSHIN, YU. M. (1961). Input Language for automatic programming systems. Computer Centre of the Academy of Sciences of the USSR, Moscow.
2. YERSHOV, A. P. (1959). What must the next programming program be? Dokl. predstavlennyi Vsesoyuz, soveschch. po. vychisl. matem. i. vychisl. tekhnike (Reports presented at the All-Union Conference on Computer Mathematics and Computer Techniques, Moscow State University, November 1959.
3. KOZHUKHIN, G. I. and YERSHOV, A. P. (1960). Plan for programming programs of the Institute of Mathematics of the S.O. of the Academy of Sciences of the USSR. Reports presented at the Conference on "Constructing programming programs on the basis of the ALGOL language". Moscow State University, December 1960. (Appendix 1 of this book.)
4. PODDERYUGIN, V. D. (1961). LUCh—A Control program for the computer STRELA-3, Computer Centre of the Academy of Sciences of the USSR, Moscow.
5. YERSHOV, A. P. (1958). Programming program for a high-speed electronic computer. Academy of Sciences of the USSR, Moscow.

6. YERSHOV, A. P. and KIM, K. V. (1961). PPS—A programming program for the computer STRELA-3 (Users' manual), Computer Centre of the Academy of Sciences of the USSR, Moscow.

7. KAMYNIN, S. S., LYUBIMSKII, E. Z. and SHURA-BURA, M. R. (1958). Programming automation by means of a programming program. *Problemy Kibern.* 1, Fizmatgiz, Moscow.

8. KOROLYUK, V. S. (1960). The Concept of the address algorithm. *Problemy Kibern.* 4, Fizmatgiz, Moscow.

9. PERLIS, A. J., SMIT, J. V. and VAN ZOREN, H. R. (1961). IT—a programming program for the computer IBM-650. *In* "Programming Automation" (Ed. A. P. Yershov). Fizmatgiz, Moscow.

10. YUSHCHENKO, E. L. (1960). Address programming and some features of solutions to problems on the "URAL" computer. Kiev, 1960.

11. BROOKER, R. A., RICHARDS, B., BERG, E. and KERR, R. H. (1969). The Manchester Mercury Autocode System, University of Manchester.

12. BROOKER, R. A. (1960). Mercury Autocode: Principles of the program library. *A. Rev. autom. Progrmg* 1.

13. CONWAY, M. E. (1958). Proposal for an UNCOL. *Commns Ass. comput. Mach.* 1, No. 10.

14. BULAVSKII, V. A. (1958). The symbolism of recordings in computer plans in programming automation. Izvestiya vuzov, Matematika.

15. KANTOROVICH, L. V. and PEMROVA, L. T. (1956). Mathematical symbolism suitable for carrying out calculations on computers. Report of the Third All-Union Mathematical Conference, Moscow, June–July 1956, Vol. 2.

16. MARKOV, A. A. (1954). Theory of algorithms. *Trudy mat. Inst. V. A. Steklova* 42.

17. YERSHOV, A. P. (1960). Operator algorithms. I. *Problemy Kibern.* 3, Fizmatgiz, Moscow.

18. YERSHOV, A. P. (1961). Operator algorithms, II. *Problemy Kibern.* 8. Fizmatgiz, Moscow.

19. BURKS, A. W., WARREN, D. W. and WRIGHT, J. B. (1954). An analysis of a logical machine using parenthesis-free notation. *Mathl Tabl. natn. Res. Coun., Wash.*, 8, No. 16; 8, No. 46.

20. FLOYD, R. W. (1960). An algorithm defining ALGOL assignment statements. *Commns Ass. comput. Mach.* 3, No. 3.

21. R.W.B. (1959). JAL symbol pair table. *Commns Ass. comput. Mach.* 2, No. 4.

22. MARTYNYUK, V. V. (1960). Algorithm for isolating syntax units of ALGOL 60 language. Lecture delivered at Conference on "Construction of programming program on the basis of the ALGOL language". Moscow State University, Moscow. December 1960.

23. KIM, K. V. (1959). Checking arithmetical expressions in the output information for PPS. Report of the Computer Centre of the Academy of Sciences of the USSR, Moscow.

24. YERSHOV, A. P. (1958). Programming of arithmetical operators. *Dokl. Akad. Nauk SSSR* 118, No. 3.

25. ZHURAVLEV, YU. I. (1958). Optimal algorithms of selection. *Dokl. Akad. Nauk SSSR* 121, No. 3.

26. KOROLEV, L. N. (1958). Methods for selecting the required word from a dictionary. *In* "Computing machinery", Academy of Sciences of the USSR, Moscow.

27. KOROLEV, L. N. (1959). Switching functions of table searching device. *Dokl. Akad. Nauk SSSR* 125, No. 3.

28. YERSHOV, A. P. (ed.) (1961). SOAP 2. *In* "Programming automation". Fizmatgiz, Moscow.
29. ISAACS, E. J. and SINGLETON, R. C. (1956). Sorting by address calculation. *J. Ass. comput. Mach.* **3**, No. 3.
30. KOROLEV, L. N. (1957). Coding and compression of codes. *Dokl. Akad. Nauk SSSR* **113**, No. 4.
31. LAVROV, S. S. (1960). Memory allocation. Lecture delivered at the Conference on "Construction of programming programs based on ALGOL language". Moscow State University, Moscow, December 1960.
32. VELIKANOVA, T. M., YERSHOV, A. P., KIM, K. V., KUROCHKIN, V. M., OLEINIK-OVOD, YU. A. and PODDERYUGIN, V. D. (1961). PPS—a programming program for the STRELA computer. Report on the All-Union Conference on Computer Mathematics and Applications of Computer Machinery, 3–8 February 1958. Baku, 1961.
33. MARTYNYUK, V. V. (1961). Separation of chains in the algorithmic scheme. *Zh. vychisl. Mat. mat. Fiz.* **1**, No. 1.
34. SHLYAKHOVAYA, T. M. (1958). Allocation of memory for vector systems. Kiev State University.
35. SHTARKMAN, V. S. (1958). Block of working location economy in PP-2, *Problemy Kibern.* No. 1.
36. YERSHOV, A. P. (ed.) (1961). (UNICODE). *In* "Programming automation". Fizmatgiz, Moscow.
37. CARR, J. W. III (1959). Recursive subscription compilers and list-type memories. *Commns Ass. comput. Mach.* **2**, No. 2.
38. DERR, J. I. and LUKE, R. C. (1956). Semi-automatic allocation of data storage for PACT I. *J. Ass. comput. Mach.* **3**, No. 4.
39. A Manual of the DASK ALGOL Language, ALGOL Bulletin Supplement, No. 5 (November 1960). Regnecentralen, Copenhagen.
40. LUKHOVITSKAYA, E. S. (1959). Block for processing logical conditions in PP-2. *Problemy Kibern*, No. 1.
41. LYUBIMSKII, E. Z. (1958). Arithmetical block in PP-2, *Problemy Kibern.* No. 1.
42. TRIFONOV, N. P. and SHURA-BURA, M. R. (eds.) (1961). "System of programming automation". Fizmatgiz, Moscow.
43. BAUER, F. L. and SAMELSON, K. (1959). Sequential translation of formulae. *Electronische Rechenanlagen* (Electronic Computers) **1**, No. 4.
44. BOTTENBRUCH, H. (1958). Translation of algorithmic formula languages into the program language of computers. *Z. math. Logik* **4**, No. 3.
45. BÖHM, C. (1954). Digital Computers, Decyphering logico-mathematical formulae by the machine itself in program formulation. *Annali Mat. pura appl.* **37**.
46. LOOPSTRA, B. J. (1956). Processing of formulas by machines. *Nachrtech. Fachber.* **4**.
47. MCGINN, L. C. (1957). A matrix compiler for Univac, Automatic Coding. *J. Franklin Inst.* Monograph No. 3.
48. SHERIDAN, P. B. (1959). The arithmetic translator-compiler of the IBM Fortran automatic coding system. *Commns Ass. comput. Mach.* **2**, No. 2.
49. WOLPE, H. (1958). Algorithm for analysing logical statements to produce a truth function table. *Commns Ass. comput. Mach.* **1**, No. 3.
50. KAMYNIN, S. S. (1958). Block for readdressing in the PP-2 program. *Problemy Kibern.* No. 1.
51. HEMPSTEAD, G. and SCHARTZ, J. I. (1956). PACT loop expansion, *J. Ass. comput. Mach.* **3**, No. 4.

52. WILKS, M., WHEELER, L. and GILL, S. (1961). Compilation of a programs for electronic computers. Foreign Literature Publishing House, Moscow.
53. DIJKSTRA, E. W. (1960). Recursive programming. *Num. Math.* **2**, No. 5.
54. Automatic programming: The A-2 compiler system (1955). *Computers Automn* **4**, No. 9, 10.
55. "FORTRAN II". Reference manual for the IBM-704 data processing system. IBM Corporation (1958).
56. MELAHN, W. S. (1959). A Description of a cooperative venture in the production of an automatic coding system, *J. Ass. comput. Mach.* **6**, No. 4.
57. KITOV, A. I. and KRINITSKII, N. A. (1959). Electronic digital computers and programming, Fizmatgiz, Moscow.
58. MOCK, O. R. (1956). Logical organization of the PACT I compiler, *J. Ass. comput. Mach.* **3**, No. 4.
59. KALUZHNIN, L. A. (1959). Algorithmization of mathematical problems, *Problemy Kibern.* No. 2.
60. KULAGINA, O. S. (1959). Operator description of algorithms of translation and automation of their programming processes. *Problemy Kibern.* No. 2.
61. BRACKEN, R. H. and OLDFIELD, B. G. (1956). A general system for handling alphameric information on the IBM-701 computer. *J. Ass. comput. Mach.* **3**, No. 3.
62. GELERNTER, H., HANSON, J. R. and GERBEICH, G. (1960). A Fortran compiled list processing language, *J. Ass. comput.* **7**, No. 2.
63. GELERNTER, H. (1959). A note on syntactic symmetry and the manipulation of formal systems by machine. *Inf. Control.* **2**.
64. GREEN, J. (1959). Remarks on ALGOL and symbol manipulation, *Commns Ass. comput. Mach.* **2**, No. 9.
65. GREEN, J. (1960). Symbol manipulation in XTRAN. *Commns Ass. comput. Mach.* **3**, No. 4.
66. LISP I. Programmer's manual (1960). Computation Center and Research Laboratories of Electronics, MIT, Cambridge, Mass.
67. MCCARTHY, J. (1960). Recursive functions of symbol expressions and their computation by machine. Preprint, MIT, Cambridge, Mass.
68. NEWELL, A. and TONGE, F. M. (1960). Introduction to information processing language V. *Commns Ass. comput. Mach.* **3**, No. 4.
69. PERLIS, A. J. (1960). Thornton, Symbol manipulation by threaded lists. *Commns Ass. comput. Mach.* **3**, No. 4.
70. PERLIS, A. J. and SMITH, J. W. (1958). A command language for handling strings of symbols, Paper 30 presented to 13th National Meeting of the ACM, Urbana, 111, June 11–13.
71. Proposed standard flow chart symbols (1959). *Commns Ass. comput. Mach.* **2**, No. 10.
72. SHAW, J. C., NEWELL, A., SIMON, H. A. and ELLIS, T. O. (1958). A command structure for complex information processing. Proceedings of the Western Joint Computer Conference, Los Angeles, Calif. May 6–8, 1958.
73. VOORHEES, E. A. (1958). Algebraic formulation of flow diagrams. *Commns Ass. comput. Mach.* **1**, No. 6.
74. BROOKER, R. A. and MORRIS, D. (1960). An assembly program for a phase structure language. *Comput. J.* **3**, No. 3.
75. BROOKER, R. A. and MORRIS, D. (1961). Some proposals for the realisation of a certain assembly program. *Comput. J.* **4**, No. 1.
76. KATZ, C. (1957). Systems of debugging automatic coding, Automatic Coding. *J. Franklin Inst.* Monograph No. 3.

77. DENISON, S. J. M. (1960). Further DEVICE interpretive programs and some translating programs. *Rev. autom. Progrmg* **1**.

78. GREMS, MANDALAY, PORTER, R. E. Algebraic interpretive coding system. Digest of the Boeing Airplane Co., Physical Research Staff, Boeing Aircraft Co., Seattle.

79. WOODGER, M. (1960). An introduction to ALGOL 60. *Comput. J.* **3**, No. 2.

80. ZEMANEK, H. (1959). Die algorithmische Formelsprache (Algorithmic formula language). *Electronische Rechenanlagen*, **1**, 72–79, 140–143.

81. MCISAAC, (1960). Combining ALGOL statement analysis with validity checking. *Commns Ass. comput. Mach.* **3**, No. 7.

82. KNUTH, D. E. (1959). RUNCIPLE—algebraic translator on a limited computer, *Commns Ass. comput. Mach.* **2**, No. 11.

83. BAKER, C. L. (1956). The FACT I Coding system for the IBM type 701, *J. Ass. comput. Mach.* **3**, No. 4.

AUTHOR INDEX

Numbers in parenthesis are reference numbers and are included to assist in locating references in which the authors' names are not mentioned in the text. Numbers in italics indicate the page on which the reference is listed.

SUBJECT INDEX

The index includes terms defined in the chapters of the book (it does not include terms used in the appendices). The pages given are those on which a particular term—usually printed in italics—appears. In the case of the blocks of the ALPHA-translator, every page on which there is mention of a particular block is given.